Myth

&

Meaning

AUSTRALIAN FILM DIRECTORS IN THEIR OWN WORDS

Myth & Meaning

AUSTRALIAN FILM DIRECTORS IN THEIR OWN WORDS

CURRENCY PRESS
SYDNEY

First published 2001
Currency Press Pty Ltd,
PO Box 2287
Strawberry Hills 2012
www.currency.com.au
enquiries@currency.com.au

NATIONAL LIBRARY OF AUSTRALIA CIP DATA
        Malone, Peter (Peter J.).
        Myth & meaning: Australian film directors in their own words.
        Includes index.
        ISBN 0 86819 609 6.
        1. Motion picture producers and directors – Australia – Interviews. I.
            Title.
        791.430233092294

Designed by Robyn Latimer
Set by Currency Press
Printed by Hyde Park Press

Contents

ACKNOWLEDGEMENTS

The directors interviewed, for their time and interest in reflecting on their films and their values.

Nick Parsons, Deborah Franco, Margaret Leask and the staff of Currency Press for taking on the project and helping with contacts for interviews.

Belinda Johns of Kennedy Miller, the staff at HLA Management.

Phyllis Coffey for her accurately attentive listening in transcribing the interviews.

Introduction

Nick Parsons

When Peter first approached me, some years ago, with the idea for this book, the first thing that impressed me was the breadth of his material – at that point, over seventy interviews. Then I read an extraordinary list of names: A Who's Who of Australian directors.

Towards the top was Bruce Beresford, and as I scanned the first paragraphs I realised that here was something different. This was not a director plugging his latest film, nor was there a focus on salacious industry gossip – although there is some of that. Here was a mature film-maker discussing in depth the meaning of his films, his intentions when making them, and frankly admitting to failure as well as success. Perhaps Peter carries with him something of the atmosphere of the confessional, but all the interviews are characterised by this disarming, sometimes startling candour. Here in a definitive collection, a group of Australia's most prolific and significant directors consider the meaning, or otherwise, of their own careers. What is it that makes these ruminations so fascinating? For me, it's that these are the people to whom, through our funding bodies and private support, we have given the power to make stories about us. If there is an Australian vision, it will be seen in their work.

Perhaps more than any other group, these directors are conscious of being part of a cultural project. As George Miller remarks, somewhat provocatively, film has taken over the role of the Church:

> It was really through the practice of film-making that I had this awareness of the collective unconscious and I sensed its power in some way. I realised that, as film-makers, despite our personal vanities, as storytellers we are the servants of the collective unconscious ...

Scott Hicks remarks on the same feeling when Peter points out the number of recent films, including *Shine*, that deal with mental disturbance:

> *Angel Baby, Cosi, Lilian's Story, Bad Boy Bubby* ... It's a curious thing, isn't it? I don't know what it's to do with, but you could point out things like the collective unconscious, the Jungian notion that somehow these

ideas are present and somehow they get discharged through different forms of expression.

Many of the Australian New-Wave directors have backgrounds that make them sensitive to the Zeitgeist. Gillian Armstrong began in documentary and continues to direct her famous series on the lives of several working-class Australian women that began with *14's Good, 18's Better*. Donald Crombie and Tim Burstall also began in documentary. Esben Storm's first film, *27A*, is a docudrama about institutionalisation. Michael Thornhill in his early days was a reviewer for the *Sydney Morning Herald* and the *Australian*. 'I saw my position as pro-active on two fronts: one was fighting censorship and two was trying to do anything to help get an Australian film industry established.' So from the time when these directors first became interested in feature films, they were already actively engaged in considering and analysing their politics and culture. As Stephen Wallace remarks: 'I suppose I always like those stories of people standing up for their rights ... on the fringes battling ... I think they're the heart of our life.'

UNDERDOGS

Wallace is not alone in being drawn to these characters. The working-class, disenfranchised outsider is a protagonist of almost universal appeal in Australia. Almost all the directors in this book build their films around this character. Beresford's *Barry McKenzie* movies, his *The Club*, *The Money Movers*, *Puberty Blues* and *The Fringe Dwellers* all fit this mould, as do the secondary characters in *Breaker Morant*. Donald Crombie's films – *Caddie*, *The Irishman*, *Cathy's Child* – also centre on working-class characters. Peter Malone himself points out that, since *Bad Boy Bubby*, all Rolf de Heer's films have focussed on 'people on the margin'. Michael Thornhill is the exception that proves the rule: his only working-class film, *FJ Holden*, 'was probably the one people liked the most'. Esben Storm says a recurring theme in his work is 'that of someone trying to break out, someone feeling trapped within themselves, trapped within the system.' Nadia Tass, too, sees herself as a constant questioner of authority:

> Sometimes, as in bureaucracy and in the establishment, we create rules for the sake of simplicity ... for the sake of what? More harmonious bureaucratic functioning? Right. But not for people. It's at the expense of the individual. It's at the expense of human nature.

Frequently, these films have a theme of disenfranchisement, as in *Don's Party*, *Cathy's Child*, *In Search of Anna*, *Breaker Morant*, *Mr Reliable*. Nadia Tass remarks that the only bad review she got for *Malcolm* was from the *New York Post*, on the grounds that it was immoral: 'Malcolm and Frank had robbed a bank and got away with it'. In Australia such criticism is absurd because most Australians do not feel, and have never felt, that they truly have a stake in their own institutions, public or private. Her next film was not so well received in Australia. '*Rikki and Pete* was the one that was recognised most in America. The reviews there were glowing ... and I think it's because it deals with the middle-class platform'. Americans identify with the middle class, which they see as the average. Australians do not.

Stephen Wallace could be speaking for all Australian directors when he remarks:

> Someone said, 'You're always showing dignified people maintaining their dignity no matter what'. I think it's really about ordinary people who are battling in life, who find a way through, because that's how I see myself: an ordinary guy battling my way through to find a voice, to say something in the society, to be important. They aren't extraordinary people, but they're trying to be part of society and be decent people ... I feel that very strongly in Australians: that's ... their greatest quality. Like my mother ... She thought she was ordinary but she was a very insightful, strong character who was – she always used to say about her family – poor but honest.

Our films are a narrative response to our cultural icons, which because of our history, tend to be working-class, or at least social outsiders. Tim Burstall, talking about *Eliza Fraser*, sees Australians as descended from the John Bull Englishman portrayed in *Tom Jones* and other 18th-century novels. Our true nature is ocker, crude, uncultivated. We reject European high culture, but have been trying to create our own ever since. Where we encounter class we tend to lampoon it. Our film portrayals of the upper class are almost universally pasquinades.

Conversely, Australians find it hard to build successful films around characters that are not low status. Simon Wincer has directed two films set in the 1880s: *Quigley* and *Lightning Jack*. The former, about an American in the outback, did well in the United States but failed in Australia. 'The film was well reviewed in America, particularly in the trade magazines, because they thought it was a frontier classic. It did pretty well theatrically ... So I was really disappointed in the way it was just dismissed in Australia.' Australians are used to Americans telling us what to do, and are sensitive about it. Quigley himself, despite his profession, is a high-status character who would always be able to handle himself.

By contrast, *Lightning Jack*, about an Australian in the Wild West, was inspired by 'the third cowboy on the left [who] gets away ... the sort of mystery guy who's an underling in a bank hold-up ... That was where Paul [Hogan] really took it from. He wanted to poke gentle fun at the Western genre.' The film worked in Australia.

It follows, of course, that Australia has never been a classless society: there have always been those on the side of authority and those on the side of the common man. Simon Wincer nominated *Phar Lap* as his favourite film because:

> there was something about that horse: he came from the wrong side of the tracks ... he was a working-class horse, if you like. He became an icon because people knew they could go to the course and put a bob on Phar Lap and they would get their money back. I think that has very deep roots in the them-and-us thing, which has always been big in Australia. I suppose that goes back to the convict days because not only was Phar Lap trained by a battler and half owned by a battler, but the other half owner was Jewish and American to boot, so that was really shoving it up the establishment and the squattocracy.

It was the Irish convicts that created the spirit of the country. Their sense of injustice and rebelliousness was in time transformed into Australian nationalism. Phil Noyce remarks, 'I think that Australia and the Australian character has been formed through the confrontation between Irish Catholicism and Anglicanism and of course these are, at least in part, seemingly irreconcilable philosophies.'

The first generation born in Australia was referred to as the 'Currency' – from the erratic hotch-potch of regional money and defaced Spanish coins circulating in the colony – as opposed to the British 'Sterling' that always retained its full value. While the Currency lads and lasses struggled to form a national identity of their own, the Sterling and their progeny and imitators identified strongly with an overseas ruling elite. Their greatest need was for respectability, which in essence meant acceptance by members of their class overseas. The character of the ocker exists in direct opposition to that idea. He is determinedly crude, undignified, cynical, because this is the most effective way of establishing his difference.

Nadia Tass: '... American comedy is different from Australian comedy. It is broader. American audiences enjoyed [her first U.S. feature] *Pure Luck* ... I would like to have put a lot more pathos and pain into it. But they wanted a comedy for America'. We don't respond to comedy unless it's painful. Convict humour was cruel: boxing matches between amputees, each supported by an able-bodied man behind him, for example, were a favoured pastime. This tradition has been carried down to films like *Muriel's Wedding* and *The Adventures of Priscilla, Queen of the Desert*.

HARD MEN

With the possible exception of Stephen Wallace, Australian directors are universally unsentimental. Gillian Armstrong recalls that she was offered

Little Women because they 'didn't want to over-sentimentalise it, didn't want it to be a *Color Purple Little Women*'. Sentimentality has at its core the belief that human sensibility is of intrinsic value. That's not the experience of most Australians, who believe that personal sentiment is only of value to the person feeling it. Our abhorrence of sentimentality is thus linked to our taciturn nature. The legacy of a brutalised past is that Australian men are afraid their feelings will be ridiculed, and are consequently ashamed of them. Films like Wallace's *For Love Alone*, that openly discuss characters' feelings, tend to fail in Australia although that film did well in France. Wallace had similar trouble with his war film *Blood Oath*: 'A lot of people criticised it, I think, because it wasn't as accurate as it should have been – and it was a bit melodramatic ... In America and in Japan they didn't criticise this at all; in Australia they did'.

Our fear of ridicule is symptomatic of our inability to trust, which manifests in a certain cynicism, particularly about those in power, but including ourselves. Discipline under the convict system was sustained by a network of informers. Consequently loyalty was highly valued among the convicts; a quality we have retained to this day. 'Mateship' is one of the unassailable values of our nation – to the extent that our Prime Minister attempted to have it enshrined in the preamble to the Constitution. But its converse, treachery, is also a strong theme in Australian film.

Gallipoli, *Breaker Morant* and *The Club* are all films in which the protagonists devote themselves to an ideal – and that devotion is ultimately used to betray them. But in both *The Club* and another Beresford film, *Don's Party*, the protagonists also betray themselves. Don's mates yearn for a Labor victory leading to a Socialist utopia, but betray that ideal in their own lives. In doing so they stand for the Australian public that for so long (in the paradigm of the film) voted against its own interests. Similarly, in *The Club*, the position of the principled coach is threatened by businessmen and big money with the assistance of turncoat board members. In another David Williamson script, *Petersen*, directed by Tim Burstall, Petersen is an electrician aspiring to a university education. Burstall himself sees it as a class film in which Petersen, by returning to what is familiar, really betrays himself. The message is clear: Australians cannot even trust themselves.

In fact, in Australia the only sphere of endeavour that is considered morally pure is sport. In *The Club*, *Phar Lap* and even *Puberty Blues* achievement in sport is an ideal that transcends the more sordid action in those films. In *Gallipoli* the running race is an extended metaphor for the innocence of Australian youth.

From the days of the Rum Corps Australians have retained a suspicion of any achievement that may be attributed to money or connections; sport is the arena in which the rich have no apparent advantage over the poor. The high moral fibre we require from our sporting heroes, as opposed to our politicians, testifies how strongly we identify with them. We are suspicious of our intellectuals because historically they have come from the middle and upper classes – and still do, despite years of universal free education. Too much education is a sign of class treachery. The only kind of intellectual we respect is the autodidact, the working-class poet.

America's first settlers arrived in search of religious freedom. They fought a war of independence for political freedom, and they believe they fought a civil war to free African-Americans from slavery. Having won, they have earned the right to aspire to the best that their society has to offer. We, on the other hand, have always felt excluded from privilege. Because we never had a war of independence we never established an aristocracy of our own. Our notion of Australia's ruling class has historically been an essentially ersatz English one or, more latterly, as a new elite base their power on the communications revolution, ersatz American. Either way, for the average Australian, too much aspiration is akin to class treason.

LOST IN THE DESERT

For a country founded as a penal colony it is remarkable that 'freedom' as an ideal has so little place in the national psyche. But in a sense Australians have always had a good measure of freedom. Very few convicts were actually imprisoned; the lack of housing stock in the early colony made this almost impossible, and in any case, the hostile country bounded on all sides by sea was in itself a prison. A convict's primary punishment was his or her exile. Consequently the theme of deracination is much stronger in our culture and our films than that of imprisonment, although the latter certainly has a place. *Picnic at Hanging Rock*, *The Getting of Wisdom* and *My Brilliant Career* are all films that reflect the theme of exile. It is the juxtaposition of Australian bush and English dress and manners that forms their basic conflict. All these films are about young women, at odds with their environment, but finding themselves.

Hand in hand with deracination is the notion of being lost, physically and spiritually, and this also is a powerful theme in Australian film, as it is in art and literature. *Evil Angels*, about the disappearance of baby Azaria Chamberlain, is the story of innocence swallowed by the desert – our most potent, if subconscious, national myth.

But this myth appears in many forms: Tim Burstall's *Alvin Purple* and its sequel are a comic reversal of the idea: the timid Alvin lost in a wilderness of sexually aggressive women. Rolf de Heer's *Bad Boy Bubby* is also the story of an infantilised man emerging into a hostile environment. His earlier film,

Dingo, is about a boy who has to go to Paris – away from the culturally sterile desert – before his musical talent is recognised. Scott Hicks describes *Sebastian and the Sparrow* as 'a kind of junior buddy movie with the theme of two people who envied each other's life': the sense of not belonging where they are. Schepisi says that Jimmie's terrible fate in *The Chant of Jimmie Blacksmith* is caused by 'the Churches' belief that ... they're going to go and save the heathen and take them out of that world'.

In the same interview Peter Malone rhetorically asks, about *Evil Angels*, 'Would it have made such an impact if the Chamberlains were not Adventist, if it had not taken place with dingoes at Uluru? That's why it stayed in the Australian psyche'. Schepisi can only agree. Religion in Australian film is almost always portrayed as a form of blindness. Rolf de Heer remarks, '*Bubby* became a film about belief systems: spiritual, religious, scientific, interpersonal and how, by clinging to them in order to try to make sense of the world, we are actually prevented from making sense of it.' Religion made the Chamberlains less trustworthy to the average Australian – in the United States it would not have been an issue.

Yet despite this, as Peter Malone himself points out, although we might think of Australia as a secular society, 'the census would indicate that it's not'. We are in fact fairly religious and the movies of these film-makers are highly influenced by the Biblical themes of faith, betrayal and the wilderness. To take the work of just one director, Fred Schepisi, religious themes or characters appear in *The Priest*, *The Devil's Playground*, *The Chant of Jimmie Blacksmith* and *Evil Angels*. By contrast in his American movies, *Barbarossa*, *The Iceman*, *Plenty*, *Roxanne*, *The Russia House*, *Mr Baseball*, and *IQ* they are hardly in evidence. So why do we have the impression that Australians are irreligious? Perhaps it's not so much that we don't believe in God; we're just angry with Him.

Esben Storm's forthcoming *Subterano* is a sci-fi movie in which a child kills people with remote-controlled toys. 'One of the themes is: if there is a God, what if that God is a prick; what if that God is just a bastard? For one of the characters, when he thinks that, it all makes sense.' Gillian Armstrong's *Oscar and Lucinda* shows us God and gambling as twin obsessions of the Australian character. Eventually this becomes God as gambling, expressed through the wager over the glass church and the love story. In other words, God cares for us as much as random fate.

John Ruane, on *That Eye, the Sky*, perceives: 'Ort is cursing, saying that his dad is better than any other dad, so why was he taken away? It's at that moment, when he goes outside, that the light appears ... It's as if it's the father, whichever father, answering the little boy with a miracle or a visual message that only the little boy receives'.

INNOCENT ABORIGINES

Being preoccupied with our own banishment and innocence, we become uncomfortable around the subject of the Aboriginal inhabitants. Because Aborigines have been genuinely disenfranchised they make a good subject for drama and are consequently over-represented in Aussie films despite the fact that Australian audiences have an aversion to Aboriginal stories. George Miller refers to our current Prime Minister John Howard's conviction that the 'stolen generations' are better left in the past:

> Australia is never going to be a grown-up country until it can deal with its indigenous history in a mature way ... It's clear that something has been greatly lost. It's not unique to Australia and has happened in all the continents ... But, in all those cases, they have been able to confront the past ... in Australia we haven't.

Esben Storm believes the same thing:

> The whole colonisation process and the invasion and stealing of the land from the indigenous people is a weeping sore. I think the country needs to come to terms with this or else it will never be able to move on. The present government probably takes the attitude that, if we starve them they'll die out and there won't be a problem any more, which is pretty much how civilisation works.

In *Deadly*, Storm consciously attempted to treat racial politics within a popular genre:

> Clint Eastwood ... All his movies are set in the mid-west with rednecks, bounty hunters. The majority of cinema-going audiences love Clint Eastwood movies. So I was trying to make this kind of movie ... If I had a sort of Clint Eastwood-y lead character, who starts as a racist, then basically we're saying this guy is the audience. He goes on a journey and by the end of the film he's holding a black man's hand, he's sort of fallen in love with a black woman and has found within himself the capacity to see that these people are just like him ... Racism and prejudice are very subtle, insidious. So it was a conscious thing to make a film that would play to the heart of the problem.

Storm correctly identifies his audience. Racism has always been more prevalent among the working class, and in the country, than it has amongst the middle class and the city. This may originate from the fact that Aborigines originally enjoyed a better relationship with colonial authorities than the convicts themselves; in fact they were used as an unofficial police force, bringing back escapees. Official policy has always had as its aim peaceful coexistence. Even the notorious policy of forced removal of children, disastrous for so many families, had as its aim the integration of Aboriginal people into mainstream Australian society – by the standards of the day, radically liberal.

But Clint Eastwood, no matter how well disguised, is not an Australian icon. He is too sophisticated, too high-status. Storm's hero is further undermined by the fact that the film judges his racist views from the start. His personal journey becomes predictable. As Storm himself admits, Australians don't think of themselves as racist, and consequently did not identify.

Bruce Beresford also tackled Aboriginality in *The Fringe Dwellers*, despite the warning, 'Nobody wants to watch a film about a bunch of Aborigines':

> It's about a group of very recognisable human beings. It is not political, dogmatic or didactic and it is free of all the usual clichés and political posturing. The treatment of Aborigines over the years ... has moulded the Aboriginal character and is largely responsible for the way they present themselves today, but the past – colour, racism, mistreatment and all the rest of it – is not a central theme of the film. It is implicit but, to me, the story is one of a family, their relationships, struggles, aspirations.

All our favourite Australian characters appear, as it were, in blackface: strong women, colourful, comic losers, handsome independent working-class young men, feisty young girls. Yet despite good critical response the film failed to catch the popular imagination. (By contrast, Beresford's other film about colonisation, *Black Robe*, about European missionaries in Canada, had more success. In this case, however, the dynamic is reversed: the Indians have much more power than the missionary, Laforgue.) White Australians cherish the mantle of the underdog and don't wish to surrender it. Once Aboriginal characters take this role, white Australia is cast as their oppressor – a role that is anathema.

Nevertheless, as George Miller says, only when we can face Aboriginal Australia squarely and apologise will we be setting ourselves on the road to maturity.

PRESERVATION OF INNOCENCE

Being grown up, however, is not something Australian characters do easily. Phillip Noyce, discussing *Heatwave*, comments, 'He, as a working-class boy, of course, was now forced to confront the moral implications of his own success and how that affected other people.' Even though this may be closer to the truth for most Australians, we prefer stories of powerless, abused, abandoned, but guiltless protagonists. Scott Hicks says of *Shine*, 'Part of the story, for me, was about failed rites of passage, of someone who is not allowed to grow up'. And reflected also in the story of the father is the disenfranchised migrant in a hostile place. Talking to Geoffrey Rush about the role of David Helfgott, Hicks told him:

> 'Well, it's about redemption. It's about someone who can go through terrible experiences in his life but emerge on the other side, in love, playing music and accepted for who he is.' That sparked something with Geoffrey. He felt there was a big theme behind this, not just the playing out of an everyday story.

In a way Hicks could be talking about almost any Australian film. *Babe* has the same story, as does *Strictly Ballroom*. Miller's *Lorenzo's Oil* takes into an American context the theme of innocent and bewildered characters facing a hostile universe.

Discussing the Gallipoli campaign, historically seen as a 'blooding'of Australians, a rite of passage to maturity, George Miller remarks, 'There is something particularly Australian once again about a war where men die heroically but somewhat foolishly, heroically but innocently. They did not glorify warmongering but glorified sacrifice.' Peter Weir's *Gallipoli*, taking exactly this line, was enormously successful, while Stephen Wallace's less heroic *Blood Oath* was not: 'We found that young Australians weren't very interested. They didn't want to know about the War. They didn't want to know about the Japanese. The film didn't do all that well here but it did very well in Japan. The Japanese soldiers at Ambon came to see it, had a big dinner and they said they were very glad the film had been made.' The film deals with an Australian war-crimes trial in which Japanese military leaders are let off the hook, while a young Christian Japanese soldier becomes the scapegoat. Our own purity is sullied. In Beresford's *Breaker Morant*, the court is British and the Australian soldiers morally, if not literally, innocent victims.

Our troubled relationship with authority is often expressed in characters' relationship with their fathers. *That Eye, the Sky* is about a young boy whose father falls into a coma and whose family is, consequently, impoverished. The film (and book) is about reconciling this situation with the idea of a benign God (more or less the theme of *Oscar and Lucinda*). Another of John Ruane's films, *Dead Letter Office*, is about a girl searching for her father. Nadia Tass says of *Rikki and Pete*: 'What they were questioning initially was their father. It was through their father that the system was represented very strongly'. Stephen Wallace's *The Boy Who Had Everything* is about a boy achiever who gives everything up to do drama. This film did well in Europe, but 'Everyone in Australia hated it'. Aussies don't identify with achievers. John Duigan's *The Year My Voice Broke* and *Flirting* are also coming-of-age stories, but with a working-class outsider at the heart. These films were much more popular.

OUR OWN STORIES

Unquestionably, on the evidence, there is an Australian vision. It derives not so much from a set of common values as an evolving set of assumptions about how society functions that originate with the traumatic birth of our colony. This vision is reflected, sometimes successfully, sometimes not, in the films of the directors interviewed here. What it means however is less important than the fact that it is ours. The best films, the films that justify government support for an otherwise expensive industry, are culturally specific. Stephen Wallace comments:

> Scott Hicks had made two or three features before *Shine* and Rolf de Heer had made two before *Bad Boy Bubby* ... All of a sudden, out of the blue, they make a film which startles everyone. It's just extraordinary. And my question is: why? What's happened? Something different has happened for them. It happened to Bob Connolly in documentary. He had been working for years at the ABC ... All of a sudden he made *First Contact*.
>
> Basically, what happened with Rolf de Heer and Scott Hicks is that they decided they would make a film they really cared about, that came from their hearts, came from inside themselves, and they weren't going to compromise. They would wait years to make it, if necessary. I think they found their voice ... And once you do that, you've got something special and people respond to it.

This in itself has created a dilemma for Australian film-makers. Their subject matter is national, regional, local. But private finance, the lifeblood of our film industry, is global, borderless, and investors expect films to recoup in a global marketplace. There is growing pressure on film-makers to produce stories that are acceptable to an international audience. And to a degree this approach can yield success. Australian characters are populating world cinema as our directors continue to make films outside Australia. Phillip Noyce's *Clear and Present Danger* takes the naive central character, out of his depth, into the context of an American action adventure. Jane Campion and Nicole Kidman paralleled this achievement in *Portrait of a Lady*. But is it enough for Australians simply to acculturate their archetypes in this way?

The locally successful and critically acclaimed television series *Wildside* was recently axed because it failed in the international marketplace, despite the fact that it clearly spoke to the Australian audience for whom it was intended. Australians have never been great supporters of their culture, even if they are enthusiastic consumers of it. More and more our ruling class is becoming part of a global community of business elite, and their sympathy and loyalty are principally to them. Lip service is paid to the old egalitarian values but the gap between rich and poor continues to grow and competition for work increases. Alliances have changed, of course: America and the global marketplace are the new mother country; the economic elite argue that our future is 'globalisation' just as their forefathers once argued that our future was to be the breadbasket of Great Britain. As borderless technology reaches more and more deeply into our homes, will globalisation inevitably mean conformity? Will we finally become a nationless people? Or is the Aussie character sufficiently robust that, regardless of all intrusions, our primary allegiance will remain to our own tribe?

As I write, demonstrators are disbursing from around the World Economic Forum. Their protest was coordinated via the Internet – borderless technology in defence of borders – and images of violent protest have been flashing around our globalised media. Whatever our leaders may claim, there is a long way to go before globalisation goes beyond economic theory and takes root in the common mind.

It is a question that exercises our film directors in this book, poised as they are between their Australian natures and their global careers. I live in hope that, despite the odds and despite its curious diffidence, the Australian character will survive. It has survived two hundred years; and, given the scepticism with which the average Australian regards the world at large, it is likely to survive two hundred more.

Gillian Armstrong

Gillian Armstrong with Bruno Ganz, *The Last Days of Chez Nous*, 1991.
(Documentation Collection, ScreenSound Australia.)

My first short was *The Roof Needs Mowing*, my Swinburne graduation film. After I'd been out in the wilds working as an assistant editor for a year, I was accepted into the first year of the National Film School, and in that twelve months we were given the budgets to make three short films. The brief for the first was to choose a short story by a well-known Australian writer. They had approached a number of writers for ideas and Alan Marshall had sent an excerpt from his book, *How Beautiful Are Thy Feet,* which was *One Hundred a Day.*

The second film was meant to be a documentary, but I was quite pigheaded about wanting to be a drama director. I actually went to the Head and said, 'I've only got three films and I really want to keep going in drama', and he suggested doing a dramatised documentary. One of the people I was sharing a house with at the time, Stuart Campbell, told me about this event in his life and we partly re-created it, *Satdee Night*. It was really one of the first gay films in Sydney. I structured the film so you knew it was a big Saturday night out and the audience was meant to feel that he was going out to find a young woman: he was getting ready, he was nervous, then, when he finally gets to this dance, it's an all-male dance. We did film at a real gay dance at Glebe Town Hall. It was a very big deal in those days to actually allow a film crew in.

I thought the story had a lovely comic-tragic twist because, after this build-up, which actually did happen to Stuart in real life, he got so nervous and drank so much before he went to the dance – these dances used to be held every two months, so it was very hard for young gay men to meet each other at that time and he built his hopes up so much that when he got there, he passed out in the first five minutes, woke up next morning on the floor, locked in the empty Town Hall under all the streamers.

That was a true story and I thought it had a lovely poignancy, so we re-enacted it with Stuart playing himself and really getting drunk and really filming at a gay dance. He has run into many people over the years who've said it was quite a seminal film, one of the first films where they saw an Australian gay young man, his pain and problems.

It turned out to be quite hard to make three films in one year; we were very busy and I was desperately looking for a final script, so I went back to the original pile of Australian authors and chose a Hal Porter short story, which was 'Gretel'.

I think David Stratton selected *Gretel* for the Sydney Film Festival and *One Hundred a Day* was in the Dendy short film awards at the Festival, which was pretty amazing. It won Best Cinematography and Best Editing. So those films and the profile, I suppose, that they gave me really kick-started my career.

2

You won the Dendy award for The Singer and the Dancer, *another Alan Marshall story.*

Alan had been a delight to work with on *One Hundred a Day*. At the film school we were very privileged to have access to these wonderful writers. He was very encouraging and told me the details because he really did work in a shoe factory as a young man in the 1930s, so he gave me great background details to think about for visualising it. But I always felt that, as a story, it was very filmic because it was written in a rhythm, the rhythm of the factory. So we struck up a friendship and he was very happy with the film.

After I graduated at the end of that year, I worked in art departments, for Tom Cowan's *Promised Woman*, and worked with John Duigan as his designer on *The Trespassers*. Then *Gretel* was selected for the Student Film Festival in Grenoble. It was the first time Australian student films had been submitted because we were the first year of the National Film School. Phillip Noyce and I were chosen. So we both did everything we could to make sure, as we got the fare to Europe, that we could go and see the world.

So Phillip and his then wife, the producer Jan Chapman, and I backpacked around the world for a year. It was a wonderful thing because we met all these other student film-makers at the festival and we visited them in their countries as we were on our little Eurail passes. We met a film-maker again in Vienna and someone else in Munich and what we realised at that time was how lucky Australians were that we had this Experimental Film Fund, as it was called then, for money for short films. But all the time we were away, there was all this talk that there was going to be a change in government and that Labor would be out and all the grants would go. So Phil and I both decided by the end of the year that we'd better get home and we'd better make something fast.

When I got back, I started working on a number of scripts and Alan had actually sent me another story that he thought I might like. It was about old Mrs Bilson – it was even called 'Old Mrs Bilson'. I liked the central part of the story and the character of the woman, but I really wanted to do something contemporary because both *Gretel* and *One Hundred a Day* had been set in the past. I rang him and said, 'What if I make this a story where she meets a young woman and this is really the beginning?' He said, 'That's fine, but I can't write what the young woman would say. I'll write what the old woman would say; you write what the young woman would say.' And that's what we did. I came up with the characters who went to the country, Charley and a boyfriend, and we mingled that with the story that had always been there about Mrs Bilson. You find out about her past through the story.

It was a great insight into those women of the country, the changing times and their stubbornness. Ruth Cracknell personified her.

Yes, it was funny because Ruth played older then – she was actually quite a young woman. Part of the plot was that she had to run down those hills; she used to sneak out and have a feeling of freedom as she ran. The real story was that Neva Carr-Glynn was going to play Mrs Bilson. I met her and talked about it and the next day it was in the paper that she'd died. I was actually the last person to see her alive, and I got such a fright because the last thing I'd said to her was, 'Now, you're sure you'll be all right running down those hills?' Imagine what would have happened if we'd all been out and she'd died running down the hill. I would have felt it was my fault forever!

After that I thought it was too risky and I'd better look for someone younger. Then I met with Ruth and she has such an extraordinary presence and power. It's funny that all those years later she became famous playing in *Mother and Son*, because we made her look that age in *The Singer and Dancer*. I'm very proud of Ruth's performance in it. I think she did a wonderful job.

The Smokes and Lollies *series?*

The South Australian Film Corporation had set up a unit in the early 1970s. It was called the 'One-to-One Unit' and it was to encourage women film-makers, subjects about women, with women on the crew. They got special funding because it was helping the employment of women. I went down and was actually assigned a project. I didn't have any say. 'We want you to do this one about what it's like to be 14 today', and I know they chose me to do that one because I always looked so young for my age – I had a big, round baby face!

I had a researcher who had started work and it was pretty open about what sort of 14-year-old we would have. The first night I was there she said she'd found out about a youth drop-in centre in an inner-city area and asked, would I be interested in coming along. So we went together. Kerry, Josie and Diana were the only three girls there, if I remember correctly. But there were forty Greek and Italian boys and three girls, because it was an inner-city area in Adelaide that had quite a big Greek and Italian population and they weren't going to let their daughters out, even though it was a government-run youth drop-in centre. Anyway, the girls came up and started chatting to me because they thought I was coming to join – so Penny Chapman's instinct about my baby face paid off – and they thought the researcher was my mother.

Because we were discussing age, they said, 'Well, how old are you?' And I said, 'I'm over 21'. I think I was 24. The first thing they said to me was, 'Are you married?' And I was really quite surprised, because part of the brief –

4

what I think we originally all thought the film would be about – was the new 14-year-old, the more modern, liberated 14-year-old. And I said, 'No. When am I meant to be married by? Am I over the hill at 21?' And they all said, '18'.

I was telling Penny this the next day and she said, 'They sound great. Go for it'. So I went back to them and said, 'We're making a film about what it's like to be 14', and they all thought about it and said, 'We'll be in it but we only want to be in it if it's honest, if it's really what it's like to be 14'. I said, 'I want you to be honest. That would be great'. And that was the beginning. They were fantastic subjects and they let us follow them around.

That film had an extraordinary effect that I was very proud of. It was run at places like the Institute for Adolescent Studies, Children's Hospital in Melbourne. The feedback I got was that they were using it as a teaching tool because it's so hard to actually get the real feelings and opinions of young girls for psychiatrists and doctors to really know what they're thinking today. Because I had spent the time with them and they had got very relaxed with me and they had also decided the whole point was to be honest, it became a very important teaching tool.

As time went by, I thought it would be really interesting to go back and see what happened to them. I've always been interested in time and what happens to people over time and I thought, 'I've caught them at 14 and they talked so much about being 18, why don't I go back?' Hilary Linstead became my co-producer and we went to Film Australia and managed to get the money to do *14's Good, 18's Better*.

Once I'd shot the second one and we'd cut the two together, I realised how lucky I was, capturing people growing up, talking about the hopes and dreams, because the three – well, especially two of them – had done a lot of living in the four years, more than most of us, so there was great story material there: the time gap, their physical changes, how their faces had changed. That was the first time anyone had ever done anything like that. I had no idea about *Seven Up*. I think it came out in Australia about the time I was going back to do number three.

It had an extraordinary effect; people were really moved by it. I remember I went to Canberra to lobby for the film industry – we went to have dinner and Bill Hayden, Susan Ryan and so on wanted to ask me about Josie and the blonde girl in the old car, and I felt very pleased. They said they had really learned a lot about people's lives. And you think, 'Well, these are the people who are making the decisions about health and welfare and education', and I felt fantastic that by just having a chance to get to know some people intimately it broke down a lot of the clichés; the clichés of the school dropout or the unmarried mother. And, of course, once I'd done the two, I had the tremendous pressure of, 'You've got to go back. Everyone will want to know what's going to happen to them next'.

5

You went back almost a decade later?

After I did the 18-year-old one, I thought that normally the most significant age in life is 21, but since that was only three years away, I thought I'd come back when they were 25. But I was shooting *High Tide* that year, so I actually went back when they were 26. That's how I ended up with the seven-year thing, which starts paralleling *Seven Up*. Because Diane had the new baby at the end of *14's Good*, when we came back it was her 7-year-old's birthday, so we got into the pattern of seven.

Then, of course, I wanted to come back when that baby was 14, the very age her mother was when we started. None of us ever thought that in such a short span we would get that cycle and see another adolescent generation.

There is great change from the 1970s to the 1990s. You were surprised when they initially asked about getting married. You've seen their marriages, the break-ups and the families. Not 14 Again *is very optimistic in terms of their having a life and having dealt with the problems of the past.*

Yes, it's a great advertisement for being in your late thirties. All of them have really come of age and found themselves as people and are very comfortable with who they are and what their lives are. They've all still got the normal ups and downs, things that aren't necessarily easy: Kerry's husband with his bad back and he may have to give up work; Josie trying to make ends meet with the pub and a young family. But I felt that as people they had really matured and were very happy with themselves in their lives.

With the last film we had some money from the BBC and they were completely amazed. 'This just doesn't happen in England. People from poor families, you don't suddenly see them with nice houses and nice clothes.' And I said to the English producer, 'But listen to their stories, how hard they've worked'. In that middle time Josie was working two jobs and Kerry delayed having a family until they could put the deposit on the house: they've worked very hard.

The films capture so many changes in Australian society in that 20 years, from the food we eat and consciousness of diet and health to the male role in a marriage. Two of the families have done complete back-flips where the woman has become the breadwinner and the father has been the one looking after the children, and there's no longer any guilt or a problem. I think it shows a very positive side for all those fathers: how they've been much more involved in the bringing up of their children than the generation before.

You're lucky to have been asked to be a chronicler of almost a quarter of a century of Australian society.

Yes. It went by very fast. And I was very lucky that the girls and their families were so generous to have been part of it.

My Brilliant Career was a landmark film and important for you.

I find all my films are very painful for me to look at, because I just see either my creative or my technical inadequacies. Certainly there are moments – and all the actors' performances – that are a joy. If they're ever on TV and I'm walking by, I may stop because I remember that wonderful moment with Ruth or with Judy or with Claudia. I don't think I've seen *My Brilliant Career* for ten or twelve years. I think it was on Australian television maybe about ten years ago and I thought, 'I'll just have a look at the beginning to see the quality and whether the print looks all right', and I did get caught up in watching the story again: 'Oh, look at Judy, she's so young, so beautiful. It's sad'. For me, it's like watching old home movies.

There are a lot of things that came together. I was very privileged to have Don McAlpine as cinematographer and Luciana Arrighi as the designer, and finding Judy and Sam. But all the cast were great. Robert Grubb and Aileen Britten and Patricia Kennedy and Wendy Hughes: they're a wonderful cast and that's what I enjoyed when I watched again: watching them, and also remembering how much humour was in it.

After Picnic at Hanging Rock *(dir. Peter Weir) and* The Getting of Wisdom *(dir. Bruce Beresford), a criticism emerged that our cinema was going back too much to stories of our past.*

At the time Margaret Fink had a hard time raising the money because they said 'Australians don't want to see another film set in the past'. She fought and we all fought and said, 'We think it's not the same as the others. It's got something very contemporary to say'. I've done interviews in recent years with American journalists who were probably still at primary school when it opened, and it sounds pathetic when you say that, at the time, it was actually extremely radical that at the end a heroine did not end up in the arms of the hero, riding off into the sunset together; that was considered to be so brave and outrageous.

It probably did a lot for the independence of women.

I have met women journalists in America who started their career because of that film. You feel humbled. At the time I had letters from people saying, 'I was so affected by it and I went home, talked to my mother and then took my mother to see the film'. A woman even interviewed me on the set of *Little Women* and she had a high-quality Victoriana antique magazine and she said, 'I opened this magazine after seeing *My Brilliant Career*. It was so beautiful and I've always loved Victoriana'.

When you make a film, you hope that it will work, that it will touch people, but it's certainly even more wonderful if it has had an effect on people's lives.

Myth & Meaning

There was a message in the film that says 'You've got to find what you love and what you're passionate about and you should search it out'. It has had that effect on a lot of people. It's also had an effect that for the last twenty years everyone has thought that that character is me and that that character is Judy! She finds it a greater chain around her neck than I do, but they think that we are Sybilla.

Your three Australian-made films from 1982 to 1992 have contemporary settings.

I went looking for something that was contemporary after *My Brilliant Career* because I was showered with scripts from America and everywhere and I realised how easy it was to be categorised: endless scripts of the first woman to fly a plane, the first woman to ride a camel, the first woman to climb a mountain. I was suddenly the director who does women achievers in the past. *My Brilliant Career* was a book that Margaret Fink found. It was her passion, then I read it and fell in love with it and wanted to do it. But I always thought that I didn't want to spend the rest of my life doing films that were only about young women battling to achieve. There are a lot of other parts of me and there are a lot of other types of cinema that I like.

I think I was developing something that was set in the near future or a futuristic world when I heard through friends about Stephen McLean's script for *Starstruck* and they all said, 'You've got to read it, it's great'. We chased after David Elfick and his reaction was, 'Oh, she's that director that does lace'. It was very lucky that I met Stephen McLean separately and found out he was the writer. I told him how much I loved his script and then he spoke to David and put in a good word for me.

But I did see *Starstruck* only two months ago on Los Angeles TV on a Sunday morning. I was flicking channels, there was Jo Kennedy doing 'She's Got Body, She's Got Soul'. I was so thrilled. I didn't know who I could ring to tell them because it was Sunday morning in Los Angeles. It looked good, it had stood the test of time better than I thought. It was a good print and sounded good.

Inner-city battlers, family and joy?

I always thought Stephen wrote with great love of his characters. He actually grew up in a pub in Port Melbourne and his mother was a barmaid, so in some ways it was a tongue-in-cheek take-off of Mickey Rooney and Judy Garland, 'Let's put on a show', but it was also a sweet story of a brother and sister and how the brother was the brains and the sister had the talent; how they had been an inseparable duo who, finally, will be pulled apart. And it's funny because all the people who wanted to categorise me, that my only focus was women achieving, immediately said, 'Oh, now she's done this film with another redhead; she only likes redheads who are trying to achieve'. I related to the brother-sister story. It's Angus's story. Jackie's certainly the star, but it's Angus's story. I suppose it's very loving about fighting to get there – in a show-business sense – as they do.

Is High Tide *about a non-achieving woman?*

Yes, definitely, and she hasn't got red hair.

What brought you to High Tide?

I went to America, did *Mrs Soffel,* which was the first American script that was sent to me where I was hooked and really felt connected to the story. I knew it was based on a true story about a middle-aged woman who fell in love with a prisoner, left her husband who was the warder of the jail, and helped two prisoners escape. The thing that fascinated me in that story was why. Why would she do something that was so immoral at that time?

And she was such a biblical person.

Such a biblical person, and it was the fascination with that sort of great passion that they had for each other that the writer and I felt. We read all the research. After the break-out the press all thought that they would find them separately, that she was obviously used and would have been dumped. The thing that was incredible and that attracted both Ron Nyswaner and myself was that they stuck together. This was the suicidal thing to do, because she slowed him down, and they were much more easy targets. So it was the fascination of what happened between these two people who were so disparate, a very conservative, God-fearing woman and this terribly handsome, charismatic prisoner and poetry writer that Mel played.

Then I came back to have my first child. Even though I had a lot of other offers from America, I thought it was a whole new world dealing with the studio system, a much more stressful one, suddenly having ten bosses and a committee and all the politics that are involved with a film with a higher budget, working with the studio system that just doesn't happen here when you've got an independent film and one or two producers to answer to.

I didn't know how I was going to manage to still make films and be a mother, and I thought the number-one thing is to try to do it with a team of close friends in an un-stressful environment. Film-making is stressful because nothing ever goes right, you never get the right weather and so on – it's battling the compromises every day. I'd met Laura Jones – she and I had worked on developing *Clean Straw for Nothing* which was never made because it was deemed too expensive.

We went to the wonderful Sandra Levy who had been our script editor and said, 'We want to get something made and we're going to try and make it a very small film to keep the budget as low as possible'. It's very hard starting from nothing, thinking you're going to write the great film, because by the end of two weeks you feel like all you're doing is, 'That's not good enough, that's not good enough'. So we said, 'Let's pretend we're writing a tiny, tiny film; it's just going to be very small and doesn't really matter'.

I had stayed at a caravan park years ago, driving between Sydney and Melbourne with my sister. It was in the Eden area and I thought it would be a great setting for a film: the people who are permanent dwellers in caravan parks. I had also, as a teenager, been quite interested in and followed surfing culture and always thought it would be great to do a story there. At that time the adoption laws had just been opened up in Australia and there were a lot of stories about people finding their birth mothers. I remembered I had cut out an article about a woman in her sixties who had found her mother in her eighties and how much it meant to her. I was intrigued by that: the strength of that blood tie.

It was originally written for a man, a surfer who came to a small south-coast town, and in the water he got to know this young girl who's surfing. She turns out to be his daughter. We had raised the money with Hemdale and we'd started casting and looked at a list of twenty men's names. Then that night I saw *Wrong World* (dir. Ian Pringle) at the Chauvel. I rang Laura and Sandra and said, 'You know, it really worries me about the alienated drifting man being affected by the truth and honesty of a young girl. I feel we've seen it before and I just saw it last night in *Wrong World*'. It was my partner who said, 'Why don't you just change it to a woman?' And I was saying, 'No, no, everyone thinks we're going to do something about women because it's a woman producer and a woman writer. We don't want to do something with women. We're going to do something with a man'.

We went in the next day to cast with Liz Mullinar and I said, 'You know the man in his early thirties? Well, that's now a woman in her early thirties'. And she said without a blink, 'Then you know who there is. Here are our four best leading actresses and one of them is Judy and, if you want Judy, I know she's been offered a play in London and she has to decide by tomorrow.' They all looked at me and said, 'So, do you want Judy?' And I went, 'Well, I suppose there's nobody better'. So we had to send Judy the script and say that the main character called John is the one we want you to play, but we will rewrite it around you. Laura and I went to meet with her, 'Look, it's totally open. Do you want her to be a working-class girl or middle-class or whatever?' And she said, 'Well, actually I've never played middle-class, close to myself'. I knew she had been a back-up singer after she left high school and went around Asia with a tacky little band. Because we needed a reason for her to be drifting, going from town to town to run into the daughter, I said, 'Why don't we make her a back-up singer? Wouldn't that be great?' So that's how we wrote the script.

Gillian Armstrong

When I was doing *Little Women*, working with crew and props people and they are telling people what the film is and who they're working with, a lot of them said to me, 'I told them about *High Tide*, everyone knows *High Tide*. They all saw it on cable'. So even though we all wish our films would be shown on the big screen, you feel thankful for cable and for video, that at least they're found.

The Last Days of Chez Nous and working with Helen Garner?

Jan Chapman approached me because she'd had a relationship with Helen for the play they did for TV, *Two Friends*, with Jane Campion. This was Helen's first screenplay. She wrote it as a film. I really loved it because I love Helen's writing. I think she has incredibly acute observation of people and wonderful poetry in her writing. I did think the biggest challenge was that so much was in one house, but I took that on board and thought, 'Well, we'll just have to do everything possible to make people still feel they're watching a movie'. After all, the house is also a character in the story.

You could see up the street, the spire in the distance.

And it was a house where there were comings and goings. You saw people walking by in the street, in through the front door and so on. We did a couple of drafts, Jan and Helen and I together, then I went off to America to do *Fires Within* and then came back and, because *Fires Within* went on and on – it was actually recut for almost six months and what they basically did was take out a lot of the politics – when I came back, I had to literally get off the plane and start location surveys for *The Last Days of Chez Nous*, which in a lot of ways was very good for me because it had been such a horrendous experience with the film being recut and all the fighting and backstabbing.

It was wonderful just to get back and make another film because, once you go through an experience like that, you begin to think, 'Maybe it was my fault that the film didn't work in the beginning', so it was nice that I had to sort of get back into the car after the accident and work with so many old friends again. Actually, Jan and I had never worked together. Over the years I had seen her work on ABC TV, and I was a great admirer. She was a wonderful producer to work with, very supportive and encouraging. The key thing was to cast the two sisters. Then we had to search for our Frenchman.

We actually cast Lisa Harrow from meeting her in London; she did a screen test we sent to Australia. Kerry Fox was here. I had both their tests on video and had to try and move the two TV screens together because I couldn't actually put them in the one room. We really wanted to make sure there was going to be a feeling of sisters. Then we went to France and tested for our Frenchman, and the thing was that none of the Frenchmen were likeable. We actually had a fantastic reaction. We met some wonderful French actors – you know, the man who was in *Betty Blue*, who is actually only three feet tall, Jean-Hughes Anglade! He came in with this long coat and entourage and everything. I mean, he does have charm and he's an incredible actor, but he wouldn't be up to Lisa's kneecaps!

Helen's point was always that she felt the woman was at fault in this relationship. She really was exploring the situation she felt. Here was a woman from a generation that had to fight for freedom and had to help try to turn the tables, but from all those years of having to assert herself, she'd actually started to become too bossy for all the people around her and being a big sister with her younger sister. She had been too controlling of their lives and they were beginning to break away from her. So, even though the story is about a husband who has an affair, it was a delicate balance.

The point was not that the husband necessarily was a villain. Jan and I felt, having seen all the Frenchmen, that people would think the film was completely anti-male, because there is this thing that a lot of the French actors have: this in-built arrogance.

As we were in London, we thought we should perhaps widen our brief and see some of the other leading European actors. I've been a huge fan of Bruno Ganz for many years. Anyway, he came in and we both thought, here's someone who you could forgive, because he is so adorable. But the French never forgave us for casting him. We were not invited to any French film festivals. It didn't get a release in France. They were very upset that Bruno was playing a Frenchman.

The journey with Lisa Harrow and Bill Hunter in the desert was very strong.

Yes, I thought Bill did a fantastic job. I'd never worked with him. I think he's really underrated as an actor. He had to age himself twenty years for us. I can remember he put the wardrobe on and just walked into the rehearsal. I thought it was my grandfather walking into the room for a second. Once he had those clothes, he just became that man.

You enjoyed making Little Women?

I had a wonderful time on *Little Women*. I was very nervous about going back to America again because I'd had that bad experience. It's a different system and you have to accept it if you go and make a film in an American studio. It is going to be a whole different system and there are going to be a lot more people who are going to give you notes and make comments. I realise that I was very lucky on *Mrs Soffel* with Edgar Sherrick, my producer, who fought for and supported me in my vision of the film. What went wrong on *Fires Within* was that I had inexperienced producers who panicked.

So, when I was approached about *Little Women*, I said, 'Well, I'll come over and I want to meet with the studio'. A key thing that I learnt from my bad experience was that you have to make sure the film you want to make is the film the studio wants to make, otherwise you're kidding yourself – it's that, 'I'll marry him and change him'! With *Fires Within*, I always loved the political and moral dilemma of this triangle, but the studio thought, 'This can be a hot sexy story set in sexy Miami'. The two were never going to meet.

The female executive at Columbia who had developed *Little Women* had actually been trying to make it for many years and was very passionate about it. I met and talked to her and I felt that she was both very bright, and other people said so, and had very good taste and didn't want to over-sentimentalise it, didn't want it to be a *Color Purple Little Women*. The producer Denise De Novi had been Tim Burton's producer for a number of years. I also felt that she was very experienced and knew the game. Anyway, we all seemed to be very much in sync.

The final thing – because Winona was attached – was whether or not I thought Winona was right as Jo, and I wouldn't have done it if I hadn't felt she was right. When I met her, I felt there was a whole side of her that we hadn't seen on screen; that, as a person, she was very passionate and alive and quite strong and, because she has a sort of haunting beauty, that had been the side of her that had most often been shown. Because of her pale skin and dark eyes and hair, she has quite often played poetic, enigmatic characters. And my instincts about that were right.

Actually, it was a very tight-budget Hollywood film. They allowed me to bring my Australian team: Nick Beauman the editor; Geoffrey Simpson came over and shot it. We finally did get it through the studio. Amy, whose project it was, had by then gone. By the time we finished the film, she had moved on to head Turner's company and we had a whole lot of boys, but I have to say our one argument was that they kept saying, 'This is a kids' film and we'll put it out at Christmas for families', and they made this really corny poster. But after they saw the film, actually they all cried and I was thrilled. Not only did they cry, they turned around and said, 'You're right, grown-ups like this, but how are we ever going to get them into the film, especially men?' But they worked very hard to do it and we got fantastic reviews. And it was a box-office hit for a film of its size, so everyone was very happy.

Oscar and Lucinda was a very ambitious project.

Yes, very ambitious. Peter Carey used to live in Birchgrove and I was in Balmain. He and I had known each other for a number of years because I tried to do one of his short stories, and we'd sort of kept up a friendship because I was the young film-maker, he was the young writer, then I did my first film, then he did his first novel...

When he gave it to me to read, I really did think it was too ambitious. 'We'll never ever raise the money for this in Australia.' I said, 'Peter, I love it, but I don't see how you can ever make it'. We'd spent three years with Pat Lovell on *Clean Straw for Nothing* and, in the end, they said to us, 'It's so expensive shooting in two countries'. That's why the budget was so high.

Then *Oscar and Lucinda* was published and I read in the paper that Robin Dalton had bought it for John Schlesinger and I was very pissed off and thought, 'What a fool I was. Of course, it can be a co-production. Why should I be thinking about how to raise the money? It's not my job anyway'.

I've told this story before in print, but because Luciana Arrighi, who designed *Mrs Soffel*, *My Brilliant Career* and *Starstruck* for me, is an old friend and she also does a lot of Schlesinger's films, I really just said as a joke, 'How's my *Oscar and Lucinda* going?' I didn't know Robin at all, but I said, 'If you're ever talking to Robin Dalton, please tell her if John changes his mind, I'm waiting in the wings'. And lo and behold, eighteen months later I got this call from Robin Dalton, 'They've done a number of drafts and they feel it's beaten them, the adaptation and the budget, and John Schlesinger's booked up for three years of operas and things now and he's let it go and said, "Good luck"'. She was coming out to see family here, so I said, 'Let me introduce you to Laura Jones, who I think would be fantastic and who loves it as much as I do'.

So we started work on it. This was way before *Little Women*. We were writing that script for five years on and off.

You're back in the nineteenth century again. You also explored many aspects of Australian Christianity.

Yes, Peter does. It's there in the book.

The Plymouth Brethren sequences were striking.

I had to study it. We all had to do our crash course in theology. There's still the Brethren movement and one of them came to speak to us, to the cast, in rehearsals. Peter did actually base it on a famous naturalist member of the Brethren whose son wrote a book called *Father and Son* about his life growing up in Cornwall with his father and the division. On the one hand there's scientific interest and on the other hand there's complete belief in a faith that's absolutely based on the Bible and the facts of the Bible. He took this as his inspiration for the relationship with the father and the son.

But Peter's real inspiration is ... that this person becomes a gambler.

Even Oscar's decision to become an Anglican rather than something else was a gamble. But that ingrained, very strong puritanical streak underlies it: the Christmas cake, being cut off by his father, the fear of the sea. Then the transition to an Anglican tradition, the priest who takes Oscar in and his own destructive gambling, Oxford...

The tragedy for us was how much we had to leave out. Peter's insight into those characters – there's a terrible cynicism: this boy with his Puritan faith, moving into a house where really all that man thinks about is money. They are very, very poor, though Betty came from a wealthier family, so he feels the burden of their poverty, that they're completely hopeless as farmers. Everything goes wrong, and they're losing the congregation to Oscar's father, who's such an impassioned preacher; they're losing their livelihood as well. It's wonderful writing.

The great black irony is that when Oscar really feels such guilt about his sinning and feels he must go away and start afresh – wants to be pure and save his faith and go and save the Aborigines – he gets put in a church at Randwick, next to the racecourse. I mean, that's the wickedness of Peter Carey's storytelling, which is so wonderful.

Oscar goes to this land where he thinks he can get away from the evils of gambling and, of course, Mr Carey brings him to the country where gambling is like a national pastime. Even the Bishop is gambling.

And the elegant lady, Lucinda, is also gambling. Oscar's confession sequence, his sitting, praying in the glass church, is a powerful confession sequence.

It's interesting that the people who didn't like the film – the main criticism – said it was cold. But when Ralph did that confession, which I thought was so simple and so true, we were crying standing there. The boom-holder, the entire crew, we had tears in our eyes because it was so effective. Also his final word was 'To my father', and a couple of members of the crew had actually lost their fathers in the last year or so, so they found it particularly devastating. So it just amazes me when somebody says it was cold.

And then at the end, with the contract in the box, to think that this whole folly, transporting the glass church, was a gamble and these two people who were certainly so right for each other, destroyed everything with their weakness; that one devilish weakness they shared. It was the thing that brought them together and the thing which finally killed Oscar. I thought Cate was completely devastating in that scene.

In terms of religion on screen – there's the beginning of Carey's Bliss *(dir. Ray Lawrence), of course, but* Oscar and Lucinda *has the Brethren and the atmosphere of nineteenth-century Anglicanism. With the symbol of the glass church, there is a spirituality that Australians acknowledge, even if they're not religious.*

Yes. It was interesting here because, I suppose, there's so much baggage about the film – Peter's book, then it was going to be made into a film, 'What's she going to do with it?' and so on, and Ralph Fiennes was here – somehow or other, no one actually talked about the content. Even the reviewers talked about whether or not they thought Ralph was any good. No one talked about the content. It really disappointed me.

Both in England and America we had incredible reviews and articles. I remember talking to one journalist for hours and so did Ralph. He said it's so wonderful because you're not seeing this in films any more, films that are actually dealing with faith and with spirituality. Peter's story works on so many levels. It was a huge challenge to bring off. My biggest regret is that we couldn't have had even a little bit more of Oscar's childhood, but it was already a very long film.

Australian Feature Films

1975 *Smokes and Lollies* (Documentary)

1976 *The Singer and the Dancer*

1978 *My Brilliant Career*

1980 *14's Good, 18's Better* (Documentary)

1982 *Starstruck*

1987 *High Tide*

1991 *The Last Days of Chez Nous*

1996 *Not 14 Again* (Documentary)

1997 *Oscar and Lucinda*

Bruce Beresford

Bruce Beresford with production crew and Indians, *Black Robe*, 1991.
(Documentation Collection, ScreenSound Australia.)

WHEN YOU WORKED in Nigeria in the 1960s, did you ever dream that there would be an Australian film industry?

You know, I don't think I gave it any thought. No, I always assumed there wouldn't be because no one had shown any kind of interest. When I was at university I felt that I was almost alone screaming that there should be a local film industry, with local movies and directors. No, I don't think I thought it was ever going to happen.

But The Adventures of Barry McKenzie *was one of the first breakthrough films. How did that happen?*

It's so long ago. I was working in London and I read in one of the English papers about the Film Commission being set up in Australia. I said to Barry Humphries that we should do a script from the comic strip because they had money available to make films, but it hadn't occurred to them that they had no one to make them. I said, 'I don't think they've thought about that, but if we whip back to Australia with a script, with you starring in it and we're all set to go, we have a good chance of getting the money. There wouldn't be all that many going for it'. And that's more or less what happened. When I came back, I remember I had a meeting with the Film Commission and they said, 'We can't give you the money because you haven't directed a feature'. And I said, 'Well, who has? Nobody'. Except, I think, Tim Burstall had. I'd done a lot of short films and I'd had about twelve years in the film industry. But somehow it happened. I loved working with Barry and we're still close friends.

What influence did it have on the way people saw Australian films and Australian comedies?

I'm not sure what influence it had. Personally, it was a massive mistake for me to do it; a massive mistake, because the film was so badly received critically. Instead of getting me work, even though it was successful commercially, it put me out of work.

But the sequel?

That was an even bigger mistake. I couldn't find anything else to make because the films were so reviled critically that I thought that, with these two films, I'll never work again. Luckily Phillip Adams saved my life by offering me *Don's Party*. But that was a couple of years later. I thought the Barry McKenzie films were very funny but the reaction was so hostile that I realised very quickly that I had made a massive mistake. They were the wrong films to do. What I should have done was something that was going to get better critical reviews.

Bruce Beresford
Bruce Beresford

You did it with Don's Party.

Yes, *Don's Party* saved my life. The play was extremely acute and perceptive and the film didn't do anything the play didn't do. It analysed the groups of friends at the party who were an interesting cross-section. The film worked because it was lively and very well cast.

The Club?

The Club was nowhere near as successful. Football movies are hard to do. In fact, sports movies are hard to do unless you're doing boxing, because then everyone understands what's going on. Other games are very difficult.

The best way to look at The Club *seems to be to see it as a political comedy with a struggle for power.*

It was and, on that level, it quite worked. People went to it, if they went at all – certainly people who weren't AFL fans – went expecting that they were never going to understand the football game or that they would hate the game. But the game itself wasn't that important.

The Getting of Wisdom *was quite a different film.*

Well, that was actually the film I wanted to do first. I had read the book when I was about fourteen and I always thought it would make a wonderful film. When the Film Commission got going, it was the film I wanted to do. But I thought that maybe it would be better to do a popular comedy, something that makes some money and gets me some credibility and then I can make a film like *The Getting of Wisdom* which would be a much harder film to make and to sell. But I miscalculated terribly. My whole line of reasoning was wrong. It would have been better to do the artistic film, even if nobody saw it. And got good reviews.

Germaine Greer, when asked to contribute to a series in the Daily Telegraph in London about the most influential novels of the twentieth century, chose The Getting of Wisdom.

Well, I think it's a great novel. I don't know if anyone reads Henry Handel Richardson these days, but I thought she was a great writer. *The Fortunes of Richard Mahony* is a complete masterpiece.

The film is a fascinating look at religion and education in the nineteenth century.

I think it was fairly accurate. I based the script, not just on the novel, but on her autobiography, *Myself When Young*. She covered the same ground. There were things not in the novel that I put in the film. I always thought it would be fascinating to make a film with virtually an all-female cast. It turns out now I've done a whole lot of them.

In Leonard Maltin's TV Guide you are listed among the directors, but Money
Movers *is left out. Has it been overlooked?*

Well, it's a pretty terrible film. Perhaps that's why it's overlooked. It was a
kind of stop-gap thing. When I signed a contract to do some work with the
South Australian Film Corporation, I originally signed to do a film that I never
actually made for them, *The Ferryman*, a script I'd written. Then, after I'd
signed, they said they didn't want to do that. I said that I understood that
that's what we were going to do. They told me to have another look at my
contract. They said they were going to do a film with me but not *The Ferryman*.
I re-read it and saw that this was in fact true. They had a number of other
projects, none of which I liked, and we finished up with *Money Movers* as a
sort of compromise.

It worked as a thriller?

No, nobody went to see it. I went on the opening night in Melbourne and there
were three people there and me. I was sitting up the back wondering what
time the session started and then the film came on. I thought, 'This is going
to be a disaster'. And it was.

Breaker Morant *was a significant film.*

Yes, but, again, it was a film that nobody went to see. But it was an important
film. In terms of actual audiences, nobody saw it. Critically, it was important,
which is a key factor, and it has kept being shown over the years. Whenever I
am in Los Angeles, it's always on TV. I get phone calls from people who say,
'I saw your movie; could you do something for us?' But, they're looking at a
29-year-old movie. At the time it never had an audience. Nobody went,
anywhere in the world. It opened and closed in America in less than a week.
And in London, I remember it had four days in the West End. Commercially, a
disaster, but ... It's a film that people talk about to me all the time.

*What do they talk about? The war situation, the character of Breaker Morant, the
trial?*

I think it's the moral conflict. It's a good story. I read an article about it
recently in the LA times and the writer said it's the story of these guys who
were railroaded by the British. But that's not what it's about at all. The film
never pretended for a moment that they weren't guilty. It said they are guilty.
But what was interesting about it was that it analysed why men in this
situation would behave as they had never behaved before in their lives. It's
the pressures that are put to bear on people in wartime. Look at the atrocities
in Yugoslavia. Look at all the things that happen in these countries committed
by people who appear to be quite normal. That was what I was interested in
examining. I always get amazed when people say to me that this is a film

about poor Australians who were framed by the Brits. That was not what the film was about for me. And I never said that.

And Puberty Blues?

Well, I'd almost forgotten it, actually. It was quite a popular film. I was very taken with the novel when I read it. It was written by the two girls when they were at school; one of those privately printed things, or printed by one of those small presses. I bought it while I was waiting for a bus in North Sydney. I went to get a chocolate or something and I saw a pile of these things sitting on the counter. I thought I'd buy one and read it on the bus going home. It was remarkable; a very well-expressed book. And the girls were only fifteen. It was a sort of insight into the way of life of those kids, which was a revelation to me. I've no idea what that film would look like now; probably not very good. Kathy Lette was a real livewire and so was the other girl, Gabrielle Carey.

From a religious point of view, Black Robe *was quite significant. What appealed to you in Brian Moore's novel and its themes that led you to direct it?*

It was my idea to make the movie. No one approached me about the film. I read the novel when I was passing through Los Angeles in 1985. I had always been a great admirer of Brian Moore's novels. This is a historical novel quite unlike his others. It struck me for a lot of reasons. One was simply the novelty of it. I knew nothing whatever about pioneer life in Canada in the seventeenth century and suddenly to read this story about these insanely savage Indians and these brave, courageous French voyagers trying to colonise them was very striking. In particular the priest, Laforgue, was significant, trying to convert the Indians to Christianity and baptise them. He travelled right across the known world to try to convince the Indians that they were living their lives all wrong because they've got to go to this place, heaven, which doesn't even exist.

Looking back from the twentieth century, this seems, in many ways, a mad thing to do. But they had their own approach to the world worked out and in terms of seventeenth-century views, they thought they were doing the Indians a great favour. It is fascinating that someone's faith could be so strong.

What interested me really about *Black Robe*, apart from the fact that it's a great story, is that clash between the European and the native American cultures. Period films are always hard to do. The further back in history you go, the harder it is. Everything changes: the look, the manners, the thinking, everything. You have to understand the way someone like Laforgue thought. He had an obsession with getting everyone into heaven, a concept which few people these days take seriously. My job is to convince the audience that this is important.

In Australia your films had comparatively little explicit religious material. But you went to the United States and made Tender Mercies, *a fine portrait of Southern Baptists.*

I think I can tell you why this is. Religion plays a much bigger part in the life of the average American than it does in the life of the average Australian. When I met people like Horton Foote who wrote *Tender Mercies* and Brian Moore, I found religion was a fundamental part of their lives. Horton Foote grew up in the American south where everybody goes to Church on Sunday. Everybody goes. In fact, if you are arranging to meet people, you always arrange to meet them on Sunday because everyone assumes you go to Church. Brian Moore had a Catholic background in Ireland. Religion was part of his life. In Australia it's not – and it does not come in so strongly to our films.

And King David?

Some time ago I was in Los Angeles, having dinner with Barry Humphries, and he said, 'You know that film of yours, *King David*? It is nowhere near as bad as anyone would have you believe. There are many, many good things in it. I think the fact that it was a disaster has been somewhat self-perpetuating'. I had a look at it again on video and I think there are a few things in it that are interesting. But, I think there are so many things that are wrong. We never liked the script, whereas I think we basically got the script of *Black Robe* right.

In *King David* we never really caught the friendship between David and Jonathan. There weren't enough scenes between them. And David, himself – I think Richard Gere was miscast. He is a wonderful actor but he is much better in contemporary pieces.

The screenplay's use of the Psalms of David for voiceover seemed to get to the spirit of the times and the religious development of the characters.

That's interesting to hear, because that was something I added, quite apart from the script writer.

You tackled Aboriginal themes in The Fringe Dwellers.

A number of people told me: 'Nobody wants to watch a film about a bunch of Aborigines'. So I dropped the project until I had enough clout to do it.

It's about a group of very recognisable human beings. It is not political, dogmatic or didactic and it is free of all the usual clichés and political posturing. The treatment of Aborigines over the years by successive governments and by whites with whom they came into contact is something that has moulded the Aboriginal character and is largely responsible for the way they present themselves today, but the past – colour, racism, mistreatment and all the rest of it – is not a central theme of the film. It is implicit but, to me, the story is one of a family, their relationships, struggles, aspirations.

At the end of Breaker Morant, *Peter Handcock declares that he is a 'pagan'. Perhaps many Australians would identify with that stance. Which means that* Black Robe *could seem quite alien.*

Perhaps Australians not being so religious could make it more attractive to audiences. I'm not particularly religious myself, in fact, and I think my philosophy agrees more with that of the Indians in the film, especially the dying Indian who says, 'Look, the world is a cruel place, but it is the sunlight – and that's all there is'. This is my feeling too. But, at the same time, it's impossible to research a film like *Black Robe* and not come out without immensely admiring the Jesuits and their beliefs.

I read thousands of the 'relations', the letters the Jesuits wrote back to France. These men were extraordinary. They were courageous, and they did everything they could to understand the Indians. They wanted to help. They were so well intentioned.

The film is a critique of the missionary methods of the past, methods that were taken for granted even thirty years ago but are now being re-assessed in terms of 'inculturation' of Christianity, not just going out like Fr Laforgue and speaking 'the truth'. Black Robe *seems to be a helpful and respectful critique of the past.*

Yes, I think it is. I was chatting to a publicist and she said, 'What they were doing was cool, wasn't it?' Yes, but not by the standards of the times. We have only started to re-evaluate this kind of society in the last twenty or thirty years. To the people of those times it did not seem like that; this was not an issue.

At a Melbourne press preview, some reviewers breathed in audibly or laughed at some of the expressions of faith by Fr Laforgue. Some people seem somewhat embarrassed that he was so intellectually convinced of the truth of what he said and that the Indians had to believe this truth and, if they were not baptised, they would not go to paradise. This would not be a Catholic approach these days although some of the fundamentalist churches still take this stance.

Certainly some of the Churches I saw in the American south would. But it was part of the way Laforgue and those like him thought. A number of times in the film he says to the Indians, 'Let me baptise you and you can go to paradise' – and there is another point, a lovely line, when Laforgue says to the Indian, 'When I die I'll go to paradise; let me baptise you and you will go there also'. And he fervently believes this. That is why I was so keen to get Lothaire Bluteau to play the role: to get an actor who can convincingly portray faith, the hardest thing to portray on the screen. You can portray anything, but religious faith is very difficult to fake. Unless I could get an actor with Lothaire's conviction, the film would have been a farce; people would have laughed at it.

He was impressive in Jesus of Montreal (dir. Denys Arcand). One of the difficulties is that, while we can admire his absolute conviction, he is very hard to empathise with as a person. Perhaps it's a reaction to the old-style missionary effort. But you took us on his journey of faith, from an utter intellectual conviction of truth to a love and service where Laforgue remained with the Indians.

Yes. But the audience would not have noticed this at all had Laforgue been a different sort of person at the beginning.

I think that, even if you have no religious faith whatever, or even if you despised the Jesuits, you would still find it an interesting story. It's a wonderful study of obsession and love. And it is a wonderful adventure of the spirit and of the body. What those people did, going to a country where winters were far more severe than anything they had known in Europe, meeting people who were far more fierce than anyone they had ever encountered ... having to deal with these people, shows us something of humanity at its greatest. It's the equivalent of today's people getting into space shuttles and going off into space. It takes unbelievable courage to do this.

When Laforgue farewelled his mother, he knew he would probably never see her again. And missionaries died young. They were full of zeal and faith.

Yes, it's obvious from reading the Jesuits' letters that the fervour they had was colossal. When I was in Africa making *Mister Johnson* I met an American missionary who was a Baptist. His group had been going out to Africa for many, many years. He himself had been there for 27 years. He told me that, of course, in West Africa everyone can have anti-malaria tablets now, but he told me that in his Church records, the average life of a missionary in the past was under six months.

Many have commented on the violence of Black Robe. Catholics in the past were brought up with the stories of the martyrdom of Jesuits, Isaac Jogues and Jean de Brebeuf (contemporaries of Laforgue). Words have their impact but to see the torture on screen, however briefly, is much more frightening.

Well, of course, you're right. The story of de Breboeuf and the other martyrs is so famous in North America that to try to tell the story of this period and not to convey a sense of the violence that was part of it would have been a travesty.

People make comparisons with The Mission *(dir. Roland Joffé).*

It's years since I've seen *The Mission* now. I think that the main difference between *Black Robe* and *The Mission* is that in *Black Robe* the Indians are major characters, have a large proportion of the dialogue and are the main focus of the drama. In *The Mission*, they are a group of people being argued about by the whites. My Indians play leading roles. When I read Brian Moore's book, I thought 'This is what it was like in 1634' and I believe it – absolutely believe it.

What drew Australian financial and artistic interests into such a collaboration on such a theme?

I think it was purely a business thing. When I was trying to raise the money with the help of the Canadian company, Alliance, who owned the rights to the project, the head said to me one day, 'Are you aware that there is an Australian-Canadian co-production deal? So that we can make films collaboratively that neither of us could afford by ourselves?' So I contacted Sue Milliken who, in fact, had produced *The Fringe Dwellers*, and she investigated the arrangement.

We sent a copy of the script of *Black Robe*. After a lot of discussion, the Australian Film Development Corporation said, 'Yes, we'll put money in on the basis that we use a number of Australian technicians and two Australian actors'. There was employment for Australians; otherwise the film would not have been made at all. I think that any wider ramifications, like the similarities between the Indians and positions on Aborigines – and there are some – were really not an issue at this stage.

More recently Paradise Road *took up the themes of war and women.*

Paradise Road was the most disastrous film I ever made.

But it did well in Australia.

No, not really. A little bit. It was one of the worst reviewed films of my career, including *Barry McKenzie*. The American reviews and the Australian reviews were dreadful – a few good ones but mostly they were terrible. And the worst of all were the English reviews. They were just lethal.

But I liked it. When it was finished, I thought this was actually pretty good. But I was quite taken aback by the reviews. They were the worst I have ever had.

You wrote the screenplay yourself?

Yes. The original idea was brought to me by a couple of guys in Western Australia who had actually written a script. In retrospect, I probably should have filmed it. But they hadn't done any research, didn't know anything about it. They based it on old movies, which was pretty silly. So I went and read a lot of diaries. A lot of women in the camps kept diaries. They're now in the war museum at Lambeth. You can read them up in the dome and I spent some time there reading and making notes. That's where I got the information. There were also some published diaries as well.

It was a great idea to present the women's memories of the War and the camps. So much had been presented from the men's perspective.

That was one of the key things that made me want to do it.

Your cast was excellent, Glenn Close portraying goodness in a credible way.

Yes, and Pauline Collins was marvellous. Johanna Ter Stege was also a wonderful actress, really down to earth. Yes, that's what they were like. The music was great.

Speaking of music, you directed a segment of Aria, *but you also direct many operas. What is your special love for opera?*

Well, I've always loved opera. I first heard it when I was about 16, I think, and I just became completely fascinated by it. It's enormously dramatic and you have, or you should have, good stories mixed up with fabulous music, sweeping everything along, and this great wall of emotion. I find them terribly powerful. They affect me and I could watch them over and over and over and never get sick of them.

The Imax film on Sydney?

Well, I didn't actually direct that one because I was working on a film in America and it went way over schedule and I couldn't get back to do the Imax. It was directed by Geoff Burton. All I did was come in and help with the cutting and the voiceover. I worked on the script with a couple of other people but it was very difficult, actually. It's about forty minutes.

A history of Sydney?

It's meant to be a history of Sydney but it's not really. It's very slight. One of the problems was the council who were putting up some of the money. In fact, there were some things in the history of Sydney that they didn't want in it. 'Well, you can't mention convicts' – but it's pretty hard to make a history of Sydney without mentioning convicts. They said 'Convicts aren't important'. They had a whole list of things. So, by the time you got in things they okayed, there wasn't much time for anything else. They really only wanted aerial shots of the harbour. They didn't want mention of anything that was unpleasant. They didn't want mentioned the fact that people came out in chains, that the

Bruce Beresford

Aborigines around the harbour died, anything that looked to be rather ghastly. The result is rather bland.

A nice little film for the year 2000?

Yes. It's quite a pleasant little tourist film.

Of your American films, do you have a favourite?

You know, I've never seen any of them again. In fact, I never watch any of the films I've done again. Just my memories of them. My guess would be *Driving Miss Daisy* and *Black Robe*. People do like *Driving Miss Daisy*. I think I get as many comments on that as I do on *Breaker Morant*.

Australian Feature Films

1972 *The Adventures of Barry McKenzie*

1974 *Barry McKenzie Holds His Own*

1977 *The Getting of Wisdom*

1977 *Don's Party*

1979 *The Money Movers*

1980 *Breaker Morant*

1980 *The Club*

1981 *Puberty Blues*

1986 *The Fringe Dwellers*

1991 *Black Robe* (co-production with Canada)

1997 *Paradise Road*

Tim Burstall

Tim Burstall (left) with Sylvia Change and John Phillip Law, *Attack Force Z*, 1980. (Courtesy of Tim Burstall.)

YOUR BACKGROUND IN film-making in the 1960s: what started you on the path to being a director?

Really, I started out wanting to write. I remember it being in the old university days where we all used to think in terms of what we called 'the big vehicle'. The big vehicle was the 250-page novel, the three-hour play or the ninety-minute film. In those days it was thought very difficult to get up a ninety-minute film from Australia. Somehow or other that was something that was done by the Yanks.

I tried a novel; that's how it began, though, at the same time, I was always very interested in film and I was a foundation member of the Melbourne University Film Society. We were all trying to get hold of 16-mm equipment at that point. My first job after university was at the National Film Library which, I thought, might lead to getting into the Commonwealth Film Unit as a writer. But they were doing nothing but docos, so I got out of that fairly rapidly.

I did found a film society at Eltham, but I really began by making a film on the weekends. I'd seen a film by Lamorisse, *Crin-Blanc*, about a boy and a horse and how he tames the stallion. Eltham was almost rural in those days and I had a few goats and geese and my kids were young. The lead in my film was six and the girl next door was five, so I made the story about a boy and a goat. We put it into an overseas film festival, Venice, got a prize with it, and distributed it through Screen Gems. It got a release here through British Empire Films as a support. That floated me and I got some backing from an old school friend and we formed a company called Eltham Films and away we went.

You made documentaries in those years as well?

When you say 'documentaries', I really was not interested in documentary. I remember hating the very idea of documentary – perhaps this is from my period in the National Film Library. The Grierson-type documentary is my idea of total boredom. It was nearly always 'from forest to newspaper print' or you followed some industrial process. It had that dreary socialist colour, too. It was always collective Man, never a story. So, after the prize I made a set of art films because Arthur Boyd was a very close friend and I knew people like Nolan and Charlie Blackman fairly well. They belonged to the same bohemia we all lived in.

I sold them to the ABC and some of them won prizes. Of course, when I say art films, they weren't documentary in the style of the usual art film; they didn't say, 'Here is the painter. What are his great thoughts?' They just looked at his pictures. I eliminated the painter. I just took the thematic material. In other words, I wrote a ballad, say, about Ned Kelly and fitted that to the pictures. They were like mini-cartoons almost.

Tim Burstall

In the case of Arthur Boyd, he did a series and I called it *The Black Man and his Bride*, which was really about Aboriginal integration, an Aboriginal shearer wanting to marry a half-caste bride. But I turned it into a narrative or into a mini-narrative. The thing I was interested in was drama, fiction material. I was interested in the theme business.

The other things I did were kids' films. We were just trying to find a market, trying to find a niche. The series of kids' films was called *Sebastian and the Fox*, made with Peter Scriven who had done *The Tintookies*. That was a puppet film: one puppet and the real world. They were like early Chaplins, meant to be comedy for kids but using the same principles Chaplin practised.

After that I had a Harkness Fellowship, one of those wealthy American fellowships that took you to America for a couple of years. You could study where you liked. That made it possible for me to work with professional actors at the Actors Studio and work on a couple of feature films. I came back, then, ready to make some features.

The release of 2000 Weeks *seems a long time ago.*

It sure is. About thirty years ago. I still look on that as part of my apprenticeship. It's written up in the histories as if it was an important breakthrough picture, but to my mind it wasn't. The current wisdom was that nobody could compete with Hollywood except countries with a language of their own, like Sweden or France. They could have small industries of their own but nobody else could and, if you were English-speaking, you were really in a problem situation competing with Hollywood.

Anyway, this fellow from United Artists said, 'But you could still make adult pictures, say in Sweden or France or Australia. What does it matter? You know, there's a hundred thousand in the art-house market. You should be able to make a picture for that,' and so on. So the intent was really to make a sort of universal art-house film, something that would work globally in a small way for the art-house circuit.

I didn't know enough about writing. I didn't know a lot about a lot of things and I personally think the picture didn't work. I look on my professional career as starting with *Stork*.

The themes were interesting. It took a theme which I dealt with later on in *Petersen*. Whereas *2000 Weeks* was about a journalist who wanted to be a writer and who felt that Australia was in a colonial situation – somebody was making a series and he doesn't get the chance to do it – by the time I got to *Petersen* three years later, he was converted to an electrician who aspired to go to university. I was able to make much more use of the class element in *Petersen*. Anyway, in *2000 Weeks* it didn't work for the audience and for me that was pretty important. I didn't think it was any use making pictures that didn't work commercially or work for an audience.

Stork is considered your breakthrough film.

Well, it was the breakthrough historically. First of all, I took exactly the opposite advice that I'd been given in the States, the advice which led to *2000 Weeks*: to take, as it were, a kind of universal theme – it's safer – and aim it at a market that is art-house. With *Stork* it was unashamedly, very heavily, Australian and was based on a play written, of course, by David Williamson. One of the points you have to make is that it was the first thing that the public heard of from him.

This play was put on at La Mama. I saw it and thought, 'We can convert that to a film'. And it had a kind of gaiety and brio. It was good-natured and it celebrated our own lives in a very straightforward way. It wasn't precious or arty. It was Australian comedy of a pretty straightforward sort, but also pretty well observed and accurate. And David has emerged over the last thirty years as a very prolific comic writer and a very shrewd observer of the Australian scene, I think.

You wrote an article in The Bulletin *in 1977 in which you categorised our films and you talked about the 'ocker comedy'. Did* Stork *herald the emergence of the ocker comedy?*

I don't think it did. It preceded the Barry McKenzie stuff, which is much more condescending, both more brutal and genuinely ocker – I mean ocker in a very cartoony style. But it's also seen through the prism of Humphries' idea of what's funny. I mean, Barry was a Camberwell boy looking down on Moonee Ponds, which is a different colour from what *Stork* was trying to do. Although there are parts of *Stork* that are ocker, the general feeling is robust. Stork is a virgin and he's also a hypochondriac. There are characters in *Stork*, whereas the characters and the colours in *Bazza MacKenzie*, well, they're poster colours and they're much more caricatures than genuine characters.

A useful distinction is the difference between a larrikin and a hooligan: the larrikins are attractive and hooligans are brutal.

Yes, I could buy that distinction.

In that vein, how does Alvin Purple *fit?*

After *Stork* I formed a company with Roadshow called Hexagon. The deal was that our production company and their distribution company could have a veto on any sort of project. In other words, they wanted a say in what kind of pictures we made, and we wanted a say in what sort of pictures we made. So if either party, the creator or the distributor disagreed, then the project was vetoed.

My next film was, in fact, *Petersen*. That's the one I commissioned from David and which we were working on, but I couldn't get it up in time for Roadshow – they wanted a picture straightaway for that Christmas. The R-certificate had just come in and they'd run a very successful Danish picture called *Bedroom Mazurka* (dir. John Hilbard). Now, I'd never seen a sex comedy in my life, literally, and Graham Burke, in charge at Roadshow, said, 'Have a look at it'. So I did and I said that if we couldn't do something better than that ... It didn't seem to me a particularly difficult thing to do.

I then wrote off to a vast number of Australian writers, asking whether they had any ideas for a sex comedy. I got ideas back from people like Michael Boddy and Bob Ellis, probably thirty ideas. But one of them was a fully-written screenplay which had been written originally in England by Alan Hopgood for Tigon Films. Anyway, I read this thing and I thought what it was getting at was really the joke of sexual therapy, where the therapist gets off with the patient.

It started off as comedy then, halfway through, it turned into a serious sort of *Four Corners*: 'What is the nature of this? This isn't really so funny, is it, chaps?'

I thought the Hopgood thing was a one-joke idea but, if our film was to be a comedy, then this was clearly the story that had more mileage in it than any other. But all the serious part, I thought, 'We've got to throw that out'. I tried to get Hoppy to do certain things with it but, in the end, I wrote quite a lot of it, using almost every schoolboy joke that one could remember. I suspect it was because we were seeing our Australian girls in the nude for the first time and it was R-certificate – actually I haven't seen it for so long, probably for 25 years, so I don't really know how it would seem now – but it was intended to be good natured.

I would imagine you'd feel rather odd seeing it in the days of AIDS because it's suggesting full liberation. But it was phenomenally successful. We took, I think, four million dollars in the days when it was two-fifty a seat. It was seen by something like one in ten Australians. I think it was the business of getting your rocks off and it being okay, the end of puritanism, something like that. But it was laughing at liberation more than urging it upon us, I hope.

Graeme Blundell's Alvin was good natured.

I remember Burkie saying, 'You've got to cast somebody like Jack Thompson'. I said, 'Absolutely not. You've got to cast somebody who wouldn't, on the surface, seem a stud or even particularly attractive'. I actually thought that Alvin wasn't, that the comic element was connected with having a Woody Allen or a Dustin Hoffman figure who is not very obviously sexually attractive and the girls rushing him. This becomes much funnier than if he was a stud figure. Anyway, that's history.

And Alvin Rides Again?

I didn't direct that. We wanted to make a follow-up *Stork* but Roadshow wanted, for commercial reasons, the follow-up *Alvin*. It was directed jointly by my cameraman Rob Copping and Peter Bilcock, the editor. And, really, I don't think Graeme Blundell wanted to do it except on terms which to some extent endangered the premise: a double-identity thing. There was the real Alvin and then there was a figure called Balls McGee, a sort of horrible crim. Part of the joke – again it's a sort of Woody Allen-ish idea – was him being mistaken for one and having to front as the other.

But when it came to the crunch, Graeme didn't distinguish between Alvin pretending to be Balls, and Balls. I think the comedy was lost and the audience identification with Alvin didn't work properly. But *Alvin Purple* had been so successful that it still worked commercially.

You also directed the short segment, 'The Child', for Libido.

Actually I made that straight after *Stork.* At the Producers' and Directors' Guild of Melbourne we cooked up the idea of a portmanteau film with different themes. I suggested, together with the committee, that we bring in the writing talents of people who normally never worked for film. The idea was to get somebody from the Patrick White-Randolph Stowe area – the mythic, epic side of Australian writing – and we'd throw in somebody from the new theatre: David Williamson. Hal Porter came in. I recommended him very strongly, but I must say when I was given his story, I had problems with it.

Hal was very cross with me because I changed the nature of the story fairly radically. I've got the original story and my shooting script and a piece in *Overland* on it with my comments on how I did it and why I made the changes I did.

Your company was successful?

Well, all those films were. *Stork* made money, both the *Alvins* made money, *Libido* made money. The first six pictures all returned their money and gave a return to the investors. They didn't make that much money for me because we had our arrangement with Village that we put up half the money. So, in fact, we were taxed on what the films had made and then we had to put up the next chunk of money. *Stork* provided me with enough money to put up my share on *Alvin*, then *Alvin* provided enough to do the next. Unlike the bulk of the early Australian film-makers, we were actually financing our operation. We were protected in the sense that we had a distributor, but we were penalised by being the entrepreneur as well.

Then Petersen.

I was surprised by how heavily attacked it was on the grounds that it was pornographic but, when I saw it again recently, I wasn't that surprised. It was very much more of a commercial for sexual liberation than *Alvin* ever was.

When David and I were talking about it I can remember saying it was important for us to kick him off showing a warm domestic side: the marriage relationship. We then show him on with his mistress, Wendy Hughes, the lecturer. Most romantics say, 'Well, it's fine to have a wife and a mistress'. But the next move was to show him in what I described as 'the public fuck', which was the deal at the university where he's performing as a political act.

However, we then follow him up with a pass or a pseudo-pass being made at the wife of his best friend. That's when they go off on the holiday. The girl in question says, 'I've had this dream about you'. And Johnny Ewart finishes up saying, 'To make a pass at your best friend's wife is pretty crummy'. But the last we see of him, he's putting in power points in somebody's bedroom and it's quite clear he's going to get off with her, and now he's become a kind of sad case. But it really hammers the notion. It surprised me that in the States they retitled the picture *Jock Petersen*. That wasn't what I chose.

This is again pre-AIDS. But for my money, when I saw it again I thought it really is more of a sexual affront than I thought it was at the time we were making it. I thought that we were striking a blow for all the things that should be said. I really wanted to say that there was every range of colour sexually. There was the romantic love of the girlfriend as against the one-night stand. Most people know all the different colours, and sex can be as deep and meaningful as you like at one end of the spectrum and it can be as shallow at the other. But it's all human.

I was also surprised when I saw it again because I thought, one, we were making a point about class and, two, I thought we were making a point about examinations. At the time they'd done experiments with various examiners and discovered that there were huge discrepancies, certainly in arts subjects, in the results being given. That also seemed rather important to be saying: that there was a sort of corruption in academia.

I think I probably would take a very different line now. I'm pro-examination and I also think ranking is terribly important. I think there's a discipline – but, heaven knows, I shouldn't go into that.

However, I still think that *Petersen* was about an important subject. Also, it was about – irrespective of whatever Jack did with the role – the idea of somebody who had been an electrician and did think there was more in life than putting in power points and crawling around underneath people's houses putting in wires. It was about the aspirations of a working-class hero for more, for knowledge, for making more of his life, finding more meaning in it. I think some of that came through, anyway.

Bud Tingwell is Petersen's father, the minister, standing in his pulpit, groping for faith or meaning in the 1970s.

We thought that was a very critical thing. My preamble should be that, when I was at Geelong Grammar, we had Manning Clark, who had all sorts of odd mannerisms. He was an interesting mentor figure. I wanted the Bud figure to be robust but exactly where he'd gone ... ? I knew a man called Father Coldrey. He used to be at the Brotherhood of St Laurence. He was active and strong and rather impressive. But I myself am an atheist and, in fact, that figure says, 'I don't know if I believe in Him'. That sort of priest interests me a lot.

Keneally and Fred Schepisi did interesting things with that kind of struggle in their Libido *story, 'The Priest'.*

Yes. I thought it was interesting but I thought it was more despairing than I would have wanted, and it was sort of morbid. It seemed as if it was anti-body, anti-sex, anti-things. Do you remember him looking in the bowl as he washed his things in the washbasin? I think it was a little bit despairing for me. See, Tom is not despairing at all; he's the opposite of that. Schepisi's not. The great thing about Fred's contribution on the Catholic stuff, to me, is that it comes out of Italy, so you don't have this awful Irish puritan thing. There's a sort of robust thing about the Catholicism of Fred. Fred's given it up, but you get the feeling that it's central. I may be misjudging the Irish thing, but I've always had the feeling that the Irish priesthood – perhaps I'm judging by Joyce, by my perception of Mannix – to some extent had something morbid and hellfire-ish.

Look, I'm ignorant on the Church, but I know in terms of my own experience, one of my closest friends, Brian O'Shaughanassy, was brought up a Catholic. Although I went to an Anglican school, I probably had more Catholic friends than anyone else. And if I was ever to be religious, I suspect that, in fact, that would be the only one I'd go for. But since I can't come at the very notion of God, it's a problem. I'm one of the very few people I know who was actually brought up an atheist. My parents were English. My father was a scientist, an engineer, professor at Melbourne University, and my mother was a biologist. I've never had a religious phase in my life. But I've always thought it's all much more mysterious than religion suggests.

End Play: *was it just a thriller?*

After all the ocker criticisms, I certainly didn't want to be locked into doing only ocker stuff and I also wanted to see whether the public would buy a whole range of other things. I suppose everybody else was trying to do the same thing at that time – we're speaking of 1974. We were all trying to widen the scope of what the public would come at.

Russell Braddon's a good writer. I have always been a consumer of detective stories and that sort of thing – murder thrillers ... though I suppose *Macbeth* or *The Brothers Karamazov* are thrillers. The brothers' struggle was part of *End Play*, but it really was just something that was midway between one film and the next. We were doing two a year at the time.

Do you look back on Eliza Fraser *affectionately?*

I had originally written a version back in the 1960s. The first film I wanted to do was something called 'Man in Iron', which was Ned Kelly. The next one was *Eliza Fraser*. I don't know whether that was the influence of Nolan, who'd done versions of both those stories, but they struck me as connected to our mythology. I would have seen Ned Kelly as a sort of *Viva Zapata!* (dir. Elia Kazan) rather than a psychopath. The magical thing is that mad armour, which visually and in terms of what it's saying, looks backwards towards knights in armour and forwards towards robots and space stuff. Visually it's so weird. It's a fairytale: to make a set of armour out of ploughshares is a very funny and curious idea.

What interested me about the Mrs Fraser story were the different accounts that had been given of it. The original screenplay that I wrote in the late 1960s was a kind of *Rashomon* (dir. Akira Kurosawa), each person telling a different story, because two different convicts claimed to have saved her. And her own story. When she went back to England, she performed in a sideshow tent, 'I was nearly raped by an Aboriginal chieftain', all that sort of thing, a highly sensationalist account. She was a younger woman married to a much older sea captain, but it made you feel that she was a totally unreliable witness.

Then there was the story that Bracewell gave. Bracewell was an escaped convict from Moreton Bay and who was living, like Buckley, with the natives. He is supposed to have saved her. She promised to get him a pardon. They walked back. When they arrived at Moreton Bay – he led her back there – she then said, 'Out dog, out cur!' He then has to fade back into the bush and she goes back to England to tell her absurd stories.

Now, in fact, it was Graham rather than Bracewell who did do the rescuing. So it's the different accounts. I was sure, and certainly David Williamson was, that the Aborigines were given a very bad press and, of course, we wanted to correct that. I think the account of the Aborigines in *Eliza Fraser* was probably something new in Australian film.

People talk about Australians as being ocker. The Brits now feel we are sort of vulgar. There's a way in which, when I go to Britain, I have the feeling they can't actually place you properly. They certainly feel our directness is crude. I think the ocker thing is just the John Bull Englishman of the eighteenth century. We are descendants of the John Bull Englishman. Think of *Tom Jones* – the ocker characteristics are the characteristics of an Englishman in the eighteenth century: very vulgar, very straightforward, very robust, very direct. And the wenching and the drinking. Any society is strongly influenced by its first founders. The Yanks are descended from the seventeenth century. Really the Roundheads were the ones who won in America, whereas the cavaliers won in England. And I think that the parts of America that I'm continuously reminded of and feel strange about are the seventeenth-century parts, whereas I think we are the eighteenth century. I certainly had in mind Tony Richardson's *Tom Jones* when we were doing it. I wanted it to have some elements of a romp. The story itself is an extraordinary story.

Did the audience respond to the satiric interpretation?

I don't think they did. I think the real problem was the story wasn't well known. It would have been known amongst a few people. Sid Nolan and Patrick White knew it and a few historians might have known it, but the general public really had never heard of it. To work a satirical angle on something which is well known is fine, but if it's not well known then the satire is to some extent lost.

A lot of people complained that they didn't know whether the picture was a drama or a comedy. But when they accept what the mix is, they like it. The picture did quite well, but the reason it didn't do very well was the cost. It cost $1,300,000. Interestingly enough, it was not my company. I wanted to do it with Wendy Hughes and Frank Thring. My theory in those days was that you couldn't get more than $300,000 back from the Australian market. All the other pictures had been under $300,000. But Roadshow really saw it as very big. They had what we call in the business 'a touch of the Hollywoods'. They insisted on overseas stars and all that sort of thing.

You went back to a smaller budget for The Last of the Knucklemen. *And the ocker thing.*

One of the funny things is that again it was pretty misunderstood in Australia – or maybe they just thought it was ocker stuff. I was trying to take the ocker stuff and cross it, as I think John Powers' play did, with anthropology. Before I rehearsed the cast, I got them to read *The Territorial Imparity of the Native Aid*. I wanted it to be seen not just as ockerism but as anthropology. But the only people who got that were the French. It was bought in France and it's done terribly well there – much better than it ever did in Australia.

There are a couple of pictures which haven't worked here but which have worked elsewhere. I'm sure the French are missing something, but what they're getting is something which we never got here. Mind you, it never had a decent run. I don't think they knew how to market it. A lot of women said to me, 'I'd never go to a picture that had the title *The Last of the Knucklemen*'. But nobody ever looked at it as an analysis of the way men work. It's a right-wing view of unionism.

After that, there was Duet for Four.

That was a script I commissioned straight after *Petersen*. Roadshow didn't want to make it and I was left with the script. Later we talked about it. I was going through a mid-life crisis of some sort and thought – 'What is the nature of work? Have I wasted my time? Am I doing the right thing?' That sort of thing. And toys was the industry we decided to use because it was being taken over by the Yanks. It was a sort of image of what was happening in film at the time. I don't think the picture works very well.

And Morris West and The Naked Country?

I was a hired gun there; I didn't choose the material. He wrote it in 1945 and it really was a potboiler. It had the rudiments, the beginnings of land-rights issues, but I took this and converted it absolutely into a land-rights thing. I thought the business of Stanton versus the Aborigines was okay. But there were indigestible lumps in the script, like the adultery. And the Ivar Kants character was too melodramatic. I had to make him a mercenary from South Africa.

You took over Attack Force Z *after it had gone into production?*

The picture was made by Fauna, Lee Robinson and John McCallum. It was the first co-production in the East that we'd done, and the Australian Film Commission was very keen on seeing it happen, even though the director – in this case Phil Noyce – had fallen out with the production company. He wanted to make it a sort of national-liberation film. It was a story set in the Second World War and, although we shot it in Taiwan, it was really meant to be the Dutch East Indies but with a Chinese population, obviously.

The man who wrote the original screenplay was an Englishman who had done *The Avengers*. It was competent, like a mini *Guns of Navarone* (dir. J Lee Thompson): people sent off on a very difficult mission. I was very interested in this Z Force. I'd known some of the people who were in it. It's all very well going off and being a spy in a European war. But if we are in the Second World War here, those people who were sent off to operate within enemy territory were so obviously European and stuck out so hideously that, for the most part, they were nearly all wiped out. Those missions were highly dangerous. Some of them worked but, although we sent lots of people off, a vast number of missions were aborted. And a lot of the people were beheaded in rather horrific circumstances.

I was talking to Lee about it when I first got there and he said, 'Well, the guys were given a number on each other – that is, if there were four in the party, if so-and-so gets hurt, you have to shoot him'. Each person had the job of shooting one other of the group if they came to grief in any way. So I said, 'Let's put that on the nose of the picture: let's have five instead of four and let's bring in somebody who's almost a star'. So we brought in Johnny Waters and I shot him in the first ten minutes of the film. Mel has to shoot him because his knee is buggered which, of course, used to happen. That was our real attention-grabber.

It was an exotic war picture of a small size. It sold all over the world and got its money back. And it did perform the task of getting some co-productions going with the East, which was useful and very important. But it's always awful when you take over from somebody else – and Phil is a friend – but he really wanted to do something quite different and I was regarded as much more of a whore, I suppose.

But you had your own control?

Well, I work half the time as a hired gun on other people's projects and the other half I try and do my own work, but in either case you're working through narrative that has to be intelligible pretty well first-up with an audience. It seems to me that it's an art which you can't be too precious about. I'm very interested in making a picture as professionally and as well as I can, but I think you've got to work within what your audience can absorb.

That's why, in one sense, films that you see forty years later seem so odd: it's because you and the audience have moved on – the battlefield's somewhere else. So you often wonder, 'What was it? Why was it so important?' Of course, it doesn't mean it wasn't important, but its importance was connected to when it was made, the people who made it then, the people who saw it then.

You had planned Kangaroo *with Helen Mirren and Leo McKern.*

Originally we were going to make *Kangaroo* with the New South Wales Film Corporation. Their bankers had all the money and they were prepared to make it – the budget in those days was $4,500,000. But in 1981 there was a slump and their bankers could not deliver and the picture collapsed halfway. I'd already hired and we'd begun on pre-production. I had Leo McKern for Kangaroo. He would have been marvellous, though a little bit old. But by the time we finally did make it, which was four years later, he would definitely have been too old. It would have been hard to see him getting on a horse, I think. But he would have been absolutely perfect ten years before that.

I finished up with Hugh Keays-Byrne who was a very good Kangaroo. I had originally seen and met Hugh when he came out here with the Royal

Shakespeare Company. But I discovered that his father had been a general or a brigadier, quite high up anyway, and was rather contemptuous of Hugh becoming an actor. So Hugh had some understanding of certain sides of Kangaroo, and I think his English background gave him that extra colour.

I didn't want an Australian writer for the picture. I wanted somebody who was seeing Australia for the first time, in the same way that Lawrence did, so I hired the writer of the screenplay for *Wake in Fright* (dir. Ted Kotcheff). His name is Evan Jones and he's Jamaican, not English. He also did a lot of screenplays for Losey, like *King and Country*, a terrific screenwriter. Anyway, he was the one I fixed on to do that job, and I think he did it very well.

The novel is a shambles as a structure, but once you compress it, it can work. But the real difficulty, the indigestible credibility problem is the nature of the Kangaroo figure. It stands or falls by whether you pull that off. And I'm still unsure. I know a lot of people think it's impossible to pull off. I think Hugh did very well in it.

The dramatic initiative is between Kangaroo and the Judy Davis character, Harriet – that is, Lawrence's wife. She kept opposing the private life to meddling with politics and getting into social questions. But she has all the dramatic initiative and I think the best sequences of the film are really her encounters, her arguments with the Lawrence figure.

I like what Colin Friels did. It was difficult to do and certain people did criticise. Colin's people come from Glasgow. His notion of the sort of accent to use was a bit wavy now and then. Lawrence came from somewhere near Nottingham. But in arguments and when he was getting angry, Colin still finished up with a sort of miner's dialect: 'tha', a version of thou – 'Tha shalt not', that sort of stuff. But you'd have to be a real nitpicker, I think, to worry about what Colin did. His is a recessive role but it's very important. We see the whole picture through him.

The D. H. Lawrence Society sent me a long thing saying that they had decided it was the best version of Lawrence as a film, apart from *Women in Love* (dir. Ken Russell). They thought *Women in Love* and *Kangaroo* were miles better than any of the other versions, which is interesting.

Fascism in Australia and the origins of the colonies and Australian attitudes towards authority?

Yes, alongside the democratic egalitarian tradition there does exist a Nietzschean tradition which you can see as early as Henry Handel Richardson. She and, certainly, Patrick White, were always interested in the individual alone, the great individual, the great leader figure. I think there's an authoritarian streak amongst most of the organisations, in the trade unions and in the Labor Party, a very strongly authoritarian streak.

If we ever got a fascist movement in Australia, it's much more likely to come out of a Labor Party. Remember, Hitler was a national socialist and a great populist. I think it would be national and I think the emphasis would be on the collective as against the individual.

The idea for Great Expectations *and to make the mini-series was your son's idea?*

We were talking one day, he and I, about *Great Expectations* and the idea of making it. Because we're Australians, obviously the person who interests us, and the only figure who was an Australian in the whole of Dickens, is Magwitch – although Dickens does send Micawber to New South Wales and he sent a couple of his sons to Australia. I think of Dickens as the greatest nineteenth-century novelist. I suppose you've got to put in Tolstoy and Dostoevsky, but Dickens is up there with the greatest. With Magwitch, the interesting thing is that, as soon as you start saying, 'What did happen to Magwitch and why was he fixated on this kid? Why did he want to turn him into a gentleman?', you get into that class stuff, into certain sides of Australia which I think are interesting.

When Tom made the suggestion, I immediately thought of all the business of emancipist versus colonist, what he must have gone through, this figure.

Although the novel was written in 1862, Dickens seems to have based it on family. There's a fair amount of evidence that Dickens' grandfather – his father was a rather feckless figure – is supposed to have actually embezzled some money and was on the run and lived in the Isle of Man. And it has been suggested that perhaps this crazy old grandfather, the wanted man, is a memory of Dickens' childhood, this figure visiting him, visiting the family. It's a possibility, anyway.

The other thing was the premise of the story that had a convict return to England where he would have been hung, killed or disposed of. But that was no longer true in 1862. There are a number of indications that Dickens set it much further back, in the 1830s. So that meant that we had to ask, 'Where did Magwitch go? What happened to him?' When I started reading around it, the most interesting book was Price Waring's, *Tales of the Old Convict System*. I used, for instance, the part where Magwitch becomes the hangman. That's taken directly from Price Waring.

Of course, one of the things that interested me a lot was Dickens' descriptions of convicts in England, then the descriptions of the convict experience in Price Waring. One realised that they were all part of one system. And you also realise from reading Price Waring that what we think of as Dickensian, melodramatic, a moralistic way of looking at things, was in fact the nineteenth century, the world they all lived in. It was quite seamless.

As soon as you say, 'The hero is not Pip, the hero is Magwitch', it does turn everything around. I originally had the same ending as the novel. The rules that I worked to were that I could write anything provided it fitted with what Dickens had written, but I couldn't cheat and alter what had happened. So, even if Magwitch survived, he had to appear to die in the hospital.

As soon as one investigated the novel in any detail, it was interesting how complexly and how intricately developed Dickens' plots and subplots are. For instance, Compeyson was the lover of Miss Haversham and jilted her. Miss Haversham's ward is the daughter of Magwitch – that is, Estella is the daughter of Magwitch and Jaggers' housekeeper.

That's in the novel, it's all true. And she is supposed to have been a murderer, to have murdered somebody on Houndside Heath. Miss Haversham's brother is, I think, ruined by Compeyson, and Compeyson has to go to Australia with Magwitch. Anyway, to me it was a very interesting exercise. It's lovely working with great writers – I mean, a writer like Dickens or a writer like Lawrence, so enormously rich. They were great.

Australian Feature Films

1969 *2000 Weeks*

1971 *Stork*

1973 'The Child' in *Libido*

1973 *Alvin Purple*

1974 *Petersen*

1974 *End Play*

1976 *Eliza Fraser*

1979 *The Last of the Knucklemen*

1981 *Partners*

1986 *Kangaroo*

Donald
Crombie

Donald Crombie composing a shot with DOP Gene Moller (left) and First
AD Peter Fitzgerald, *Flipper*, 1996. (Photo courtesy Donald Crombie.)

WHEN YOU BEGAN your film-making career in the 1960s, did you ever imagine you would be part of an Australian film industry?

I never thought – I imagine I wasn't alone – that there would ever be a feature-film industry in this country. I never thought I would ever make a feature film. I always thought it would be nice. Through the 1960s I was working at Film Australia doing documentaries. The only reason I started doing drama was that I had been to NIDA – not as an actor – it was a technical course and it fitted you for stage management and for directing plays. But it demystified the actor, so when there was a demand for dramatised documentaries – and they were public-service training films – Stanley Hawser, who was then running Film Australia, thought I could do it because I'd been to NIDA. So I got to direct, along with others. Peter Weir did one too, and a couple of other directors who went on to do feature films.

So, when the renaissance occurred in the 1970s and I got my chance with *Caddie*, I never thought I would ever make another one. In fact, making one was almost enough. I thought, 'Oh, well, that's fine', and I'd done it. When it actually worked and was successful and people went to it, Tony Buckley, the producer, said, 'We've got to make another one'. I said, 'How do we do that?' I mean, we were very naive.

The other thing that was amazing: it never occurred to me then to go and work in America. Today directors seem to make one film and they're off to Hollywood. Of course, now the reverse is true: the Hollywood industry is very, very interested in looking for new talent, wherever it comes from. But in that era I don't think they were so interested in taking on Australian directors. It was quite some years before even people like Peter Weir got offered a Hollywood film as opposed to going there. I think we were seen as an exotic species. I remember we went to see a man – he was an agent, I think, in America, but he represented Warner Bros here – and he had the box-office returns for every day. He could just look and say, 'Oh, yes, such-and-such did so-and-so in Melbourne'. So they were watching us and they knew about us, but they didn't rush to us with offers. It was strange. Then I think they realised subsequently that the best thing to do is just hire Australians and away you go.

Do I Have to Kill My Child? *and* Who Killed Jenny Langby? *What attracted you to these docu-dramas?*

Jenny Langby was for Community Welfare in Adelaide. Basically what they wanted was a film that said, 'Look over the fence. The person who's living next door to you could be in trouble', à la Jenny Langby, who was obviously going under with a multitude of personal and social problems and no one knew. The message in the film is in the neighbour coming and looking after the kids. After the event, of course; it's all too late to save the woman.

That's where I met Anne Deveson and where we first worked together. We brought her in to front it. It was written by myself and Greg Barker and Anne came in because we were sort of faking it as a documentary, a dramatised documentary presented as a genuine story. At that time Anne had the profile of being a front person.

I think Anne Deveson and I instigated *Do I Have to Kill My Child?* Anne came up with the idea because she had a personal interest in child abuse – 'baby bashing' we should call it – as opposed to sexual abuse. That was just being discovered. It was really creepy that there was virtually nothing written about it; it didn't happen. I don't think I'm revealing a confidence here, but when one of her children was born very premature she found herself not coping and her feelings of anger and losing control had frightened her.

So, being Anne Deveson, she started to explore and discovered there was this hidden syndrome in society. The research that Anne did was quite extraordinary: women admitting that they would literally lock themselves in a room to stop them getting to the kid. Pretty horrific stuff. And you realise when you get out into the suburbs, or not even the suburbs, there are people with immense loneliness and huge problems that no one knows about.

Around the time the film was made, it was just starting to come into medical literature; it really was ground breaking. So she and I decided we would try and do a dramatised film. We went to Film Australia and they put up some money and our friends at Channel 9 put up the rest, which is amazing when you think of Channel 9 today – they wouldn't touch a film like that with a barge pole, being a one-off for a start and an hour-long drama. Anyway, we made the film and it was hugely successful. I think it rated 40 in Sydney and something similar in Melbourne. It did numbers you only get with test matches and big one-off sporting events today! Anne received huge mail from that one film. She said the people rang in and wrote that they thought they were unique, that they were monsters, and then they realised they weren't. So that was an extraordinarily satisfying experience. It really worked.

We tried to do another one after it. Anne wasn't involved in this one. I was asked by the Tasmanian Community Welfare to make a film which we called *Slippery Slide*, basically showing how, if you send a kid to boys' prison, the slippery slide means he will end up in jail, or a very strong likelihood. I went down and read copiously. I was given access, which is apparently pretty rare, to the Community Welfare files on these kids, and some of them were just shocking. You could start at the back of the file and go forward and come to the kid at 18 in Risden Gaol.

We made the film and again Channel 9 took it. But it didn't rate nearly as well because we realised that, with *Slippery Slide*, you tend to say 'It's somebody else's problem; that wouldn't happen to me'. So it didn't have a wide appeal.

You have often stayed in the suburbs with your feature films. How does Caddie *seem in retrospect?*

A long way away! What can you say about *Caddie*? It was fascinating because it was a period in Australia I didn't know about. I didn't realise what went on. I suppose there are similar themes: a woman who was left on her own had to make do with two kids before the era of social services. It's so long ago, I suppose I should look at it again one day.

You created an atmosphere of inner-Sydney suburbs; the pub atmosphere.

Yes, we got that right, apparently. I think the nearest I ever went to that was in Adelaide, where they still had six o'clock closing. I never saw the six o'clock swill here. By the time I was able to have a drink, it was back to ten o'clock. But I remember going to Adelaide with Film Australia and experiencing something of it, but perhaps not quite as frenetic. We did the research and talked to plenty of people who remembered it. We got the whole craziness of men ordering ten beers and then drinking them as they were shouting, 'Time, gentlemen, please' and the girls behind the bar, what they went through. We spoke to barmaids who gave us quite a bit of background.

You got a real feel for the women and the rapport between them.

With Helen Morse and Jackie Weaver again; Melissa Jaffer.

And the Greek connection.

Yes, this was based on the book. The Greek was killed in real life. I'm not quite sure where he was killed, whether it was here or in Greece, but Caddie's life was very sad: a battler story.

You said you weren't expecting to make another feature film, but you directed The Irishman.

That's because, as I say, we were naive and just thought, 'That's nice, we've done that', and then Tony Buckley's saying, 'You've got to get out and what will we do next?' We didn't have anything. I had read *The Irishman* some years before and I had liked it. Because my family came from western Queensland, I've always found the Australian outback very evocative. I really like working in the outback and I love those sorts of stories and people. Tony read the book and we wrote the script and away we went and raised the money.

Strangely, it wasn't easy. I remember Matt Carroll saying to us because of *Caddie* being successful, 'You'll be able to write your own ticket. You'll be right; you can make anything you want'. Well, that wasn't true. It was as hard to raise the money for *The Irishman* as it was for *Caddie*. People didn't rush forward with money and investors didn't come out of the woodwork to give us money. But I think it was a film that was pretty true to the era that it was set in, and to the characters. Again we researched fairly carefully what life was like in that particular era.

I went up to north Queensland. *The Irishman* is a true story; that's what actually interested me about it. It's based on Elizabeth O'Connor's husband's father. She wrote it at a place called Forest Home Station, in the Gulf, just out of Georgetown. I went to the place where she wrote the book and sat on the verandah. She had just sat there and written what she could see. I can't remember the fictional name of the station, but it was actually Forest Home, and her husband Phil was the manager and his father was the teamster.

I found out later that it had a better ending in real life, but I suspect it wouldn't have been satisfying in the cinema. He had the fight with the boy. Since horse teams were coming to an end, motor transport was running him out of the Gulf. He went down and started working in timber – which was in the movie – but he ended up pulling cane trains. The last use of a horse team in north Queensland was pulling cane wagons, and the old man ended up there.

Phil, the son, who was Michael in the story, when he was 24 or 25, I think, went to look for his father. He found him somewhere around Tully and they went and had a drink. They had the one drink and the father said to him, 'Well, I suppose you've got something to do'. He interpreted this as meaning, 'Don't wait around', so he went and never saw him again. He died in Brisbane. It wouldn't have been a very good ending in a movie; it's probably better he fell over a cliff. But it was, I thought, a very human story where they actually did meet up and the old man cut all his ties with the family.

And family ties in Cathy's Child?

I was commissioned to make it. The producers came to me with a script, so I didn't have anything to do with the writing or the evolving of the project; it was just a directing job. But I actually liked that. I think, of my feature films, it's probably my favourite. It was probably the most successful for me, mainly because I think we were extraordinarily successful in creating that character, Cathy Bikos. Michelle Fawdon is obviously not Maltese, but she pulled that off brilliantly, I thought. The accent, I'm told, is perfect. She lived with a family and that's how she achieved it. It was a very good project to work on.

Based on newspaper stories?

Yes, Dick Wordley was still alive. It's an absolutely true story. I think that was his first, but he made a bit of a profession out of chasing runaway kids around the world after that. He never gave up. He was a typical journalist: a drink problem and a few other problems. I did meet him.

It raised issues of post-War migration and inter-cultural and multicultural problems: such a contrast between Australia and Greece.

It was that Greek patriarchy thing, wasn't it? The father believed he had the absolute right to take the child and go wherever he wanted. She was a strong woman in the sense that, once she went, she had to do it all on her own.

The Greek focus in The Heartbreak Kid *(dir. Michael Jenkins) is patriarchal Greek dominance sanctified by the Orthodox Church, and in* Head On *(dir. Ana Kokkinos) there is the same kind of strong Greek family focus. It would be an interesting study to look at those films and see what they're telling the Australian audience about multiculturalism. So* Cathy's Child *would be significant in that development.*

I hadn't thought about that, but you're right. A Greek in *Caddie*, a Greek in *Cathy's Child*.

Then you went back to social questions in The Killing of Angel Street?

That was a labour of love. That was the film we really cared about and wanted to make. It was very difficult to get going, to raise the money. We went through several writers. Michael Craig ended up writing – he and Evan Jones, the West Indian writer who wrote *Kangaroo* (dir. Tim Burstall) and *Wake in Fright* (dir. Ted Kotcheff). He came in in the end. I went to England. I wanted Julie Christie to play the lead and, by this stage, we thought with *Caddie* behind us, and *The Irishman*, we had a bit of a chance to attract a star. And sure enough we did, we got Julie Christie, but unfortunately she came at a price that the market wouldn't wear. We went to America. We actually did the whole waltz through the studios and I discovered for the first and only time the expression 'vehicle dependent', which described Julie Christie: unless Spielberg was directing or she had a big male star with her, they wouldn't back her. The money that her agent was asking was just too rich, so we eventually had to let her go.

Then we offered it to Helen Morse and she said she would do it, but she didn't like the script and wanted it changed, so that's why we brought Evan Jones out. We sat up in a motel unit somewhere on the North Shore for weeks getting the script right and then, on Christmas Eve, she withdrew. It has never been explained why she withdrew. Helen, I think, had her own demons about film so she pulled out. But of course, with her went the money. So we then had to start all over again.

I think Elizabeth Alexander did a good job, but you just lose your judgment. Originally, Bill Hunter was going to be in it and, for some reason, I felt that Bill and Elizabeth didn't work as a combination, so we had to let Bill go, and he's never spoken to me since. And maybe he was right, maybe he could have worked, but I felt John Hargreaves and Elizabeth worked but Bill was designed for Julie Christie.

John Hargreaves was always very good with the larrikin side of things.

Yes, he was terrific in the film. I'm quite pleased with the film. I think it worked and it did what we set out to do.

The background of Sydney politics?

Again, we researched it pretty thoroughly and we got fairly close to the beast, I think. We were peculiarly warned off by a senior politician, who's a judge now, I believe. He rang Tony Buckley and said that this film was a bit close to the bone and – talking about me – he said, 'He's got young children and he should be thinking a bit about what he's doing'. It didn't put us off, but you did look under the car for about two days afterwards because you thought, 'Hang on a minute, what's all this about?' ... And the nexus between government and big business and crime. They're very comfortable together.

Did Heatwave *(dir. Phillip Noyce) have the same problem?*

Yes, *Heatwave* and *Angel Street* came out at the same time – a bit unfortunate because I think they're quite different films. I remember having almost a physical altercation with a character in Berlin because *Angel Street* got taken to Berlin. I was bailed up at a party by a journalist who'd had a few wines too many and he started abusing me because the wrong film was in competition, and I was saying, 'Well, I'm sorry. What can I do?' And he lambasted it, said how dreadful it was, that it was a disgrace, that *Heatwave* was a masterpiece and hadn't been recognised. And I thought, 'Talk to the festival director, not me'. This bloke was pushing me and being very aggressive and I thought, 'This is all crazy'. But *Heatwave* is very different. Some people prefer it to *Angel Street* and other people don't.

So then it was Kitty and the Bagman?

That probably shouldn't have been made. It was a bit of an aberration. That only got made because we were flush with funds. That was when it became ridiculously easy to make films. There were better things we should have been doing with our time. I don't have any great brief for it now. What was interesting about *Kitty* was that it was our own particular crime scene. I was very annoyed to hear that the American distributor had put on a frontispiece to the film, a card or something, that said that it was a homage to the Warner Bros gangster films of the 1930s. And I thought, 'Absolute bullshit! How dare they?' What they were really saying was that we didn't have a crime culture of our own in Australia, therefore, in some sort of weird way, they were trying to make it more palatable to American audiences – which didn't work. It didn't do any good in America.

It had a touch of the Damon Runyans!

Phil Cornford: he's a writer whose byline you see a lot in the *Herald* now, but when we were doing that, he worked for Mr Murdoch. He and John Birney were both hardboiled old newspapermen. Phil Cornford was a man who shouldn't have been born in this century. He was a buccaneer. He did things like dressing as an Afghan and crossing into Afghanistan, doing crazy things to write about. He loved that era and the way those women ran their crime empires and were at each other's throats. It was probably a valid dramatic thing, but I don't think the film was all that good.

The crime of last century in Robbery Under Arms?

We all knew that we were making a giant western and we would never have another opportunity like that in Australia. The budget was huge by contemporary standards. I think it was seven million then. Ken Hannam was the other director, so we just shared it. I did the first three hours and he did the last three. I had never done a mini-series before. It's probably the closest I will ever get to the experience of what it would be like making a big western in the United States. If you wanted 500,000 head of cattle, you got them!

It's a great book, great characters, and I think we cast it well. Ken and I did the casting. We found these young actors just out of NIDA, Steven Vidler particularly. The girl I thought was terrific in it, Jane Menelaus. With Sam Neill, I obviously saw the Finch style. I thought he and Finch were somewhat similar. I think the way Sam portrayed the character was pretty right as far as the book goes.

The choice of locations was interesting, doing it in South Australia. I think it was set around Goulburn originally, but the Wilpena area of the Flinders Ranges was a very spectacular backdrop for that.

Then you directed Playing Beattie Bow.

I think that worked all right. I'm amazed now, when I meet young actors and actresses who were all brought up on it. They have never heard of *Caddie*, but if you say *Playing Beattie Bow*, 'Oh, yes, we saw that when we were in year –' whatever. I think they would have made quite a lot of money out of that, the producers, because the cassette runs were huge. It was helped by being in the curriculum, which is a great start for a film.

It was a fun thing to make. And we had a very good designer, George Liddell. The set was based loosely on what The Rocks were like back in that period, and he just imagined the rest.

I haven't seen Rough Diamonds.

Nor have I. *Rough Diamonds* is something I never talk about. I should have taken my name off because this was a case where the distributor came in and altered the film without my agreement. One of the things that really annoyed me about it was altering the plot. The history of *Rough Diamonds* was that I was in north Queensland when we were doing *The Irishman*; we were doing the location survey and we had passed a road gang. The chap who was showing us round pointed out a character leaning on a shovel and said, 'That's Bill Bloggs and he owns –' some station that was 60,000 hectares of prime grazing country. I said, 'What's he doing in a road gang?' and he said, 'He's broke'. So I went into this and found that in the rural crises that come every now and again, the people who own these huge properties can actually be cash-strapped.

I thought this was the subject for a film, so I came up with a storyline which was *Rough Diamonds*, basically, and took it to Film Australia. It was too rich for them. It wasn't a feature, it was an hour – this was in the same era when we were doing *Do I Have To Kill My Child?* It was going to have Michelle Fawdon in the lead. But it went into the bottom drawer. Then some years ago Damien Parer came to me and said, 'Have you got a feature?' He was going to Queensland and they had a scheme where they would help producers, give them money, if they had a couple of feature scripts. I showed it to him and he read it and thought it was terrific, but it needed to be developed. It was a very serious story about a chap who's going to lose his property because the banks were coming in on him. Then we introduced an element that he was an untrained but good singer. He meets a girl who's a singer and who's fleeing from a bad marriage. They have a romance and end up together. He starts making some money in the country and western circuit, which helps keep the bank off his back and saves his property.

We were originally going to have Craig McLachlan; then he got a job in London, so we went for Jason Donovan. We had six or seven songs in it and away we went. The distributor, I believe, sold it as a musical and sold it very well to Rank in England. When they saw it, they said, 'It's not a musical. It's a social realist drama with some songs'. So they cut out all the bits that mattered to me, which was the whole story about this bloke losing a property. The whole reason for the film, the reason I got involved in it and developed it, was taken away by the distributor. The FFC in their wisdom backed the distributors and said, 'If they think it's got to be like this, it's got to be like this'. So I said 'Fine', and we parted company. I've never seen the film and I never will. It's terrible, I believe, because it doesn't have any heart; there's nothing there. It's never been released, thank God. But I wanted to take my name off it and I was talked out of it. I now regret that because I realise I

Myth & Meaning
Myth & Meaning

should have taken my name off it, because otherwise you wouldn't have mentioned it, and they're the reasons.

Years ago Tony Buckley, Anne Deveson and I wanted to make a film about the Ingham rapes. You might wonder why anybody would want to make a film about the Ingham rapes, but we thought there was a good story there and Anne was very keen. It certainly was a very dramatic story. I won't bore you with the details but it was ritualised rape. Basically, these men in Ingham were raping the women and, because they didn't know it wasn't like this in the rest of the world, they just accepted it. It went on over a period of years.

Anne and I went up to Ingham and interviewed people about it and there was a script written. Olivia Newton-John and I got together and we were going to do a film in America. Anyway, that fell through, so we thought, 'Olivia Newton-John: terrific idea. She'll be good'. She was looking to do a straight drama. So we went to a producer, 'Would you like to be involved in this?' and he said, 'No. That would be completely wrong because it's a straight drama and the audience will walk into the cinema expecting seven songs, because we've got Olivia'. And, of course, the same thing with Jason Donovan. I should have realised that. The distributors all went, 'Jason, he's going to sing, that's good. It will be a light entertainment'.

You have directed a number of mini-series and some telemovies.

Yes. What happened was it became increasingly difficult to finance films and easier, conversely, to do television. I really like the mini-series form. Being given four hours to tell a story as opposed to ninety minutes is actually terrific, and the few that. I've done that I like have been good. The two *Heroes* were, I think, terrific. These were some of my most memorable and pleasurable experiences making film: a really very strong story and I was quite pleased with the results.

As you can probably see with the themes, if I have a philosophy about what I do, I like it to have some meaning. That's why I've never gone to America. I just couldn't go over there and work – you look at some of my colleagues like Phil Noyce, who's gone to America: fine; that's his bag. But I've no interest in going over there and making *Clear and Present Danger* (dir. Phillip Noyce) or one of those sorts of stories.

The most successful mini-series I did was a film called *The Alien Years*. Peter Yeldham wrote the story and it was done for the ABC. It was a World War One story of Germans in the Barossa Valley, and it was actually true of the whole of that period all over Australia, where they were persecuted because they were Germans – even though they might have come to Australia in the 1840s when the first settlers came to the Barossa from Germany to escape persecution. If your name was Müller, you didn't have a very good time. A lot of it was economic bastardry: there were two bakers in town, one

English, one German. Well, it didn't take a lot to suddenly say, 'Well, I heard old Hans down the road saying that the Kaiser is great'. And the enmities that had flowed from that period were still in existence in the mid-1980s when that show was made.

It did quite well; one of the highest-rating ABC mini-series of that period. Of course, they all watched it down in the Barossa and the result was extraordinary. For a start, in Adelaide the talkback radio program they have at about nine in the morning, for three days it was just people ringing in with their own stories. A huge healing went on. Families who hadn't spoken to each other for three generations buried the hatchet, and I was invited – and I regret not going – to have lunch with the patriarch of the Grant family, the Orlando winemakers, who came out in 1840. He wanted to have lunch with me because he thought the film was so significant; what it had done for that community. That was a terrific film to do.

You also made some of The Feds *telemovies.*

I did that for money. Unfortunately what has happened is that it's got harder and harder to make what I would call meaningful television. In fact, conversely, it's now come round the other way: it's easier now to get a film up, or it seems to be, than to get a television drama up. If you have a message or you want to make something with a bit of soul to it and get it on television, it's very difficult.

You're not seeing very much now, are you? The ABC may be your only port. The commercials seem interested only in long-form series. You don't see many mini-series. Channel 7 is doing one that Tony Buckley is producing from Bryce Courtenay's *The Potato Factory*, a four-hour mini-series, but there seems to be very little of that sort of work, because the prices went up. You couldn't make a *Heroes* today or an *Alien Years* – I just don't think they would be interested. I don't think they would buy anything period.

Then you have this terrible trouble with casting, where the networks, for putting in a third of the budget – probably not even that – insist on casting control. Then they want Ray Martin or somebody to play the lead because it's the only way they think the audience will watch it. The last thing I did, that *Feds* thing you mentioned, that was a nightmare, absolute nightmare: the casting, dealing with television network executives. They have never heard of half the actors in Australia and they're not interested. They say, 'Unless you can get them on the cover of *TV Week*, that's it'. That's the way you cast them.

But, looking at your work, especially between 1975 and 1985, that's a very good body of material with a strong, humane Australian streak.

Yes, well, I'm quite pleased. And there's a couple of films you've probably never even heard of. I think one of my best was a film I made in Adelaide called *Parents*, about parenting, which was made for Community Welfare. It was just made on tape, a very cheap production, but it was dramatised. We've had four kids and had the usual problems, and I wrote this from the heart. It was designed to show to parents, when their kids get into their teens, what they're likely to expect. But no one has ever seen it, apart from community groups in South Australia.

We did another one down there, which was about sexual abuse. It was again designed for teachers – how they could recognise in their classroom a kid who may be being abused. They were quite worthwhile films to get involved in. There's no money in it, you just do it for love, but I would rather do that than make a Movie of the Week in Los Angeles.

Australian Feature Films

1976 *Caddie*

1978 *The Irishman*

1981 *The Killing of Angel Street*

1982 *Kitty and the Bagman*

1985 *Robbery Under Arms*

1986 *Playing Beattie Bow*

1994 *Rough Diamonds*

Rolf de Heer

Rolf de Heer, *The Old Man Who Read Love Stories*, 1999. (Vertigo Productions.)

Each one of the awards surprised me. We had no real expectations when we went because we thought that just getting into competition at Venice was already beyond our expectations. We liked the film immensely but had no idea how an audience would react to it.

You received the OCIC, International Catholic Award?

That surprised us no less than any of the others – and probably a little more – certainly at first. But, with a little bit of reflection, for me personally as a film-maker, I appreciated that one more than the others. It was the clearest message that the film was speaking to audiences in the way that I wanted it to speak.

How can Bad Boy Bubby *be seen in continuity with your other films?*

Bad Boy Bubby and my first film, *Tail of a Tiger*, were the most personal films that I had made. And the two that I had written independently. The second film I wrote, *Incident at Raven's Gate*, is, for me, a little bit of an aberration. This had more to do with, when it came at a particular stage of my career, what was possible and what was not.

I am attracted to material that is positive. There are a number of things that I care a lot about; one of them is childhood. The preciousness of childhood for me is important, above almost anything else. I can refer all other themes to childhood. If a plot has no bearing on childhood, for some reason it's less interesting for me. *Dingo* refers to childhood. *Tail of a Tiger* is clearly very much concerned with childhood. *Bad Boy Bubby* is very much about childhood – more, in fact, than any of the other films. So, in the broadest sense, all the issues of the world today can be related to childhood, 'What does this do to children?' Perhaps the single most important thing we can do is to love our children without abuse. The film became, for me, a plea for childhood.

What Tail of a Tiger *and* Dingo *seem to have in common is a sense of identity and some sense of vision: the young boy with the planes in* Tiger; *Dingo has his boyhood dreams, the vision of Miles Davis coming down from the plane onto the tarmac and the boy's wanting to be a trumpeter.* Bad Boy Bubby *highlights identity and growth. What was the genesis of* Bad Boy Bubby?

Its evolution is very peculiar. I was writing down thoughts, writing down ideas. I was writing them down for a very low-budget film more than ten years before I actually wrote the script of *Bad Boy Bubby*. You can imagine how over ten years the film evolves and changes, particularly in the way I work. There are elements in *Bubby* that are very much part of earlier ideas. But then other things developed – look, I had children, so that changed me very much as a human being.

Some things in the film are consciously constructed in so far as I say, 'Well, I want to do this' or 'I want to do that', but so many more of the parameters of the film are subconscious and come from who I am as a human being and what I think is important. You tend to like certain things; you don't question why you like that scene or why you want to put it in a particular place, because it's simply a function of who you are yourself. It may be taking a view opposite to your own, but it still has a function of relating to how I live my life as a human being.

One of the things I want to do is move people. Now, that can be done in a cynical way or it can be done, I guess, in an optimistic way. My sensibilities are in the more optimistic way, so that would tend to lead me into looking at the world through more innocent eyes.

The idea of a child-man emerging at age 35: where did that come from?

A number of influences. One is quite simple: in some way I wanted to make a film about childhood, about the preciousness of childhood. But, ultimately, I ended up with a decision to explore this through the dark side, if you like; wanting to deal with certain aspects of child abuse and associated issues. I was thinking that if I really wanted to deal with it in a confronting way in a really low-budget film, then it might be better to do it somehow with an adult rather than with an actual child. I was concerned about the process of doing the film with a child; I hadn't worked out what would happen to that child. I had worries about involving children in that sort of confrontational material. So that's one way that it came about.

The other way is quite peculiar: that the very first time I began to think about making this film was as a consequence of seeing a Sam Shepard play, in which a close friend of mine, an actor, played the part of the character, Dodge, a 70-year-old man. It was an extraordinary performance and I wanted to make a film with him. We wanted to capitalise on that extraordinary performance of his being an old man. But we realised that a younger actor playing an old man on stage is one thing, doing it in the cinema is quite different. It is much more difficult and much harder to get away with. So, in a sense, the first image for the film was an old man in a room, being played by this friend of mine. But, of course, that couldn't be. So then he became a younger man playing an older man. That was some kind of development – and that's where the character of Pop coming back home came into it.

Have people asked you about Being There *(dir. Hal Ashby) and the Peter Sellers character, Chance, the gardener?*

A couple of people have asked about the script and a few about the film itself. I haven't actually seen *Being There* and I read the book only well after the film was finished. Somebody said, 'You should read it', and I said, 'Yes, I know I should'. But now I can because, when I was working on *Bad Boy Bubby* and *Being There* existed as a film, I knew I shouldn't see it because I didn't want to be influenced by it. The same with *Kaspar Hauser* (dir. Werner Herzog). A lot of people have asked me about it. I've had the tape for six or seven years because somebody gave it to me and said, 'Look, you know, it's a bit like what you're doing'. Right, fine. I put it away and didn't look at it.

The religious dimensions of Bad Boy Bubby, *especially with the opening sequences: the mother seemed very slatternly, but she had a crucifix on the wall. It seems to be broken and have no head.*

That's right. It doesn't have a head. It's a flaw in the film-making that we don't actually see quite clearly that it has no head. So the mother saying, 'God can see everything you do. Jesus will tell me' has been added. This somehow empowers the image: the strength of what he feels, the fact that the crucifix doesn't have a head, and he's told that despite that, it can see everything he does.

This makes an audience ask, 'Where is this film going?' It introduces the God language that recurs during the film. What do you bring personally to the film in terms of God language and Christianity?

I was not brought up particularly religiously. At various times in my life, in some senses, I was. When we were refugees from Indonesia back to Holland, I was farmed out to a family which was particularly religious. Every mealtime there were Bible readings and so on. I remember that quite well. My father was, I guess it would be fair to say, anti-religious, although 'anti' is a bit strong – anti-religious in the broadest sense. Whereas my mother was much more tolerant. She didn't actually encourage religion, but was more tolerant than my father. I don't want to paint them as extremes, because they're not.

When we came out to Australia we lived in a migrant camp for eight months – not the best of circumstances – and various things happened. I think I was 8 at the time. My brother and I did a whole series of things for which we had ultimate cause to feel regret. I don't know what my parents said to me, to either of us, at the time, but what happened was that when we eventually moved out of the migrant camp, my brother and I independently decided to go to church. We did this for two years, I think. It was almost a question of sneaking out on Sunday mornings and Mum would give us threepence in the corner of our handkerchiefs. We had decided this was the thing to do. I guess religion faded for me after that as I began to question lots of things.

Then, through my late teens, I had three particular friends, two of whom were Catholic. So there was a sort of religious mix between the two groups. It was the subject of a great deal of discussion as we tested our theories of life, religion and other issues. At one point during this time, almost in deference to one of the friends particularly, I made a serious attempt to see if I could get myself to believe in God. Ultimately that didn't work for me either.

The next major thing that happened to me in the development of where I stand with religion was that I did a year of philosophy at Sydney University. That influenced my way of thinking about all things more than anything else I've done. Since then I've been more an interested observer in seeing how religion affects different people and its place in what people are and how they live their lives.

You tend to see what I might call 'good people' and there seems to me to be no differentiation according to their goodness as to whether they have faith or whether they don't have faith. And you see what one might call 'bad people', overall, at the lower end – I hesitate to make judgments like this but it's hard to talk about it in any other way – of what are considered by society to be bad people. There's a greater number of them who have no connection with faith at all. Then you have all the people in between. And what I find is that of the people in between who have faith, the thing that characterises them most for me is hypocrisy. But if they are people with faith who are not characterised by that hypocrisy, then they're almost always, to me, in the 'good' category.

That explains a great deal about your characters in Bad Boy Bubby. *Is Bubby's mother evil? She uses religion and God as threats.*

Yes, she does, but I don't see her as being evil. I see her as a product of her upbringing, a sadly damaged product of her upbringing. She might have been 17 and brought up in a rigorous household, protected from the outside world to a great degree. Then, somehow, she was seduced by the Pop character. And he disappeared, of course. She found herself pregnant and unable, in the society that she lived in, to reveal that she was pregnant.

She was naive and really incapable of dealing with the outside world. So she hid in that place – that cellar, effectively – and as she got more and more disconnected from society, the things that she had been taught as a child became more and more fractured. She used them and became more distant from how she used to be but she became, in another sense, a lot more focused on the little bits and pieces that she retained from her past. And in her own way, with all her difficulties – which, I think, are quite severe – not only is she in this terrible situation, but she's also quite disconnected from other people, trying to bring up this child who has nearly killed her. She has no armoury at all to deal with her problems. And, as life goes on ... there's one bed in the place, Bubby was a little baby and she probably loved him a great deal and she probably still does – but the basic situation never changes. Then as he grows up, the situation develops and she's completely out of touch. I say this because I don't feel her to be evil in any way. But once again, because of her past history, she is to be seen within the theme of childhood.

Bubby himself?

The film is about the way we judge people, usually by superficial appearances, almost always by arbitrary standards, often wrongly and unfairly.

Bubby has no way of judging people. He has met only one other person in his life: his mother, on whom he is completely dependent. He has no real basis for comparisons (no television or radio or books), so no bases for making judgments about people. He is uncorrupted by any pressure to conform. He is the complete innocent.

Using Bubby's non-judgmental view of the world, the film begins to explore parts of that world, wandering through random aspects of people and society. Bubby can begin to form some picture of the whole. And so the world is funny and tragic. It is ugly and beautiful. It is spiteful and forgiving, loving and hateful, honest and hypocritical. That is how Bubby finds it and how the world deals with him. The people in this world teach Bubby how to be. He learns how to behave.

A complete contrast: Angel's parents – when Bubby goes to their house for a meal, their walls and their sideboard are covered with religious pictures, statues and holy cards, full of religious icons.

I don't want to say that all products of a rigidly religious upbringing – whether it be one religion or another or even non-church – have severe problems. Angel herself has found her way out. One of the themes in the film is personal responsibility: how much personal responsibility do we have? You get into discussions with people about responsibility and they thump the table and say, 'Of course we have total individual responsibility'. And I say, 'Yes, right, I agree with you'. But it's a little bit too easy. You can say it and I can say it, but when you consider that the overwhelming majority of serial killers were abused as children, it forces you to think. It's not just a coincidence, is it?

But then again, not all children who are abused turn into serial killers. Angel's upbringing is fundamentally different from Bubby's, although there are many similarities. But she comes out of it one way and he comes out of it in a quite different way.

The other thing about that particular dinner scene is that, while the language differs, it's based directly on a scene that I actually experienced. It was not about religion. It was about racism. The mother is the major protagonist in that scene from *Bubby*; in the reality I experienced she was a self-professed, churchgoing Christian.

When that experience happened to me, it took me a long time to recover. I mean, I wasn't the Bubby character. I was just there. It unfolded in front of me and there was nothing I could do to change anything. It was just a most extraordinary experience.

What you have said about philosophy and your questioning seems to be dramatised in the Norman Kaye character.

Yes. Norman's character and the sequence itself highlight for me the schizophrenia that one can feel about religion. His music basically represents for me what is absolutely the best possible thing. Of course, the best thing about Christianity is not its music, but the music in the film represents what a force for good it can be.

The first sound that Bubby hears when he emerges from the cellar is the harmonised choral singing of the Salvation Army group – and a hymn continues while he is making love with the Salvation Army singer.

They are the first people who treat him with kindness. At the same time I didn't want them to be ciphers in the way that we often see the Salvation Army in the street. We don't think of them as real people. And they are and they should be seen as real people. They shouldn't be judged as puppet people who walk around in uniforms.

The second section of music, during the love scene, says the same thing. If a person is going to have a God, the relationship between that person and that God needs to change continually.

Norman Kaye's music was played on a great organ in a church, in a state of disrepair, that was being rebuilt, but dominated by a huge crucifix. The theme was brought back into focus when Bubby buried the dead cat. Bubby uses the organist's words as part of the service for the cat.

Yes, but the essence of the sequence is the music and how it affects Bubby and what that can mean for Bubby. But then you get the other side of it in the plant sequence. The engineer says to Bubby at the very end of his long speech about arguing God out of existence, 'Look, you have to shed yourself of being a subject, in a sense, and make your own decisions'. That's the area that interests me most, especially for the people in the middle ground. But there can be some excusing of one's own behaviour. In fact we're taught to do that to some degree in different aspects of various religions: that we are not always in control of our own actions. But there is also the refusal to take control of our own lives and be responsible for what we do. I know things are changing in the churches and, really, they're changing quite significantly, but you know the old way: 'You can do anything you like; as long as you go to confession and you'll be okay'. That, to me, is the most appalling thing and it teaches us that we have no responsibility.

Bubby became a film about belief systems: spiritual, religious, scientific, interpersonal and how, by clinging to them in order to try to make sense of the world, we are actually prevented from making sense of it. But mostly it became a film about questions rather than answers.

Epsilon. *It screened for the Australian Film Institute Awards in 1995. Was that before you did extra work on it?*

That was before we did extra work on it.

Is it much different from the AFI screenings version?

It plays a little differently in that it's contextualised differently. It now starts forty or fifty years further on from when the action actually takes place. There's an old woman around a campfire talking to two kids about it. Then you go back in time. At the end you find out that the old woman was the woman whose campfire the alien walked into. There's some narration by the old woman through the film. So there's been new stuff shot and there's been some stuff reduced and cut. It actually plays differently. It somehow plays a little easier, a little less intriguing, but I still like it. I like it as much as I did before. It's just a marginally different film, that's all.

There was a touch of the essay about it.

That's still there. You can't get rid of that completely.

What inspired you for Epsilon?

It was an inspiration. That's the only one I can say – it came out of nowhere. I was in post-production on *Bubby*, working by myself on a Sunday, late, at the studio in the cutting room and I started to think, right, here was a chance, the only chance I'll probably ever have, of making a film where I can do anything I want, say anything that I want in any way that I want to say it, and I haven't said any of the really important things. I'd seen some motion-controlled star footage in the previous weeks and it had really affected me, fairly profoundly. It was like a sort of a longing, a beauty but a longing and a tragedy about its beauty.

I guess it was about the earth. It was just filed away in the back of my mind. Then when I was driving to a friend's place that evening to have dinner, only a five- or ten-minute drive, and it just hit me. It was like I knew everything: how to do this film. I didn't know it in absolute detail, but I was like a man possessed. I was making phone calls and by the end of the night I knew it was going to take about a year to shoot, what its budget was going to be, roughly what the content, the set-up, was going to be, the characters and lots of things about it. Then I put it away.

Then *Bad Boy Bubby* happened in Venice. I was in Rome for a week after that because I missed my plane. I'd started to work on it a bit because I had to do something. Then and there I convinced Domenico Profacci to put up half the money. I came back to Australia. The Film Finance Corporation put up the other half and away we went.

So it's a plea for the earth? A plea for humanity?

Yes. It's not a film about childhood, but it's the one film I decided to make for my children. We stormed around the world with great resolution, all of us – the tiny crew and then the cast – feeling that we should do it. It didn't matter how hard it was; we should do it.

Then it was an epic history of stuff which was quite extraordinary. I'll write the book one of these days because of what has happened. It's just staggering, but it happened.

The whole thing was shot with this motion-control rig and I didn't know what they could do. In that sense the film was also about me finding out how this thing worked in order to be able to use it properly in the film that we were already shooting. In places it works, in other places it's a deeply flawed but, for me, a very interesting film.

It screened in Cannes in the marketplace in 1995 and the boss of the American company that had bought it was at that screening. It was jam-packed with people being turned away. He walked out after eight minutes. He's a big man. Since that day it hasn't sold a single territory in the world anywhere.

The transition from Bad Boy Bubby, *and its children's themes, to* The Quiet Room?

It was very much via *Epsilon*. *Epsilon* is not a film about childhood or children, but making it was a long and difficult process: 157 shooting days, all exteriors and all around Australia, especially in the desert, with some overseas shooting as well. When it was finished and bought, there was supposedly more work to be done on it. In the contract with the Americans, they'd set aside a large amount of money for more work if that's what I desired – not anything I had to do. I thought it was a good idea, yes, great. I wanted their suggestions. They wanted to make some suggestions and it was all fine.

But then it was a long time waiting for the money to come through and I needed to keep the crew together. In one sense that's how *The Quiet Room* was born: to make a film in this block of time, a limited block of time. We needed to be shooting in about six or seven weeks. So, we set a shooting date. What do we make the film about?

I'd been thinking about the way children think for quite some time and I'd been casting around for a project to work with children in an adult context. So here was an opportunity to make a film that didn't particularly have to be about anything, but it could be about anything. And I thought, 'All right, let's do it'. So that's really how it came about.

And this brought you to imagining the parents via the child's perspective?

Well, that was interesting. The marriage breakdown was imposed on the project part of the way through, after I'd begun to work on the ideas, because I needed various things – I needed narrative drive, I needed conflict, I needed a reason. It was about children thinking. That was my primary concern and, well, 'How do I do that?' Every film is about the way people think. So 'How do I do that more intensely? I've got to enter the girl's mind, understand what her mind says'. I didn't have it worked out exactly how I was going to do that, but I figured that if we heard what her mind said and we heard what she said as well, it could get confusing. And it's a bit of an easy contrivance, in a way.

So I thought, 'Maybe the thing is just that she doesn't speak, and the only way we can access her is through her mind'. And that then became what I decided. 'Okay, now, why doesn't she speak?' I had to find a good dramatic reason, and that's how the marriage breakdown came into it. I thought, 'I'll do that. That makes sense'.

It was finding the plot rather than the plot finding you. And finding the child's point of view cinematically with the camera?

Yes, it's part of the evolution of 'What is cinema and what makes it worth people spending ten bucks to go and see a film?' What do they need to get out of it in order for that money to have been well spent? It's a constant question for me. It could have become less focused on the child and been more of an ensemble piece. That would have removed the pressure on the child as an actor and on us to get the child right. But I thought, 'No, you see that sort of stuff on television. This has to be all or nothing; this has to be so completely and utterly all or nothing, that either we fail gloriously or we succeed. The chances are we'll fail gloriously, but only in trying to do that can we succeed'. So everything I could think of was to focus it on the child and to make it her perspective – her perspective of adulthood – because that ultimately is the thing that makes it different and interesting.

You're touching on the experience of parents of children of that age.

I thought that might be the case. But in fact what surprises me is the number of people who respond to it in terms of their own childhood. That's not something I'd expected. I mean, I should have, because a lot of it comes from my own childhood and how I used to think. But I never once thought that people would respond to it on that level. It was first evident with a couple of people on the crew. They didn't say anything to me, but one day I heard some comment between two crew people and I thought, 'Of course!'

These days, with so much surfacing about violence and abuse in families, a lot of people are going to respond to it in that way – more than they would have ten years ago.

Yes, I think so.

It's a contribution to adults really focusing on themselves and on children now.

Hopefully it is. In the end one hopes to not just entertain people.

How typical of Australian experience do you think this is?

I don't know and I can't know that. Obviously, I was very careful to not make it specific. What are the problems in the marriage? The little girl woudn't have a clue. What's important is not why they fight, but that they do. I remember standing in a yard at someone's place and hearing the people next door go at it, and being quite interested in this until I heard a child. Then it was not interesting any more; it was terrible. Yes, so the 'that' rather than the 'why'.

Was it received well at Cannes?

Fantastic. We had no expectations for anything like that at all. I mean, competition at Cannes – a ludicrous concept when we were making it. It was just a lovely film to make, because there were no pressures involved. It was just a film and us who were making it. It was great. Then, of course, it gets selected to go to Cannes. It was completely crazy. It turned the world upside down for a bit, but we coped with that. Then we actually went to Cannes and the response was really wonderful. I mean, what's good about it is that it sold very quickly on that day of the screening. The first sale was made on the red carpet on the way out of the cinema; the first deal was closed.

What that means, of course, is that those people who risked the money in the first place on the basis of an idea – I said, 'Look, I want to make this film. It's going to be sort of about a 7-year-old child's perception of adulthood. Can I have the money, please?' And they said, 'Oh, well, okay then'. And then I could make it with complete freedom. And because I could make it with complete freedom, it could be as focused as it is. People can like it or dislike it, but that's what it is.

You produced The Sound of One Hand Clapping *(dir. Richard Flanagan)?*

I was sent the script years ago and I read it and liked it a lot, but it was very wrong for me at the time. It was just one of those scripts that you like a lot and you write back and say, 'Look, very nice. I liked it for these reasons. However, it's not for me at the moment; I'm busy with this, this, this and that.' Then a couple of years later it was sent to me again, saying, 'Please reconsider'. It had been rewritten in the meantime and worked on further, and I had this intensely strong emotional reaction to it – so strong that I thought, 'I can't direct this. It's going to destroy me if I try, because I have to be really involved with the material in order to do it justice and, if I get really involved with this, I'm gone. I can't do it'.

It was one of the most clearly visualised scripts that I've ever read. I thought, 'Well, whoever has written this can clearly communicate what they want to see. And if they can put two words together with their mouth rather than just with their fingers, they ought to be able to direct it'. So I rang Richard Flanagan and said, 'Look, you should think about doing it yourself. I can't do it because of these reasons. Think about doing it yourself'. He rang back a few days later and said, 'Well, I've thought about it and I suppose I could. I've never really thought about it because I don't know one end of a camera from another, never been on a film set'.

It's the only screenplay he'd ever written. I said, 'Well, okay, you decide to give it a go and I'll stick with you. I'll give you a hand'. And that's where it started. Then in the end that has to be formalised because people start to talk about the budget and everything else, and 'Okay, he's a first-time director who's never been on a film set, doesn't know anything about film. Okay, someone like me being involved makes a difference', but then suddenly you become the director's mentor. That's where it started. Then I ended up being the producer. And you basically go along for the ride once you've said, 'Okay, I'll stick with you'. You either do or you don't. In this particular case it means I had to produce it, and it was a long and difficult and wonderful process.

And then Dance Me to My Song?

It's sort of a love triangle. The script is by two people who are complete amateurs in scriptwriting terms, but some of the material they wrote is incredibly powerful and I worked with them over a period of years to try and help them knock it into shape. But ultimately the task was beyond them at the time. Heather Rose is severely afflicted with cerebral palsy, so it was a very slow process for them to write a script. She can't talk; she can only use a voice machine. Then the opportunity came that we could do it, but the only way was if I wrote a script based on some of their material, which is what I did. They were both perfectly happy with that because the spirit of their material was not changed.

The poster says 'a film by Heather Rose', directed by yourself.

Heather originated the project. By her persistence and sheer will, she made it happen. If she had at any stage pulled back from it, it just would never have happened.

Normally you try and create an environment for actors to give of their best. But the nature of her disability mitigated against her being able to do the sorts of things that actors can normally do, to do with timing and accuracy.

The set became focused around Heather in a way that's not usual, really. But that was the way the film was going to get made best. In the end everybody felt that we were there to allow Heather to do the best she could. Then it went a step further. We realised that what we were there for was to be Heather's mouthpiece, to interpret for Heather what she'd started. I was sitting on set and talking to Heather and I just looked around and thought 'I know what's going to happen: they're going to want to put "a film by Rolf de Heer"'. To me, that was completely inappropriate. It felt absolutely like a Heather Rose film. So I said to her then and there, 'This is what we're going to do'. They did argue because I was just going to put 'a film by Heather Rose'; a number of people in the distribution area got very irritated with me and said, 'Okay, well, the compromise is, "directed by Rolf de Heer"'.

Heather Rose's co-writer suffered from chronic fatigue syndrome.

When we did *Bad Boy Bubby* I tracked down Fred Stahl, a laser scientist who specialised in miniaturising electronics. He effectively built Nick's electronic wig for us. Then, because it had some teething problems, he came onto the shoot as an assistant in the sound department. He worked on that entire shoot and had an extraordinary time because it was so liberating to him, having worked in the areas that he worked in, to work in this completely different way with different people. But, shortly after, he got chronic fatigue syndrome quite badly. Heather had a featured extra role in *Bad Boy Bubby* and she saw film-making from the inside in a way that she had never had the chance before, and it was an area she had always been interested in.

Some months later she was browsing on the common ground bulletin board that had been set up by the state government here, and she was talking to a bloke called Fred. After a while they discovered that they had both worked on *Bad Boy Bubby* and suddenly they had this real connection, this event in their lives that had been important to both of them. And that's where they began to work on the script.

Eventually Fred was able to visit her every now and then – they lived about twenty or thirty kilometres apart. But without that bulletin board, there's no way they could have got as far as they did. They wrote numbers of drafts together. I became script editor. I started to help them because they were just doing it, then I became script editor so we could apply for some money – they were both broke at the time. Then, suddenly, I had the opportunity to make a film in terms of timing. I said, 'Look, I need to do another draft of it because it's not quite ready, but shall we make this film, shooting in eight weeks' time?' They both said 'Yes, of course'. And, in the end, the final script is a complete synthesis of three people's work.

It's an extraordinary experience which most people find fairly confronting. She literally bares herself, her soul and body: an extraordinary self-revelation.

It is that, but it really needs to be seen as a performance and, if you knew Heather well enough, you would see precisely that it is. You have to put it down to shots, because with cutting you can do anything. But you look within a shot and you can see what a performance it is, how precise it is in the end and how much she understood precisely what we were doing. The character is not Heather. I mean, I encouraged them to draw upon themselves in the writing – because with new writers it's always a much better way to go – but no more than many writers do draw on their own stuff. It is in part self-revealing but, in a sense, she is using herself as a prototype of people who have cerebral palsy or other such conditions, to provide that window into their lives.

You didn't shirk anything, even in terms of sexual relationships: a very graphic revelation of what is possible for someone who is so disabled.

Yes, and again those things are not in any way directly autobiographical, but the thoughts behind this and the wish to express it are from Heather.

And Madeleine?

You are intended to have some empathy – sympathy – I'm not sure which. It was never my intention to make Madeleine unremittingly evil. I know some people will see her like that but I'm always pleased when people find they have some feelings towards Madeleine which aren't entirely hostile.

She was self-absorbed a lot of the time but, handling a range of moods in the person you're caring for, the exasperation quotient can be very high.

Since Bad Boy Bubby you've portrayed people on the margin, people who experience loneliness and isolation in a way that is not usual in cinema.

Yes, it just happened like that. I don't think I've set out to do that. In fact, I haven't. With film-making being so capital-intensive and business-oriented, it's often simply the luck of the draw. Like *Dance Me to My Song*: when I became involved it was never my intention to make the film, because I was working on a number of other things that I thought would be happening. Then, when I produced *The Sound of One Hand Clapping* and we got towards the end of the post-production process, it had been a long and interesting and difficult process but quite rewarding. But I just needed to come up and breathe and do something of my own, because the whole process of producing for someone else is so different – your sensitivities have to be so different. And this was the one project that was close by and achievable quickly, which was like a parameter. But it may just as well have been one or two of the other things I was doing, which are not remotely like this at all.

I'm doing a film based on a Tagore short story and it's just a lovely story, a lovely film. It's a lot more open than the previous few. In the end it's about fatherhood, I think. It's a relationship between a 6-year-old English girl and a giant Afghan trader. And it's a lovely story.

Australian Feature Films

1985 *Tail of a Tiger*

1989 *Incident at Raven's Gate*

1992 *Dingo*

1993 *Bad Boy Bubby*

1995 *Epsilon*

1996 *The Quiet Room*

1998 *Dance Me to My Song*

Scott

Hicks

Scott Hicks with Max Von Sydow, *Snow Falling on Cedars*, 1999.
(Photo: Doane Gregory, Universal Pictures.)

RETRACING YOUR FILM journey from Freedom *to* Shine, *what are your memories of* Freedom?

Freedom was a very mixed experience. On the one hand it was heady and exciting and intoxicating to be making your first feature film but, on the other, there were difficulties in the way the production was organised. The writer, John Emery, and I were kept separate from each other. In retrospect this was a huge blunder because the film was never totally focused in its vision and I think that's reflected a little in the sort of schizophrenic nature of the film.

Of course, it received very mixed reviews and it didn't do much at the box office. But there were elements about it of which I'm still extremely proud. And then there are things which, if we had worked this material better as writer and director together, we could have done something more substantial. So it was a mixed experience and a little scarifying in the end that it didn't work. And, you know, the director really cops it for good or ill.

You mentioned the word 'vision'. What was your vision of the film and what themes did you want to explore in the early 1980s?

It's such a long time ago now. I think at the heart of it there was a character that I liked and that I recognised; someone with enormous frustration – not unintelligent, but obsessed with cars and in some ways constrained by the unemployment experience that was so rife then and indeed is, of course, now. So it was about someone trying to break free and trying to define himself. It had shades of Walter Mitty about it as well.

I used the word 'schizophrenic' before. *Freedom* was a story that fell into two parts: one was about the whole environment, the whole milieu that Ron had grown up in; the second was about his hitting the road. When he tried to realise his dream, stole the Porsche, found the girl and did hit the road, it became another movie and I don't think those two elements were ever fully reconciled. So you had some people who loved the first half and hated the second and vice versa. When you have that happening with an audience, it's hard for it to gel.

This may be irrelevant, but I was looking for locations for *Sebastian and the Sparrow*; I drove across the Nullarbor and I stopped at various petrol stations along the way, and twice people said to me as they were pumping petrol into the car, 'So, what are you doing?' I said, 'I'm looking for locations for a film'. 'What have you made before?' 'I made this film called *Freedom*.' 'Oh, my favourite film!' So there were people out there who really got something from it but, in broad terms, it simply didn't work. Sometimes that happens.

Scott Hicks

With Sebastian and the Sparrow *you moved from themes of freedom and frustration to something for children and the family.*

That really came about as my own son entered his teens, my elder son, and I became so forcibly aware, as you do as a parent, that your kids have a life that is quite separate from yours. It's like a secret life in a way, because there's the life they live with you and then there's the life they live with their friends. So the encounter between the rich kid and the street kid had something of that expressed in it. I wanted to explore the idea – it was a kind of junior buddy movie with the theme of two people who envied each other's life. To Sebastian, Sparrow has the perfect life: nobody's on his back, he can do what he likes. It looks like glorious freedom. But to Sparrow the constraints of that life are very real. There is Sebastian with the luxury of a home, a family and a very well-to-do existence which was Nirvana to him. I love the way those thoughts could jostle together.

In part the film becomes a road movie too, because they go and search for the street kid's mother. So, probably, it was the first expression for me of the theme of family, relationship, defining who you are and how you become yourself and how you establish your own identity.

One of the things I wanted to do with *Sebastian and the Sparrow* was make the kind of film I felt I could go and see with my own son, because I felt that as an early teenager, he was neither in the *Rambo* (dir. Ted Kotcheff) category nor the *Bambi* (dir. David Hand and Perce Pearce) category. There had to be something in between and there wasn't anything filling that niche. I think there was potentially a huge audience for the film, but I simply couldn't get distributors to commit to it and pick it up properly. Where it played, it received fantastic reactions and at film festivals overseas it won several major prizes for a children's film. I distributed it personally in Adelaide and on its first weekend it out-performed Woody Allen's *Crimes and Misdemeanours* and *Tango and Cash* (dir. Andrei Konchalovsky). If only we could've parlayed that into a broader distribution, it would have been a different story, but the fact was that people didn't want to know about what they saw simply as a children's film. That was that.

The impact that David Helfgott had on you?

Well, David is quite simply one of the most extraordinary people that I've ever met. When I saw him first that night in Adelaide in 1986, I was so struck by the contradiction that was presented in him. There was this shambling, awkward, confused exterior coupled with the brilliant virtuoso who was making thousands of decisions a second about what was happening in his music. And I thought that somewhere in this gap must lie an incredible story. So it became a journey, really, to find out what that story was and, also, to develop a relationship of trust with David and Gillian that would enable me to make that story. Naturally they had concerns about the sensitivity of the material and how it would be handled. So it was the start of a long process. I had no idea how long it would actually be, but it was the beginning and it really took possession of me in a way which was very, very powerful and continuously re-motivating through the long process of trying to get *Shine* made.

In Shine *you show David having that kind of effect on several characters, Sylvia and her fellow worker, as well as Gillian herself.*

David seems to have this effect on people. He does sort of 'possess' you in a strange way. It's quite a phenomenon, but you can't fail to be moved by the experience that he's been through. This was what first fascinated me about the story: this extraordinary, unique character, and the gap that lies between this and the incredibly focused piano virtuoso that he is. Much of the dialogue is derived from conversations with David, and everything that is performed by both Noah Taylor and Geoffrey Rush is scripted. There's no improvisation. Every last word is on the page.

I think people tend to recognise elements of themselves that they've long suppressed or have repressed in the process of growing up. We bury those childlike elements. David seems to me like a person who has never really grown up, so what you're responding to is this eternal child. Part of the story, for me, was about failed rites of passage, as it were, of someone who is not allowed to grow up but, having been created by this father who decides he wants to make his son a little genius, he's then broken because this father doesn't want to share him with the rest of the world. That's the struggle at the heart of the story.

The amazing legacy, though, for David, is his music. As the father says, the music will be his only friend and, for David, it is. It's what ultimately sustains him until he finds a relationship to give him stability.

While the story of *Shine* is inspired by David Helfgott's life, in telling a story of a life in cinema, it's obviously necessary to select very carefully the fragments of that life through which you tell the whole story. Naturally there is a lot of compression. You don't have the luxury of six hundred pages to tell a story, as in a biography, so you compress and you select and you condense. I tried to keep what I saw as the important themes and find the fragments of that life which best express those themes – the power of the father-son relationship, the problem of growing up, letting your children go – and find a way to express this cinematically. Having said that, everything in the film has some basis in reality that derives from some incident or some situation that David has experienced. The film is very much David's point of view.

The music and mental collapse?

Actually, trying to play Rachmaninoff's Third Piano Concerto would drive anybody nuts, but what I was trying to show in these scenes is far more than someone simply playing the piano extraordinarily well. This is somebody undergoing a process of psychological disintegration. What it's expressing is an artist really going so far out on the edge that he simply topples over. He is consumed by the very music that he's trying to express. I deliberately did not want to become too clinical or diagnostic or psychiatric in my interpretation of David's situation. That was too limiting a way to look at the subject. I wanted it to be much more expressive and ambiguous, to show piano-playing as it's never been seen before – that, in a way, it's a dangerous thing. To express yourself like this is not a simple, dainty thing which you do in a salon or a drawing-room. It's very demanding, potentially damaging and some people get hurt.

There are not many Australian films with Jewish themes. What did you want to communicate in terms of Jewish culture, Jewish secularism and Jewish religion?

I was fascinated by that part of the story because it was a whole culture that was alien to my own. I was fascinated by the idea of this Polish Jewish father, with his family in the Australian suburbs in the 1950s and 1960s, who had actually rejected Judaism and embraced a sort of Stalinist dream and ideal and was somehow wrestling with these different forces. It's a powerful element of the story because it's so unusual. We don't hear a lot of these stories in Australia. This was an area of the story which I was terrified of, because the cultural references are so deep and so pervasive that I felt I had to be so careful not to put a foot wrong. I had to get this right.

And the tremendous response that *Shine* has had from the Jewish audiences, particularly in America, has been very rewarding because I feel that they would have been very quick to reject it if it had put a foot wrong in their cultural domain.

I have had letters, from people in the film community who are Jewish, saying how moved they were at the attention to detail, like the mazutska on the door of Rosen's house and the importance of its being there; this kind of detail that is so important to any cultural or any religious belief.

David was born in Melbourne and grew up in Perth, so he's an Australian, but his father's very much the Polish Jew and his mother's very much the Polish Jew, very much a background figure. I think that's a very broad cultural experience in Australia – not specifically the Polish Jews, but people growing up as young Australians from a family whose first language isn't English and whose first culture is not Anglo-Saxon in the way that the majority predominantly are.

The socialist background of the film is very interesting, especially with novelist Katharine Susannah Prichard.

Yes, Red Kate from the West. That was a touching relationship. Here was this elderly artist in the twilight of her career embracing a young man about to embark on his. Katharine, the writer, speaks of David Helfgott in her letters and he's referred to in her biography as being someone who really moved her with his talent and his ability. She tried to nurture that and give him some warmth in an otherwise difficult experience of growing up. So she becomes something of an icon to David.

As with many of the characters in the screenplay, the character of Katharine embraces other people – actual people who had an impact upon David's life. You can never show everybody, so you have to draw together the themes and try to dramatise them through individuals. That's why there are a number of fictional characters in the film who are essentially condensations of a number of different real people – plus a little bit of fiction thrown in. It's a creative process, all the time searching for an emotional truth, while being very much aware of where the reality occurs and how that has had its impact on the story. This is part of the challenge of telling a story inspired by a real life.

Armin Mueller-Stahl's performance was very persuasive in terms of a father living through his son. It contrasted beautifully with the warmth in the performances of Googie Withers, John Gielgud, Sonia Todd and Lynn Redgrave. Working with Armin Mueller-Stahl to create such a portrait of a father?

When I first met with Armin to talk about the character and the role, he said, 'This is a very dark character', and I said, 'Yes, there are very dark passages'. He said, 'I think he's a monster', and I said, 'No, no, he's not, and it's vital that we don't see him that way'. I said, 'Look, the writing is very dark and some of the things he does are dark, but the way you're going to play it is that we're going to read his own pain in your eyes. It's not just in the words, it's how you communicate', and I think he really took to that. You do read such a depth in his performance where we feel for him enormously. I sense him as his own victim. You have compassion, I think, for the life he has come through and the confusion in his nature: he loves this boy desperately, but really loves him too much, and that's as destructive as not loving him at all.

The father was absolutely vital to the film: a man who has indeed lost one family in the War, in the Holocaust, and is determined that he will not lose this family that he has created. He simply would not let them go. He loves them all too much. When I watch this performance, I feel for him and read his pain. I see his dilemma.

So Armin was an absolute find for the film and for the character. His explosive power as an actor was tremendous. He's like watching a fuse

Scott Hicks

burning. A lot of the time he likes to keep it like that, but I said, 'Look, Armin, there have to be a couple of explosions; you can't just be a fuse'. I don't think that Hollywood has yet discovered that tremendous power he has – or, perhaps, is a little reluctant to explore it. So in his Hollywood pictures he tends to be a rather genial, amiable, grandfatherly or avuncular sort of figure. But there's a darkness in there which is fantastic and he was able to bring so much of that to bear on the character as it was scripted by Jan Sardi.

The fact that the father didn't visit David during all those years in the institution was harrowing. Then when he came to David's flat, gave him his medal and disappeared, this was very powerful.

Actually, that part of the chronology is another example of the jostling of reality that one does. While that kind of encounter did take place, in reality it didn't happen at that particular time. I always felt that it was vital that there was an attempt by Peter Helfgott to try come to terms with what had happened or as nearly as possible try to convey his sense of regret and loss as to what has happened. But he can't find the words to express it, so you have this extraordinary scene which is, on the surface, about nothing. He comes, he opens a tin, he gives David a medal and he leaves. But in it is written the loss of these years and when he dredges up again the old story about the violin and what happened to him as a child with his father, it is tragic, absolutely tragic. And in that moment, I found it hard to retain my composure, watching Armin while shooting the scene, sitting next to the camera. This is very unusual – you're normally very much focused on the technicalities of what you're doing, but I was close to tears when he did it at the time. I found it astonishing.

And, of course, with Geoffrey Rush opposite him, the scene has great tension between the two. It's one of the huge rewards of directing when you get actors who just play scenes like that so brilliantly. One of the strange things was that this was a huge scene in terms of pages and pages of script. We really had only a little bit of time in which to shoot it. And the production office kept saying to me, 'You're never going to finish this scene on that day. Look at it, it's four pages of dialogue. You're not going to be able to do it in three hours'. And I said, 'Look, if the actors are good, we won't have a problem, and look who we've got. We've got Geoffrey, we've got Armin, we know where we're going. Don't worry about it'. And in the event, it was one of the most painless scenes to do. I wanted to keep it very simple because it was about what the actors were going to do, not about how clever I could be with the camera, just getting the camera where it was going to read those faces. And that was going to tell the story. It's probably the simplest piece of direction that I've ever done, and yet, at the same time, one of the most rewarding moments.

Noah Taylor's performance is one of his best. His playing of the Rachmaninoff and what he communicated about genius and stress was particularly powerful. There was continuity of performance between Noah Taylor and Geoffrey Rush, with the speech patterns, the verbal play and the puns.

Noah has become something of an icon in the Australian cinema as carrying our collective male dream of growing up. I think he's probably sick of that now because he's a mature man in his mid-twenties, but here he was playing another teenager through to early adulthood. But the point I made was, 'Noah, you carry the transition. You are the one who charts the disintegration'. So it's very much a transitional role but it's not just another rites of passage story. It's a failed rites of passage, which is a whole new experience to explore, and he embraced that challenge enormously.

We have a character – and this is often true of a prodigy in any endeavour, be it chess or mathematics or music – we have someone who has developed one small slice of their personality to an enormous degree – the talent to play music – but almost at the expense of everything else. And ironically, that is both their making and their undoing. Out of this you're not going to create a highly competent human being, a social human being. You create, maybe, a great artist, not a social human being. But at the end, the music has a redemptive quality for David. There's a scene which is dear to me in the film: the older David is playing the piano in the lodge where he's living; he's playing almost literally for his life because he has nothing else. As his father said to him, 'Music will always be your friend. Everything else will let you down. Everything'. We see that enacted in the frenzied piano playing with Geoffrey Rush doing all his own stunts at the keyboard. Yes, I think music can be both the making and the undoing of a prodigy.

Noah is an instinctive performer, but like any performer he's a part of a bigger picture and I found him very responsive to ideas, often very simply expressed. I think he's an actor who's probably in some ways too used to taking care of himself on film. It's very difficult for actors: they've got to come and do all this stuff. Nobody wants to be made a fool of and yet they have to do very difficult things. And sometimes it takes a while to build the trust with an actor where they realise you are not going to let them down, so when you ask for more, they're willing to give it, and I found that with Noah. If you pushed him for some more, it was there. He was going to give it, but he needed to feel confident, like anyone, that he wasn't going to end up making a fool of himself. There was no way I was going to let that happen.

Working with actors is what I enjoy, so it's always a learning process for me with each personality I deal with.

In 1995–1996, Australians saw Angel Baby *(dir. Michael Rymer),* Così *(dir. Mark Joffe),* Lilian's Story *(dir. Jerzy Domoradski) and* Shine, *all with themes of mental breakdown and institutions.*

Well, you can go back to *Bad Boy Bubby* (dir. Rolf de Heer) and it goes on and on. It's a curious thing, isn't it? I don't know what it's to do with, but you could point to things like the collective unconscious, the Jungian notion that somehow these ideas are present and somehow they get discharged through different forms of expression. I feel that *Shine* is exploring a different part of that territory.

A word that I always use about *Shine* came from talking with Geoffrey Rush early on when he asked me, 'What is it about in the end? I mean, what is it really about?' And I said, 'Well, it's about redemption. It's about someone who can go through terrible experiences in his life but emerge on the other side, in love, playing music and accepted for who he is'. That sparked something with Geoffrey. He felt there was a big theme behind this, not just the playing out of an everyday story.

Così was looking for the comedy, I think. It was an utterly different kind of expression. I also felt that we were dealing not so much with madness, which seems such – or too much of – a generic idea but, to me, David is an eccentric, is a glorious eccentric who doesn't have to be moulded into anything approaching what we call normality. If you take another line, you can say he's another manifestation of the Australian innocent abroad. You can look at Mick Dundee, you can look right back to Barry McKenzie and look at the fact that in our cinema we've often dealt with incompetent males struggling in the broad seas. So there are all sorts of different ways you can look at the thematic elements.

In Lilian's Story, *Lilian finally goes to her father's grave. Jerzy Domaradski says there is a kind of reconciliation.* Shine *also has David go to his father's grave and there is a kind of reconciliation. Part of the collective unconscious may be that there is some need in children, if parents have oppressed and abused them, that they experience a reconciliation.* Lilian's Story *and* Shine *show the possibility of reconciliation and forgiveness, where you might think it could never be.*

It's interesting because, when we shot the film, that wasn't the final scene. That scene came about ten or twelve minutes before the end. There was a whole other story element which ultimately I removed in the editing, but when I removed this story strand we had shot, the film had no ending. It then occurred to me that the cemetery absolutely was the right place for the story to conclude. It was like the coda to the piece.

Many people said, 'Finish it with the concert, with David taking a bow', and I thought, 'Well, that's the obvious place to finish it, we'll freeze on it' –

in fact I ended *Sebastian and the Sparrow* that way. It's like Mickey Rooney and Judy Garland, 'Let's put on a show', and that then is the end of the picture. But no, it was important that there be that moment where everybody gets a pay-off in the concert. You see Rosen, you see the mother, you see the family, but where's the father? Well, the answer is that he's in the soil and David has to move on. So you have this lovely moment between these two, in their own way, wonderfully eccentric people who have found each other and they're moving through the graveyard into the future.

I loved the ironies that jostled in that. It was like having a film called *Shine* which was all about rain.

Shine seems to have spoken to the Australian psyche and contributed to our understanding of identity and the resilience of the human spirit.

Look, I hope so. It's beyond a dream, really, as a film-maker, to imagine that that kind of thing can happen, but it would be enormously fulfilling to have a sense that you have contributed something simply by trying to tell a story that presented itself as being so powerful. I just wanted to share that with people and, in a way, it's been a dream ride – not without its difficulties but, you know, that's not really the point. It could've been as difficult as it was and not had this kind of effect. So yes, I hope there's something in there because I found the story inspirational.

Australian Feature Films

1982 *Freedom*

1990 *Sebastian and the Sparrow*

1996 *Shine*

George Miller

George Miller. (Kennedy Miller.)

WHITE FELLAS' DREAMING *was your overview of Australian cinema and its effect on Australian audiences. How did you begin to plan and structure it?*

I think I started with the belief that, if you look at the mosaic of cinema, particularly over a long period, you'll see definite patterns of the cinema both reflecting and distilling a culture. The films that impacted in some way did so for a reason that was more subtle and potent than the obvious ones. Looking at that and, perhaps, at a simplistic view of Aboriginal songlines, they brought their culture into being, creating myths and stories that ultimately also served as maps in the landscape, moral maps and cultural maps. I think our cinema does that as well. So, I just tried to test the thesis by looking at all the films and looking at films which in one way or another impinged on Australian culture or world culture.

You mentioned in the documentary that you were born in 1945, the fiftieth anniversary of cinema, so you lived through the second half-century of cinema. The films that you discuss are the films of your life.

Yes, exactly. The thing that was surprising to me about the renaissance of Australian cinema – or that which people like to call 'the renaissance of Australian cinema' – films made from the early 1970s – was that everyone seemed to be obsessed with historical, period films and there was no attempt to make contemporary films. That didn't seem to go anywhere. It wasn't until after I took a broader view that I saw it was Australia, a newly adult Australia after the election of the Whitlam Government, really catching up with itself – or a post-1960s Australia catching up with its history and reinterpreting its history – through the only popular cultural medium as young as the country. Theatre, opera and literature pre-dated the founding of Australia.

It was necessary in those years to look at issues of Australian identity. And it still is.

There were always academics and intelligentsia who tended to do it, did it wonderfully well and embraced it. But I think cinema did it and popularised it much more than Henry Lawson or Arthur Streeton.

The chapter headings of White Fellas' Dreaming *indicate some of the principal cinema 'songlines'.*

By looking not at individual films but at the cumulative effect of several films that impinged on basic, essential themes that Australia had to deal with, it seemed to follow the history fairly well. It was a map of the evolving Australian character, which was pretty clearly defined through film. Most historians or social historians would no doubt pick up the connection between the convict, the bushranger and the digger and, in between, the larrikin, 'the working-class larrikins', who went off to war and became the diggers. That was probably the most quintessentially Australian experience between the two world wars: the last time that that kind of old Australian was really seen.

You remarked that Gallipoli **(dir. Peter Weir)** *was the 'apotheosis of the digger'.*

For me and for a lot of people it was. *Gallipoli* is a very interesting film for me. I was growing up in the 1960s and Gallipoli was treated as a kind of joke. There was the play, *The One Day of the Year*, which was the only time when that generational dispute was dealt with. But, since Peter Weir's film, something else was recognised and it did create some kind of catharsis. It retrieved the Australian digger for Australian culture. He somehow became acceptable again. There is something particularly Australian once again about a war where men die heroically but somewhat foolishly, heroically but innocently. They did not glorify warmongering but glorified sacrifice.

'Catharsis'. You have used the word in the context of 'coming to terms with our shadow past'. Do you see that in other films, including your own?

I don't think enough Australian cinema has done this and Australians don't like to see confronting cinema. There is a hankering for a more child-like view of the world. Australia is never going to be a grown-up country until it can deal with its indigenous history in a mature way. We have a conservative government who talk about the black-armband view of Australian history – and those of us who disagree call it the 'black-blindfold view of Australian history'. When others refer to the 'stolen generation', the Government refers to it as the 'rescued generation'.

But black armbands are a strong symbolic reminder to people to mourn.

Exactly. It's clear that something has been greatly lost. It's not unique to Australia and has happened in all the continents, not the least of which is in the Americas as well as in New Zealand, our close neighbour. But, in all those cases, they have been able to confront the past, try to atone for it simply by recognising it. But in Australia we haven't. I see New Zealand as a much healthier country for having gone through the cathartic experience of popularly celebrating *Once Were Warriors* (dir. Lee Tamahori) which was one of the highest-grossing films in that country.

We, when we make films like that – *The Chant of Jimmie Blacksmith* (dir. Fred Schepisi), *Dead Heart* (dir. Nick Parsons), *Blackfellas* (dir. James Ricketson) – unfortunately, not many people go to see them. It's not that difficult a thing to do and, once it's done, we heal. I love that notion, 'You're only as sick as your secrets'. So long as you try to hide it, disavow it or pretend it's not our responsibility, then you are going to remain a bit sick. I think cinema is one of the means by which that can be properly celebrated.

There can be a great Australian film about it – I can feel it in the air; there are so many great projects around the theme of genocide. Somebody is going to end up making the great Australian film about it.

You made the point that until we face this issue we will remain 'morally and spiritually diminished'.

I'm quite convinced that's the case. One of the things that cinema does by stealth quite often is deal with these things. The most striking example is *Gallipoli*, which also helped explore the Australian experience in Vietnam. By being aware of how powerfully the Vietnam films in the U.S. helped deal with those issues – everything from *The Deer Hunter* (dir. Michael Cimino), *Platoon* (dir. Oliver Stone), *Born on the Fourth of July* (dir. Oliver Stone) and *Apocalypse Now* (dir. Francis Ford Coppola) – is why America, essentially, is a very powerful culture: because it is able to deal with those things in its popular culture. Sure, there's a lot that's dysfunctional in America but, because of their First Amendment, they're able to bring a lot of stuff to the fore. No problem telling stories about corrupt government or demonic big business: they're almost the clichéd bad guys in the movies. But that helps the culture to be healthy.

When did you first encounter Carl Jung and Joseph Campbell?

With Jung I simply read about him at university as part of medical studies. We had to do psychology and I came across him, read him with interest, but it was just an overview along with Freud. I understood him in an intellectual sense – the notion of the collective unconscious. But really, with a lot of things, I didn't get into it too seriously. It was only when I became a film practitioner that I actually had the experience with *Mad Max* of seeing that this low-budget genre film had resonances in countries that I'd never even been to and whose culture I knew nothing about. It seemed to speak to them in different ways.

Japan said Max was a Samurai and followed that sort of tradition. The French picked it up as a western on wheels and Scandinavia saw him as a Viking, as I said in the documentary. But when these things were said to me, I thought, 'This is a living example of what Jung was talking about'. It was really through the practice of film-making that I had this awareness of the collective unconscious and sensed its power in some way. I realised that, as film-makers, despite our personal vanities, as storytellers we are the servants of the collective unconscious, serving that larger mono-myth. Films like *Mad Max* should emerge out of Australia. To that extent they do contribute to that culture which some people call 'the monoculture', the broad global culture, rather than the local, specific, regional, more national culture.

The Mad Max *films could be seen as an Australian manifestation of the collective unconscious that resonates everywhere.*

Yes. What I found interesting was that here it was in practice whereas, previously, it was in theory. And, if Jung described the territory, Joseph Campbell was its consummate guide.

He provided a language to guide people and, of course, popularised the hero myth.

He did two things. First of all, he had more scholarship than Jung. Jung was a practitioner but Campbell was a formidable scholar with his study of comparative religion. He spent a long time just trawling through the material and making comparisons. His other great talent was being able to synthesise and clarify; a great command of language, a great passion for his work. It's one thing to describe and another thing to make sense of its purpose. I think he described the function of mythology in a way that nobody else has ever done.

To me, he explained most of the big questions. My life post-Campbell seemed a lot clearer. He not only explained what I did as a job, as a storyteller, but also explained to me an enormous amount about politics and about religion. So much of religion seems dysfunctional and achieves the very opposite of what it is meant to. He also explained in a way that nobody else has done for me this compulsion to understand the world through a spiritual dimension, this religious compulsion.

He had that wonderful description of mythology as being 'other people's religion', and the notion – not only his – that where a lot of religion loses its mystique and becomes dysfunctional is when we concretise the metaphor, when we take what is essentially a metaphorical expression of a powerful idea and make it an absolute. Then you're taking on a rigidity, which doesn't leave much room for wonder and awe. You become brittle. What was heroic in the past now becomes tyrannical. When you read *The Hero with a Thousand Faces* you see that it is the face of almost every hero. They love too much what they create and yesterday's hero becomes tomorrow's tyrant. If you look at politics and, indeed, the histories of a lot of religions, those two things really seem to apply.

Some Church people so hold on to their understanding of their truth that they become overly dogmatic instead of realising that they need to appreciate the good and the beautiful, especially in the imagination and storytelling.

The other thing I learned from Campbell (and I say this with humility, not out of any arrogance – in many ways it's the opposite of arrogance): cinema has taken over from the Church. When you realise that, it's a bit scary if you are a film-maker. There is a responsibility. And you'd better put all your wisdom into your work. You can't treat it casually.

In times gone by – and I think this was again Campbell who said it – as you approached a city (and still, some of the great cities of the world) the first thing you see is the cathedral because it reaches so high to the sky. Now you approach a city and you see the high office towers. But amongst them you will see the cinemas as bright and as lit-up and as attractive as once the cathedral was. You go into these places and undergo a kind of public dreaming. They are places of meditation. You congregate with strangers and you do have a shared experience. Often, if a film is very powerful, not empty-calorie kind of stuff, but stuff that resonates and stays with you, it can have a very powerful effect. For me, and I dare say for most people, the greatest sense of awe I had as a kid – and as an adult – was in the cinema: a sense of dread, a great sense of inspiration, a great sense of love.

You could argue that it's all artificial but, if you take the argument further, you can see that in fact film does work in that feedback loop with the Zeitgeist and it does distil and reflect and affirm the Zeitgeist; reinforces it and then spews it back – and that feedback loop keeps going on. So, it's not artificial. It's not imposed just by the film-makers. The film-makers are responding to what they have experienced. Storytellers respond to what they have experienced. So, in many ways, it does take some of the function of the Church away or, at least, it appears to. But, film has to have a moral underpinning, otherwise the culture is in big trouble. That's what I'm beginning to understand.

So many cultures recognised Max in the context of their myth-making. Someone referred to him as a 'Christ in leather'. Would you have seen him as a Christ figure? Would you have intended biblical or gospel overtones when you were making the films?

No, not at all. Because you are dealing with the hyperbole of a future world where you can do everything; he's not a Christ figure. He's too limited.

You referred to him as 'a lost soul who becomes an agent of renewal'.

I always think of Mad Max, especially *Mad Max 2*, as a closet human being. Basically, all he cares about is himself but, unwittingly, he becomes the agent of change. And that is true of the hero, whether the hero is Christ or Buddha or Moses or any of the great religious figures. With Christ, and this is one of the reasons He's so powerful, He is the one who exemplified this the most: the relinquishing of self-interest for the greater good. That's the classic in all hero mythology. And Max never quite gets to that stage. He never quite relinquishes his self-interest. And so he's not really a Christ-like figure. But he falls into the fairly classic hero mould and, ultimately, he is the agent of change. That's the other thing that the hero must be. He must change the established order.

I must say that Babe is much closer to a Christ figure than Max. Particularly in *Babe* (dir. Chris Noonan), he does change the established order. In fact, in *Babe, Pig in the City*, he's much more of a Christ figure because he turns the other cheek. He goes to save from drowning the one who was about to kill him. But in *Babe*, he relinquishes his self-interest in order to save Farmer Hoggett and to help fulfil the dream for Farmer Hoggett and to show that a pig can, indeed, be a champion sheepdog. He does it in part for himself but it's mainly for the farmer. Yes, he's closer to Christ – not that a pig should be Christ but he's more Christ-like than Max!

Moving to Lorenzo's Oil, *how important is that film to you?*

That's my favourite. Of all the films I've worked on, it's my favourite. In the most extraordinary way, everything you saw in that film happened. We didn't have to bend the drama very much at all. It is true life and epically heroic. In fact, I would have to say *Babe*, *Mad Max* and *Lorenzo's Oil* are all, in many ways, the same story. It's the hero myth: you enter the dark, unknown landscape and, by courage, you undergo a number of trials and endure; then, in the darkest moments, where you finally realise that it's not for yourself but for the larger good, you relinquish self-interest, you come to that understanding and return with a boon for your society. And that's exactly what the Odones did.

There are children all over the world today who are alive because of Lorenzo's oil. They continue to live normal and healthy lives. For a while the medical establishment tried to say the jury's out but the jury's well and truly in on this now. Lorenzo himself is 21 and he's still in the state that you saw him in the film. They arrested his disease but he had so much loss of his myelin tissue that now they have to find a way to put that back. But, even in that, they've given thousands of people suffering from diseases so much hope. I found that to have that played out in a suburb of Washington DC and in a small suburban house, it's an epic drama in real life and that was extraordinary to me.

As we go into the next century, are you optimistic about Australian films and about Australian audiences responding?

Some things make me optimistic but in some ways I'm nervous. And I'm nervous because Australia is at a risk of becoming a skin-deep culture. I think, for instance, when you look at *White Fellas' Dreaming*, the most interesting films came out of the times of most change or turmoil, when the national identity was being forged. So, it's not surprising to me to see films like *Sons of Matthew* (dir. Charles Chauvel) (even though it was about cutting down big trees and taming the land); like *Jedda* (dir. Charles Chauvel), which is still quite impressive on the Aboriginal problem (even though it was lurid in parts, it tried to deal with trying to preserve Aboriginal culture and the conflict in that); like *Gallipoli* and other films, that did impinge on the culture.

I was discussing this with David Stratton who is studying and lecturing on these developments in Australian and in world cinema. I asked what sort of patterns he picked up when cinema is most vital. 'It's always at a time when a culture's most under threat, the most interesting films arise'. I said, 'That's not so good for Australia, then'. He said, 'No, that's really good for Australia, because people are trying to sort out and define the culture'. That's why I think films on the Aboriginal question will come out and will be made pretty soon. But it's one thing to get them made, it's another for them to be seen by many, many people. So, the answer is, 'I would like to be optimistic but I'm worried that Australian culture is a little skin deep'.

Australian Feature Films

1979 *Mad Max*

1981 *Mad Max 2*

1985 *Mad Max Beyond Thunderdome* (with George Ogilvie)

1998 *Babe, Pig in the City*

Phillip Noyce

Phillip Noyce, *Newsfront*, 1978. (Document Collection, ScreenSound Australia.)

CLEAR AND PRESENT DANGER *is a Tom Clancy action thriller, but it seems to be an ethical film or a film that takes ethical stances.*

Yes, it has a very strong moral line. It's really about the rule of the law. One of the basic assumptions of the film is that human beings are imperfect and, as a result, we need protection from ourselves. That's why we codify human behaviour by erecting laws, by having moral codes that we are expected to follow. This is a film essentially about what happens when we don't follow those laws.

That's what America was doing in the 1980s?

It's what the whole world has been doing. It's about the chaos that results when we ignore the laws or the moral code.

This is a film for the new political era. In the post-Cold War world, the influence of the American president has become even greater as the United States is increasingly called upon to act as a police force to the world. This is a film that asks when it is appropriate for such a powerful nation to act and how should it act. Jack Ryan has to decide whether he keeps quiet and not injure the presidency, the institution he has served for so many years, or does he do something that will endanger his own career and reputation and endanger the presidency and plunge the whole country into turmoil akin to Watergate or the Iran Contra Affair.

Staying with ethical issues, what do you think Backroads *contributed to an Australian understanding of Aboriginal issues?*

I don't think it contributed a whole lot to understanding. I think it probably contributed much more to Aboriginal self-awareness because, as insignificant as this might seem, it was the first film which gave them a hero, or an anti-hero. And the film has been very popular – even now, twenty years later, it's still screened and shown all around Australia to Aboriginal groups.

I'm not sure that it had a great effect on the rest of Australia because essentially it was preaching to the semi-converted. I don't know whether it made them any more aware.

You're pleased with it in retrospect?

I think so. I mean, it was principally an artistic exercise, and part of that notion turned it into a political tract. The idea was to construct a B movie, a road movie, and then, by inviting Gary Foley – who was a known activist and spokesperson for the then strong black movement in Australia, an emerging black movement – by inviting him to be the star, I knew that there would be a political confrontation in the making of the film and that this would appear on the screen. But that was an artistic decision and, as it turned out, the film then evolved into a political statement.

So I'm pleased with it in retrospect in as much as we achieved that confrontation. We captured it on screen so the film was a weird combination of this escapist B movie and political tract, and somehow they sat together in the one strange document.

There are more explicitly religious themes in Newsfront. *In looking at, say, the presentation of the Catholic Church in films,* Newsfront *offers some significant perspectives: Angela Punch McGregor's staunch character, especially, her leaving her husband and, against the laws of the Church, actually re-marrying and giving the Church away. There were also church sequences associated with the anti-Communist referendum of 1951. What was your perspective on things Catholic as you dramatised them in* Newsfront?

You must remember that this is not exclusively my perspective because Bob Ellis was the writer of the original piece – I adapted the screenplay but he was the original screenplay writer – so he's principally the author in that respect, or it's a shared authorship in film terms, because I was then interpreting his writing and, in a sense, adapting and reinterpreting it by the characterisations and so on.

I think that Australia and the Australian character has been formed through the confrontation between Irish Catholicism and Anglicanism and, of course, these are, at least in part, seemingly irreconcilable philosophies. In my interpretation, the one philosophy, the Irish Catholic philosophy born out of the combination of the Irish experience and Catholic doctrine, is that you should not expect to inherit the earth while you're on the earth but you will later, whereas English and Scottish Protestantism says you will inherit it now and you should do everything you can to get it because it's yours. So take it and don't worry about later. We'll worry about that when we get there.

This is a film, in part, about the confrontation of those two sets of values. But it's also very much a film about Australian Catholicism, the good and the bad aspects of Australian Catholicism – the repressive aspects and the enlightening aspects. But, as we know, and as in America, the Catholic Church was also seemingly split into two extremes: one the extreme Right, the other the extreme Left. And it has always harboured these seemingly irreconcilable philosophies.

Angela Punch McGregor's character, in moving from her staunch stances to her abandonment of Catholicism, seems to represent what was actually happening with Catholics during the 1950s and 1960s.

Yes, the film principally describes change, and Australia has changed enormously since the Second World War. The seeds of those changes are to be found in that first decade after the War.

In Heatwave *we again find ethical issues. You have used the word 'confrontation' several times.* Heatwave *seems to be an ethical-confrontational film.*

Yes. *Heatwave* was the story of a working-class Protestant boy who made good. I don't know whether audiences realised that, but we had always assumed that he was a working-class Protestant and that Judy Davis's character was a middle-class Catholic girl. She, in the Catholic saintly tradition, had adopted a social cause – had set herself up as the spokesperson and protector of the working class. He, as a working-class boy, of course, was now forced to confront the moral implications of his own success and how that affected other people.

In a way, the religious and ethnic backgrounds of the two characters were just a continuation of the conflicts that we had seen in *Newsfront*, but Australia had by this stage moved from a principally working-class and upper-class society to a principally middle-class society.

That's captured in the atmosphere of inner Sydney, its buildings and the regulations of law and government.

Obviously it's a film which deals with ethics and morals and responsibilities and just like *Clear and Present Danger*, the issue of right and wrong. But it seems as though so much Australian history – and I'm talking about that conflict between Irish Catholicism and English Anglicanism – was captured in those conflicts over land development. By that time, of course, it had been embraced by groups who had come to Australia after World War Two. The English seemed to have joined with any nouveau riche who presented themselves, whether they were Czechoslovakian or Hungarian or whatever.

The most interesting thing about Australia is Irish Catholicism – I mean, it's the basis of the country. Interestingly enough, I think that it is the basis of the value system and has had much more effect – or at least it has produced the unique Australian character – much more than the English, in my opinion, simply because of its strength.

Through personalities and the public moral stances?

A great deal of that has to do with transportation, as Robert Hughes points out, as much as it does immigration. This is because of the number of radicals, whether they were political or religious or social, who were transported from the British Isles between 1788 and 1850. As Hughes points out, every single radical movement in the British Isles sent a representative to Australia.

You moved into Asia with Shadows of the Peacock *(*Echoes of Paradise*).*

Echoes of Paradise was a very different film from the one we intended to shoot, because the film was meant to be set in Bali and, at the last minute, due to an inflammatory anti-Suharto-family article in the *Sydney Morning*

Herald, all permission was withdrawn and we ended up shooting a bastardised version of the film in Thailand, which we probably would have been better off not to have shot.

It might have been much more political?

Yes, the original story was very different. It was really about the Balinese character's alienation and his coming to terms with it, coming to terms with a western influence and his traditional obligations, trying to work it all out. Wendy Hughes' character went through a very similar journey in the original story. It's just that the setting and the Balinese character were very different once we moved to Thailand.

Twice in Clear and Present Danger *there were references to East Timor – briefly in a news bulletin on the radio and in a remark made to the American President by one of his advisers.*

You did hear it? Actually it's not the radio, it's the TV earlier on – in fact, it prophesies a revolution. It's a little low, unfortunately. I mixed it too low, but in it the Fretilin have taken over the radio station in Dili.

It was a bit low, but then the President's aide or his adviser says that the situation is calm.

I put it in for the Indonesians. It's symbolic really. I thought, 'We'll put it in and we'll see if they pick it up. If they don't, well, that's one over them because they'll have this film out there throughout the country, a hundred prints all around Indonesia and a lot of people will hear it, will wonder about it and they will start some discussion. If they ban the film, then it will be really interesting, because they'll ban it on such a flimsy pretext. This itself will cause some discussion. Otherwise they'll have this sixth column element running around all the villages of Indonesia.

But I should have mixed the TV comments – it was a delicate thing – where the Fretilin have taken over the radio station, just a little louder. I was afraid that if I made it too loud, the authorities would hear it and they would definitely cut it out. But I now realise that it's just a little low.

It's aimed squarely at a building in Jakarta called the Department of Information, which is full of funny little men who do nothing else but listen to radio shows, television shows, read newspapers and things like this, so that they can ban whatever is considered anti-Indonesian. It's a whole building of Orwellian characters.

And your move to Hollywood?

I grew up watching and delighting in Hollywood movies. Hollywood is the Mecca for directors and I'm happy to work there while I can. I am interested in the content of a film rather than its pictorial possibilities. But I am also an outsider and can bring a 'South Pacific cynicism' to a film and that is a virtue. With *Clear and Present Danger*, there is an opening close-up on the American flag. I can force the audience to look at the kitsch and reflect on it. It is a portrait of American life slightly different from one made by an American, an involuntary filter placed over events. Czech Milos Forman's view of American life is different – and the U.S. liked it. Paul Verhoeven, with *Basic Instinct*, brought a combination of repression and indulgence that is Dutch. With the Jack Ryan stories, *Patriot Games* and *Clear and Present Danger*, I have a combination of escapism and reality (though some believe one cancels out the other) and audiences can be entertained and enlightened simultaneously; escapism and political relevance all rolled into one. That's the best combination.

As a director?

There are ten or fifteen superstars in the United States on whom Hollywood depends. But there are three to four hundred directors waiting for a phone call from the superstar!

The director is a ringmaster in a circus. A good circus is no good without a good ringmaster. All those good acts can fail – a big pause and someone needs to bring on the clowns, and when the clowns aren't funny, you need a drum roll. The tightrope walker begins. And you need another drum roll.

But directors are also like vampires, sucking the life-blood ideas out of everyone around them – and then calling them their own. A director needs to have a soft front, a strong back and allow everyone to speak up.

Australian Feature Films

1978 *Newsfront*

1981 *Heatwave*

1987 *Echoes of Paradise (Shadows of the Peacock)*

1989 *Dead Calm*

John Ruane

John Ruane, *The Love of Lionel's Life*, 2000. (Photo: Greg Noakes.)

THAT EYE, THE SKY received nine AFI nominations.

I was very pleased and very surprised that we got nine nominations. They gave us one for the Young Performers' Award, for Jamie Croft. It was uncontested. I think Jamie should have been nominated for best actor rather than just be given an award outright, but I'm glad that he has got the recognition for his performance.

Your earlier films were short stories, Queensland *and* Feathers.

Queensland was made in 1975. What we were trying to do then, strangely enough, was trying to imitate *Summer of the Seventeenth Doll* (dir. Leslie Norman) in reverse and to imitate *Midnight Cowboy* (dir. John Schlesinger), a sort of Northcote version of *Midnight Cowboy* – not the story, but the fact that they were headed for a dream. Their dream was Miami. Our film was obviously about heading to Queensland.

The film came from an article in a newspaper that said this guy, who was a slaughterman, had killed his de facto wife. Then he had got drunk for two days. They found her body under the bed. Now, from that grisly and unlikely tale we decided not to make him a slaughterman and not have any killing, but to see how a relationship broke up, how they parted, came back together and then broke up.

I know this sounds a bit pretentious, but the film was quite poetic in a way, especially with the final image of the man pushing the Holden uphill and trying to make it to Queensland while the camera did a big crane shot. We stumbled upon this shot. There was a big staircase and I thought this shot would be a good idea. So we bought a round of beer for somebody on the Northcote City Council and they brought the trucks to wet the road down.

Even though *Queensland* was made in 1975, it seems to be an even more old-fashioned film than that, in a weird sort of way. It's about a vanishing breed of Australians. But, then again, I suppose they haven't vanished, because there are still people who are poor, there are still people who live in boarding houses. John Flaus, who plays the lead role of Doug, always tells me it's one of Australia's first social realist films. I think there is a truth to that because we were trying to capture the way people spoke or the way those particular characters spoke. No one said what they really meant. We were trying to get some kind of subtext to the dialogue. I think we did. Recently I saw *Queensland* again. It creaked and groaned but it still stood up in a way.

But then I didn't do another film for eleven years, until 1986. That was *Feathers*, which was a Raymond Carver short story. That was a big break between lunches! I did a telemovie in 1985 called *Hanging Together* – which no one has ever seen. Strangely enough, it was a comedy. It was based on a play, a comedy about the second-last man hanged in Australia. It was a bit like

Steptoe and Son (dir. Cliff Owen) set in Northcote. I learned a lot from it. I ended up doing a bit of writing on it, but it was basically a play and we did it as a play. It was mostly set in one location. It had Gary Day in it, John Larkin and Pat Evison. It was produced for the then Australian Film Theatre.

Feathers was a big difference for me because it was the first time – I know this sounds strange – I had worked with a professional crew. With *Queensland* we were students; with *Hanging Together* we were being trained or learning on the job. With *Feathers* it was interesting to come in contact with people who got paid to do their various functions. So it was a much more efficient machine and I think I had matured a little bit – I hope I had – between *Queensland* and *Feathers*. When I say 'matured', the main difference is that I had a sense of humour. While *Queensland* was an interesting film, there was no room for humour. I was able to make *Feathers* poignant in places, but also keep the humour going, a sort of blackish humour.

Over that eleven years I developed a kind of black-cynical approach to funding bodies and how things went. I was lucky that I got two projects in a row, *Hanging Together* and *Feathers*, both of which were black. Then, of course, came *Death in Brunswick* and its black humour.

The scene in Death in Brunswick *when Sam Neill's Carl goes to Mass with his mother and had no idea about the changes in the Catholic Church after the Second Vatican Council is a very funny 'Catholic' scene.*

I think it's actually in the book: Carl standing there in the church and he says, 'What's happened to the Mass, Mother?' Mel Gibson saw the film when Sam Neill did a special screening in America. I met Mel Gibson briefly in America and he said to me, 'Yeah, you're the guy who did *Death in Brunswick*'. He said, 'There's a wonderful scene in that film. It's the funniest scene in the film, where Carl turns to his mother and says, "What's happened to the Mass, mother?"' And I thought, only he would pick up on that because he's such an ardent right-wing Catholic who thinks they shouldn't have changed the Mass.

I'm not a Catholic, but I went to that church the Sunday before to go to the Mass to see if I could pick up on anything extra. I rewrote the scene that we did the following week. I can't remember who the priest was there, but he was quite an interesting priest. I tried to put a bit of him, I think, into Denis Moore who played the priest. The microphone bit is a little over the top – but maybe it's not. They tell me some priests walk around with the microphone.

The graveyard scene and the church scene, I thought, were the best two scenes in *Death in Brunswick*. I was proud of that scene because we shot it all in a day. It's a weird kind of scene because the rest of the film was straight and that scene had what I'm always scared of: a dream sequence (with Mustafa); but I think it worked. I added some of that extra stuff about 'Amongst us today we have adulterers and we have so-and-so and we have so-and-so'. Denis Moore is a great actor. He did that role very well, the priest.

It's a strange film. In many ways it limps. Again, it's a film that works and then it falls down, then it gets itself up again. And it's a bit too long. But if the audience hooks into the film (and I can tell in the first three minutes when Carl comes into the kitchen after he has stopped the cars and he finds Mum has got her head in the oven): if the audience laughs at that point, then they enjoy the rest of the film.

I was in an audience in Adelaide who didn't laugh – one or two people laughed – and I watched half of the film with them and they didn't get it. The thing about the mum became the signpost.

Another gap before That Eye, the Sky?

After *Death in Brunswick* I wanted to do a serious film because there seems to be four years between each film: *Feathers* in 1986, *Death in Brunswick* in 1990 and *That Eye, the Sky* finished in 1994.

And, to castigate myself, I suppose, I think the mistake I made with *That Eye, the Sky* is not to have more humour in it, because the book had a lot of humour. But, unfortunately, with the novel being written in the first person, a lot of the humour comes from the little boy interpreting the events and the situations he finds himself in and that he observes. So we are party to his sense of humour via his inner thoughts. When you pull that away, you have to come up with an orthodox third person approach. I really wish we had come up with more humour.

The stage play is very humorous, certainly, but its shortcoming was that it wasn't poignant. The stage play, instead of having the father in coma and using an actor, once he went into the coma, they used a dummy, which removed him from reality. The actor who played Fat played the chook as well; a very good device on stage: you simply put a cap on the actor. It was very theatrical and it made it very funny. They also used an adult to play Ort.

With the chook in the film there was, at least, some humour early in the piece, so the film had something of that humorous flavour.

Yes, we got a bit of humour. But the film is what the play can't be: it's very visual. The countryside is quite majestic in the film. As well as working as putty between the scenes, I was hoping that the countryside would give the audience a sense of power and of beauty, of a sort of spirituality, with the ever-flowing river.

Your landscape was very dry: some water, but a desert-isolated atmosphere and countryside.

The film was shot in Wentworth, about half an hour's drive from Mildura, and the house was actually on the edge of the desert. It had previously been on a citrus orchard. The people had moved out of the house because it was built on a concrete base and the droughts, over the years, broke the concrete. Although the walls standing on the outside were all intact, inside the house was all topsy-turvy, so the people moved out. But that house used to be the centre of local social activity. It had a tennis court, its own sprinkler system. And the lady who was born there and lived there as a child, now lives up the road. When we put the house back to life, she was quite excited. But then, of course, once the crew moves out, the house goes back to its old condition and the desert has reclaimed it again.

It's a very interesting story how we found the house. We sent the production manager all around the country trying to find a house that had character. He ended up contacting friends of his, rang them in Wentworth and said he was looking for a house for the film and, if it could be near a river, that would be great. Then he asked how this particular lady's husband was. They told him that he had had a car accident and had been in a coma. He told them that that was what the film was about. So, in a way, we were guided, led to that house. I wish I had exploited the house more. It had more potential.

How were the special effects created for the house's aura?

In the book, the house has a cloud of light that rests above it, which only the little boy can see. We couldn't do a cloud of light, so we wanted to do a yellow aura that sat above the house. It should have been done by computer animation, which would have cost us about a quarter of a million dollars, but we had only about fifteen per cent of that. So Michael Bladen did it the old-fashioned way: through opticals. I think the people in the laboratories who know how to do opticals were buried in the 1950s. Everything is now done by computer animation and moving, travelling mattes. So he had a lot of trouble doing it on no money. How they made the actual light was with cooking oil – vegetable oil – with aluminium flakes in it, just shot in a tank.

I think at times the light above the house looks a bit like a 1950s movie; sometimes it's a little bit too theatrical. But I think that if people like the film, if they get into the film, they forgive some of the film's sins, so to speak, because every film has shortcomings; if they get into the story, they go with the flow.

I was always in two minds about what the light above the house represented: was it the father's soul? I suppose it's a combination of the father's soul, of hope, of faith. And when you say 'faith', do you mean spiritual faith, do you mean faith in God or ... ? So it is open to many interpretations.

The guys who were the gaffers, who set the lights up, they called it 'the mother light'; then they started calling it 'the God light'. So they would say, 'Bring God over', and they would bring this big light over the house. So, for me, it was a mixture of God and the father's soul, because the light appears only when the father has been brought back to the house and the little boy is talking to his grandmother. She is the mother of the man in the coma. Ort is cursing, saying that his dad is better than any other dad, so why was he taken away? It's at that moment, when he goes outside, that the light appears. So it's as if there's a core response. It's as if it's the father, whichever father, answering the little boy with a miracle or a visual message that only the little boy receives.

How does this compare with the light in the novel?

Of course, in the book it's much easier because, as a reader, you paint the picture of the light that you want. You imagine how it is in your own head. Also, you can say in the book that none of the other characters can see this light, although they're bathed in it, glowing, but they don't know. This is magical stuff – obviously that's why Tim Winton is such a great novelist.

When you come to the film, you have to work concretely, which makes it much more difficult. If you show the light, you've got the *Casper* (dir. Brad Silberling) situation: who sees it and when does it go? I didn't really want to have some kind of big electric switch that, once the boy went inside the house, click, it goes off, and then, if he walks out, click, it goes on. I couldn't have a backyard light going on and off. So I had to make the decision. We decided to leave the light permanently there.

In a way it's like saying there's a permanent flying saucer above the house, particularly when you show it. When the boy walks inside the house, we still see the light is there. What this says to an audience is that it is real, it's a hundred per cent concrete, because the light didn't switch off. But, at the same time, I'm hoping that the audience will get a feeling that the film is always from Ort's point of view. We are, therefore, in his story.

I think – and I'm being very critical of myself again – the film loses its focus and then drifts back again. There is a point in the film where it loses its focus from Ort's story; it moves on to Henry and then comes back. For a moment the pace of the film drops. This is a mistake. But in some ways you have to make the film to learn how to make it. It sounds a stupid thing to say, but each time you go into a film, it's uncharted water and you learn something different. The reason why I didn't want to do another comedy after *Death in Brunswick* is that, while I haven't mastered comedy, I wanted to have another challenge. I wanted to do something different. The first film, *Queensland*, was a serious film and I wanted to do something serious again.

Henry Warburton and God?

We had the challenge of having a little boy who feels that God is talking to him, from a novel that explored what this boy thought some of the stories in the Bible meant. I wanted us to feel it to a degree as, I think, the novel does.

But we extended it. I wanted audiences to feel that the stranger, Henry, when he arrives at the front door, is a fallen angel. The audience doesn't know who he is. When the little boy says to him, 'Can you see the light above the house?', he replies, 'Yes, it's a marvellous thing', but he's referring to the constellation. So there's a blurring of what he sees, and the audience is not quite sure with the music, the wind and the way he looks, the way he looks around – you feel that he may be a Bruno Ganz from *Wings of Desire* (dir. Wim Wenders) who has come from Berlin.

Peter Coyote as Henry Warburton?

Of course, one of the controversial issues was using an American to play Henry. But it gets down to two things: one, you want to make the film but the people who put money into it need some kind of safety net and, two, I actually thought an American worked because he was an evangelist and that kind of religion seems to come from across the water.

If we had made him English or Irish, I'm not sure how it would have worked. But, at the same time, I must admit I was very keen on the French actor, Tchecky Karyo. But the man we had actually playing the role of Henry, but then the arrangement collapsed, was Scott Glenn. I think Peter Coyote is in that same school of acting as Scott Glenn. They're kind of B-grade actors for the public. They don't recognise their names, but they recognise their faces.

Henry describes his religious experience. How real is it? How much is of God? How much is subjective?

The difference between the book and the movie is, I think, that the book is much more black and white. In the book, the character of Henry is much more the stereotypical tortured sinner-cum-penitent who has found God and who's more insane, given to falling on his knees and yelling out for the Lord's forgiveness.

I was motivated by trying to make all the characters totally credible, so that if an actor said to me, 'Why do I do this?' I could answer him. There's a big soliloquy that Henry delivers towards the end of the film, which is supposed to be the justification for his thoughts. Rightly or wrongly, we shot it and then we removed it. It was at the beginning of the film, when he talks to Alice on the landing. He talks about his father who was a bishop, that he was never close to his father and, when his mother died, his father had called him to him and said, 'Now neither of us has anyone in this world'. So he had gone off religion, wandered around the country – he tells these stories in the book – and he then found religion, kitchen-table-like religion, not in a church, but out in the fields and from people. So he had come back to God. But he felt that he had been given a gift which was a burden, like Paul's road-to-

Myth & Meaning
M y t h & M e a n i n g
M y t h & M e a n i n g

Damascus experience, when he had been struck down in the boarding house for three days in a fever and he feels, after he comes out of the fever, he has had a light bulb, a burning light, in his head for these three days. And his landlady says, 'God has been with you'.

So he has travelled around the countryside or around the world with this burden-gift, wanting to try, I think, to save people but not knowing how to do it. And strangely enough, if you were to say that God has to work in mysterious ways, I would say that Henry goes to the family telling himself he wants to help them. But he lusts after the daughter, Tegwyn. In a weird way it was the right thing for him to take Tegwyn away – not that their relationship would work, but he was the key to get her to move out of the house, to move on.

I think that even if he hadn't turned up, Ort would have still seen the aura. The miracle at the end, whether it's a miracle or whether it's a dream, would still have happened. But Henry does make the whole family think.

The miracle at the end – do you do it realistically or do you do it as a dream? I suppose I wanted to film it as something open-ended. I wanted it to depend on the audience's view of life for how they would interpret it. I shift ground on it. In a way, I think it's a dream and it starts when the little boy is on the seat at night, looking out into the river. I wanted it to be that it's a dream and that it's unlocked by his grandmother playing the piano. This wasn't in the book. I put it into the film, because I wanted it to be a physical thing to unlock the father as well as a spiritual thing. I had read in a book about comas that sometimes people are unlocked or brought back as people, talk to people and hold their hands. But sometimes it's early memories that are the little keys that bring someone out of coma.

What was in the book and what was in the film, earlier before we cut it out, was that from the beginning Ort felt himself the guardian of the family. He goes around at night, looks in keyholes, checks that everyone's okay. He says at one point that he hopes that Grandma will play the piano once more before she dies. So that was a key plot point which we lost, which was in the book.

Another point occurs when Tegwyn is feeding her grandmother. The story that the grandmother recites over and over again concerns Sam – Tegwyn's father – when he was a baby. She used to put him in an old wooden box on top of the piano when she played. Here's a key that I thought Tim Winton should have used himself. The little boy hears the piano and that should trigger in him a realisation that something is going to happen to Grandma. He should lay his father's head – Grandma's son – on the piano and the noise will come up into his dad's head.

I also read that people don't speak when they come out of coma; they don't come out a hundred per cent normal. Sometimes their emotions are so great but they can't express them, so they might cry. So that's why I wanted

John Ruane

to have the close-up, to show that there was a tear that came out of the father's head: the key had turned in the father. The boy goes to sleep that night and there's the big dream or the big miracle. Because you're dealing with a film that does not have an orthodox narrative; the film is rather dreamy. It's the kind of film where you need to put in some of your own thoughts for it to actually click.

I have met people who have absolutely loathed the film while some people have found the film pro-Christian. I have had distributors tell me that they wouldn't take the film on because it was too religious. I don't know quite what that means, 'too religious'. It's as if you're allowed to be religious only if it's in a controversial way. It's alright if someone vomits green bile, or a film like *Priest* (dir. Antonia Bird), about something very controversial within a church. But if you are tackling an issue which comes down to – I don't know what – I find it confusing myself to even speak about whether it's belief in something, a faith in something or whether it's a faith in an orthodox God or your own father, and how it all clicks together.

So it's a strange film. When I went into the project, I said it was not a mainstream film. It's not a commercial film. It's an art-house film and it has a very small audience.

It's the kind of film that former Age *reviewer, Neil Jillett, used to categorise in a derogatory way as mystical:* The Navigator *(dir. Vincent Ward),* Fearless *(dir. Peter Weir). Is it Australian scepticism faced with the mystical?*

Yes, but part of the interesting journey of the film is to read what people write about it. It's strange, but I feel that the print media will rubbish the film and the television critics will like it. But it will be interesting to see how the public responds if the film survives.

When Ort and his mother went to church at Christmas, the church looked like a Catholic church. Were they Catholics?

It was a Catholic church – the Catholic church at Mordialloc – with an amazing red and white interior. It could have been any denomination. But what I liked about it's being a Catholic church – in the book it's a Catholic church – is that there's a large crucifix. There was supposed to be a parallel between Christ on the cross and the little boy recognising the man suffering like his father. Whether there was a physical resemblance or not, there was a resemblance of someone in pain, someone whose head was hung down. There was supposed to be a correlation.

And when I got into the church – not that I did it very well – I was trying to show as well that there was a correlation between the saints having a glow, a halo above their head, and that the house had a halo above its head. Haloes date from way, way back, for someone who is pure, who has an inner truth or some special knowledge. Through the painting or whatever way they're represented, it is acknowledged that they have a glow of knowledge or faith, truth or whatever, above them. I didn't really get that across in the film, but that's what I was trying to do.

It would be interesting to revisit the film in years to come. If only you could correct some things in it. But some people will appreciate it, some people won't, and people always get the most amazing interpretations from films.

With Dead Letter Office *you broke the four-year pattern and directed a film after three years. What attracted you to this film?*

I liked the idea of being able to look inside someone else's culture in a way that I would normally not be able to do. I liked the fact that part of the film was going to be shot in another language. I liked the themes of home and what constituted a home and how you couldn't move on to a certain point of your life until you complete one part of the journey. Family is very important for Alice in the sense that it is very important for her until she finds her father and gets that search out of the way. It's as if she blames this for what's happened to her: that she can't carry on with her life, so to speak, except for him.

Frank is someone who has his family in a drawer. He can't put them on the mantelpiece until certain events in his past have been re-explored. So I liked all those themes in the film. You got to share them – it was a serious picture.

The Australian problem was the typical-enough broken family, whereas the Chilean problem was deeper: the destruction of family by political persecution.

Yes, which is probably stereotyped, as one reviewer said, but most likely stereotypes have some reality sometimes. I also liked the fact that it had some romance in it, but it was not an overt romance. It was all very subtle. So I like that and I like the fact that the film had a melancholy sense to it.

Alice meeting with her father was unexpected but moving.

That's the highlight of the film itself, I think: seeing the two mad Ottos in the one frame – and the fact that the father is slightly tarnished and is a disappointment. Nevertheless it's an important meeting.

It was a film that had many things happening in it: the metaphors, the pigeon threading its way and drawing everybody together, and the chance to look at the slightly eccentric characters in the dead letter office itself.

The eccentric characters highlighted themes of downsizing, privatising and the harsh aspects of economic rationalism.

I think the reason they chose me to direct was on the basis of *Feathers*. They felt it had a bittersweet quality to it and that's what they were hoping would come to the fore in this film.

John Ruane

The Chilean subtext. It was very moving when it dawned on Alice that there was a whole world of suffering she had no apprehension of: an important insight for an Australian audience.

Yes, the film is very timely in the sense that it lets you see someone else's culture, someone else's story, and you see how it rebounds on Alice. I think one of the best moments in the film is the cut from her looking at all the photographs of the people in the book to her standing in the dead letter office looking over to the picture of the mountains with 'Congratulations Frank, 10 years'. It's a good cut, that. I think that one's a very powerful moment.

Another powerful moment was also the sympathy for Carmen in the park; then when it emerged that she was a fascist, you were jolting our romantic presuppositions about migrants, and taking them a bit deeper.

That's right. Not all migrants are here for correct political reasons, or our perceived correct political reasons.

You made an arresting comment about your work in an interview with the Sunday Age.

Yes, about directing. It's like the priesthood: you don't do it for the money; you do it because you're insane. It's a calling.

Australian Feature Films

1975 *Queensland*

1986 *Feathers*

1990 *Death in Brunswick*

1994 *That Eye, the Sky*

1996 *Dead Letter Office*

Fred
Schepisi

Fred Schepisi. (Photo: Kate Gollings.)

Yes, I started in advertising. I left the monastery, the juniorate, and I finished about six months at Marcellin College. That took me through to 14. I had done my Leaving and so I decided to go to work and went into the dispatch department at an advertising agency – sort of learnt all that filing, running messages to the various places which are all part of learning what goes on at the printers and the block-makers, all that stuff. Then I went into physical production, press, did layout, typesetting and then organising all the physical requirements for magazines and press and folders.

Television came in around about that time and I got moved into the television and radio department and I was doing writing and production on radio and television commercials. In fact, for a while there, I was the only one in the department, which was pretty strange because I was only about 17. Then they put another guy in over me, because they couldn't exactly take me out to clients. But in those days there were a lot of writers in the agency, quite a little hotbed, actually. Geoff Underhill, who used to write plays and worked for *IMT* and stuff, and Phillip Adams was there and Geoff Taylor; a little haven for people who wanted to be writers, playwrights or whatever and couldn't make a living out of it here in those days.

So you worked there into the 1960s?

Yes, until about the end of 1962 or 1963, when the big recession came. Everyone seems to forget that particular recession, but it was devastating. The agency had grown and had split into two agencies within the one. Then the recession hit and they fired one side of the agency and I was on that side. I got a bit of a golden handshake and subsequently I went to Cinesound – put my age up a few years and lied.

I was only 23 at the time, so I lied like hell and got a job running the place and found out that practically everyone there was only an assistant, so I had some pretty fast on-the-job learning to do. We turned it around and in seven months it made its first profit ever. In eighteen months we were making more than the Sydney head office, and it was round about then I found out you weren't supposed to be making money – at least I don't think so. Anyway, two other guys and myself bought the company. So in February 1966 we became The Film House, and that ran for about 31 years. I closed it about a year and a half ago.

It's a long time, certainly.

Yes, it is, and frankly I would still keep it running if it was serving the purpose that I wanted it to serve, but it wasn't.

How did Libido *and your short film, 'The Priest', emerge from all of this?*

Fred Schepisi

Well, I got into the business because I wanted to make films. I thought, 'That's easy, you just go into business and you make films'. And the first thing that happens to you, of course, when you start a business ... Well, it wasn't like it is nowadays; you didn't get paid up-front or anything like that; you didn't get any amount up-front; you had to outlay everything, and most advertising agencies would take between four and nine months to pay you, because of the way they billed; then they put the money on a short-term moneymaker. So the busier you were, the more likely you were to go out of business. You just couldn't finance yourself.

So I discovered that I was making a lot of money, excepting I didn't have any, because it wasn't coming in here, but it was going out there. And that meant you had to churn the wheel faster and faster and faster to eventually get some money. It was disastrous. Then I had a couple of people who had a kind of illusion about what the money coming in meant, and they were expanding me at a rate far greater than the money coming in. And that got me into awful trouble. So you think you're going to make films, and what you find is that you're in business and, as I said, you seem to have a lot but, if you get off the wheel, it all falls over and hits you.

So it took me a while to recover from that, but in that process I was writing *The Devil's Playground*. I wrote *The Devil's Playground* over five years before I did it. I was meeting a lot of actors, doing a lot of commercials and a lot of documentaries. So I joined the Producers and Directors Guild to try and meet people working in theatre and television, to see other disciplines, as it were, because I wanted to go along and watch them direct plays and see what they did in that side of television.

Everyone in that group was not in there as a guild; they were in there just to meet one another and help one another, so we started to devise projects. One year we ran a scriptwriting competition. The idea was that we would select six scripts and they would be produced on radio, television and in theatre, although I think we kept them separate at that stage – I can't quite remember – and then we used the Swinburne students to shoot it. Well, we decided in the end that it was a terribly bad idea because we spent the whole time explaining why that bit of film didn't work because that student didn't expose it properly or ... The concentration went on the wrong things and a lot of the scripts were (not to be rude about it) of the style of the little old lady who thought she was a writer and hadn't ever had a chance.

Sometimes, of course, magic comes from that, but not en masse. So the next year we did three sets, changing the criteria each time. Finally we went out and got writers of novels, people who hadn't worked on film or television or theatre, and got them to write small pieces that we would then perform on stage, on television and on film, just to show the difference. And, of course, what that showed is you shouldn't do that.

But that was good, we didn't care, we just did it. Everybody was helping everybody and there was quite an extraordinary spirit. We got a little bit of help on the last one from the Experimental Film Fund, but we were putting our own money in and, I guess, hoping it would be a showcase, certainly understanding that they would be good training. It doesn't seem like a lot of money now, but I tell you what, it was a lot of money then.

So you chose Thomas Keneally's story?

Yes. Tom's script had come in and I just jumped on it. I just muscled my way into that because I wanted Tom to read *Devil's Playground*. He did and was incredibly kind about it. When he got involved acting in it was when I heard about *Jimmie Blacksmith*. I liked the idea of the story and I got inspired by a couple of the images from it, so a lot started from there.

'The Priest' tapped into the crises in the Catholic church at the time. In a sense it was prophetic of what has happened in the last 25 years in issues of priesthood, faith and celibacy.

In that case it's the writer; it's always the writer that makes the material, and that came deeply from Tom's experiences, although it wasn't auto-biographical. One of Tom's best books by far is *Three Cheers for the Paraclete*. It's those things that are *formed* by personal experiences, not necessarily *being* them, that probably produce the truest work. His wife was a theatre sister and a nun and Tom went right through almost to the end of the seminary course, so I think they were his deeply personal observations. And they happened to dovetail with my experiences and the questions that one comes up with.

A lot of people at the time reacted to Arthur Dignam as giving such a desperate portrayal of a priest and identifying that with Keneally, but failed to remember that he wrote Robyn Nevin's lines as the nun as well; that he actually was presenting both sides of this relationship. The background was very real: afternoon tea with the nuns, the kind of conversation about the bishop and whether he would approve ... It was so authentically Catholic that it revealed something of Church life of the past.

Yes, I think we both had a fair bit of knowledge in that area. Some of that is cinematic too; just the way you present that stuff: the politeness or the polite veneer. It was good. If anything in that film, I got a little too gimmicky visually at one point, sort of whirling the camera around. I wouldn't do that now. I would do a variation on it. The energy was already there: even though that might be what was going on in his head, I don't think I needed to reinforce it quite so much. We did that damned thing in six days.

Fred Schepisi
F r e d   S c h e p i s i

In terms of the Catholic Church presented on screen in Australia, with 'The Priest' and The Devil's Playground, *you actually enabled Australian film-makers and television makers to explore Church issues that otherwise they might not have.* Brides of Christ *might not have been, had there not been* The Devil's Playground.

Right. I met Ron Blair who wrote the play, *The Christian Brothers.* He said he heard I was doing *Devil's Playground*, so he wrote like hell to get his play finished. I think it's rather significant, by the way (I don't think this is true now, but it was true then) that many of the people doing things, writing books, plays, getting into film, were Catholics or ex-Catholics or traumatised Catholics, and it was all strictly railing against that Irish Catholic severity and obsessiveness that I think most of us saw was counterproductive to what religion really should be doing. And I don't think it's any accident. As Phillip Adams and various people have written, while not a lot of great cinema, or anything, was coming out of Australia, it was a fairly complacent society and there was not a lot to rail against.

That, of course, always brings up to me, 'What is the point? If you have a pretty damned good lifestyle, do you need it?' I know you do; please don't get me wrong. You need it in a different way. But since there is little to rail against other than, say, mental torpidity or spiritual barrenness, then there's not a lot of great work happening. Great work, unfortunately, seems to come out of oppression or deprivation. So I think at that time that area, oddly enough, was religion.

In a documentary screened on SBS you said that it was at Assumption College that you first got interested in what we used to call 'the pictures'.

Well, you had Saturday night: that was the best night of the week in a way. You had to go to a movie, although they were pretty bloody awful movies. Every kid's going to get interested in those movies. But my main stuff happened probably when I was 15 or 16, when I was working and going to night school and then I was sneaking into the Savoy or the Australia Cinema. I was hoping to see naked women. I remember going to see *One Summer of Happiness* (dir. Arne Mattsson). I remember it was on the list and, in those days, if it was on the list you weren't allowed to see it under pain of some kind of sin. I sat through the whole thing and obviously I was going for a bit of a perve. The girl took her clothes off and lay down and her breasts disappeared – that was a big surprise to me – and that was about two seconds and then she was seen in the distance in the water. That was it. And I loved the film, a fantastic film. I thought, 'Why is this film on the list? Why am I getting into trouble for this?' Of course, I found out later that they were taking the mickey out of the priest. That was entirely lost on me.

1 1 3

I saw *Wages of Fear* (dir. Henri-Georges Clouzot), *Rocco and His Brothers* (dir. Luchino Visconti), *The Bicycle Thieves* (dir. Vittorio De Sica). That was a golden era of European cinema and highly charged. I found every one of them absolutely spellbinding, albeit sometimes for the wrong reasons!

Were there any cinema precedents for The Devil's Playground, *or was it just so much part of your life?*

No, it was part of my life. I don't have cinema precedents; I just don't. I'm not stupid enough to believe that they're not absorbed, but I don't follow one style of film-maker. The material dictates its needs. The thing I would say about *The Devil's Playground* is I watered it down because, in fact, it took me five years to get the money together and over half the money was mine, and I had to put in that much money again to get it out. I had to hire the cinema. Nobody liked the film until I got it out there, which I find rather remarkable. But in remembering that I wrote it five years before, I knew if I went as far as I should go, everyone would go, 'Oh, come on, that's not on, that's not possible'. Nobody would believe it. So I deliberately pulled back on all sorts of things, so the impression was shocking enough or jangling enough without going the whole hog.

Did you draw back in the presentation of the brothers, the range of characters?

In a way. They're all real men, and combinations of two or three. If you take the main boy, what I did was this: every one of those brothers is the possibility of what he might become, depending on which side of his personality gets most influenced, whether his sexuality gets so repressed that he goes down the Francine road, or whether he's able to overcome that and be more joyful (like, say, Brother Arnold, who's quite content in the spiritual life), or whether he's the middle guy who's more realistic, split the difference. So every one of them is a variation, they're all what's inside that guy. But they're also based on real people.

But you can come across a great teacher here or there; I certainly did. There were a couple, in fact, and one very much in particular – Brother Osmond – who was very, very inspiring in every way, like music and Latin and geography and English: he made them great subjects for everybody. That can help.

Now, over forty years later and with the uncovering of repression as well as the exposure of abuse, we probably should look at it again in that light. However, even in ordinary Catholic schools, students were far more prudish in the early 1950s much less explicit in language than the characters in the film. Was the film a 1970s'-perspective dramatisation of the 1950s?

No, I held back, believe me. Believe me, I held back. See, I went to Assumption, and I was there for so long before I went to that school that I was kind of horrified by what they were doing, what was happening in that school. And at a particular time I went to one of the brothers who had been at Assumption – I went to see him and I said, 'You know, I have to tell you this because I know you'd understand', all this bizarre behaviour, this, this and this. He was pretty shocked and quite a number of people got called out, sent away. I had decided to leave at that point, and pretty soon afterwards the juniorate was stopped and the students put into an ordinary college. I don't think they really did know the extent of what was going on. I was doing it from a real belief that 'This is how it should be, and it doesn't need to be this weird. This is something like the Middle Ages'.

There were some good people around – some very good people around, good brothers too – and they were there with the sick buggers, and the rest of it was just like misguided religious zeal.

You've got to remember that the majority of those kids were going through puberty but it's all been covered up, so that just makes it twenty times as bad. I remember I sat in a theatre in Brisbane with Terry Jackman and there were nuns and brothers who had all come along to the opening night, so you can imagine what that was like. The brothers were all holding their breath and absolutely silent, and the nuns thought it was great.

I had to change my phone number. I was somehow becoming a counsellor. I know a few brothers decided to leave the order pretty soon after that. You know, the success rate of the juniorate turned out – at one point only fifty per cent of them kept going.

To Jimmie Blacksmith, *beautiful to look at and a striking re-creation of the history. Keneally's novel inspired you?*

No; there's an unknown quantity of certain things, but a couple of images strike you and they're the things you go for, fire your imagination, and they should be full of possibilities. But it did have something so terrifying and beautiful at the same time.

With The Chant of Jimmie Blacksmith *you initiated some serious reflection on Aboriginal issues in the late 1970s. However, in reference to it Ken Hall was quoted as saying that Australians won't look at films about Aborigines.*

He's right. I understand with *Dead Heart* (dir. Nick Parsons) that there was the same reaction. They won't. They won't because, you see, most Australians are nowhere near Aborigines, nowhere near in contact with them, so it's not an issue in their daily life. They can have theories on it, but they don't have to test those theories. In certain areas of Western Australia there's a lot more Aborigines – in country areas. But in most of the cities you're not in contact with Aborigines at all, and the film bites you right where they think you're safe.

I remember a psychiatrist friend of mine with liberal attitudes and seemingly intellectual character went to the premiere. When I got home I found a swear word across my front door, and it turned out to be the psychiatrist. I said, 'Why did you do that?' He said, 'Because you made me realise I was racist'. I think that's what *Jimmie Blacksmith* does for a lot of people: it makes them feel about it in a way they don't expect from it. It's a very violent film – on purpose. It was meant to be anti-violence but all those things bring home a reality.

In terms of Church and religion, the film opened with Methodism, Rev Mr Neville and his wife and Jimmie eating with them. Then he went to the initiation: another world. This gave you a hook onto the Australian audience with their churchgoing, confronting them with those issues. And at the end Mr Neville visits Jimmie in prison and finds his religious worldview inadequate.

Yes. Well, it's the cause of it, isn't it? I mean, Christianity is not the cause of it, but the Churches' belief that their version of events is right and that they're going to go and save the heathen and take them out of that world. And then, of course, the Aborigines are spiritually and culturally displaced. The world that they were being pulled into, at least at that time – and it's probably still fairly true now – does not accept them, so they're not part of that world, and the world they've been pulled from rejects them.

Then as big a question is the interracial mix, so that the person is also internally conflicted, disliked by both societies for that as well. So that's the central conflict of the whole thing: those two issues. There were a few priests who used to visit me because they had worked in Aboriginal missions.

These awful situations that they were put in: they were out there seeing the Aborigine living the life that is so particular to them, setting up a conflict in the priest trying to take them out of this world into another world, and then questioning, 'Why are we really doing this?' And then only being able to do this with the boys, because the girls were unsettling. The priests were a bit sexually interested in a way they didn't expect to be, so they had to keep the girls away from them. They didn't deal with them, or treated them badly, emotionally badly. And this guy in particular (and I know a couple of others as well) was absolutely conflicted by this: that their celibacy was preventing them from doing the right job if, in fact, it was the right job in the first place.

One of the things I always thought was strange was that there was a lot of pressure on the missionary role of a person in religious life. It was always held up as one of the great things – you know, to go off to Africa or to go to New Guinea, somewhere like that – when right round the corner was a problem larger and more important than travelling to distant places. I was always unsettled by that lack of attention to the needs of the neighbourhood, if you like.

Fred Schepisi

This particular priest I was talking about a minute ago: he was spectacular about it. He would get out in mufti, setting up coffee shops and all kinds of things for people to come in and talk. His branch of the Church hated it and stopped funding him. But the number of people's lives that this guy touched effectively I thought was fantastic, because he was really working within his own community to help cure and solve problems in a way he was never able to – they used to keep pulling him out of there and then sending him off.

This is still the problem now for the Churches: whether there is any need for the religious to go to foreign countries as missionaries, or to go, collaborating with local Churches, to build them up with the people. This is far more realistic than the old-time missionary effort. It's a different world and so it should be a different Church.

We've been into this whole thing of imposing our belief system on them, or making them replace their system.

Black Robe (dir. Bruce Beresford) dealt very powerfully with the issues of mission and inculturation. The real challenge for most people in the Catholic Church today is for the local inculturation of the Gospel. However, at the end of Jimmie Blacksmith, Jimmie is actually captured in a convent and the nuns are rather horrified because it is the Bishop's room. This seemed to be a symbolic touch about the Church and the cultures.

I don't even remember that one!

Many Australians found Evil Angels very embarrassing. It challenged the way that a lot of people had reacted during the 1980s – to Lindy Chamberlain, especially. That whole question of rumour – all those scenes of tennis parties and dinner gossip, the cousin who knew this, the acquaintance who said that. You also challenged the role of the media. That's irrespective of the core of the film and the experience of the Chamberlains.

The really interesting thing about that film was the night when I'd just finished it and I showed it to Michael and Lindy Chamberlain. And they were absolutely floored. They were in tears for ages afterwards because they had no idea of the scale of the thing, of what was against them.

They had no idea. And in it they realised how inadvertently, just by proclaiming their innocence and insisting on proving it, they realised how much they contributed to their own difficulty as well. It was something they put behind them very quickly – and probably continued to, and not incorrectly – but they were devastated. I think nobody understood.

The difficulty of making a film like that is there are no villains. It was the accumulation of so many things that just went to work against a person; at least five or six major things that contributed to the misunderstanding of those people. And conventionally, in a film, you wouldn't do that; you would reduce it. You would reduce the characters, you would reduce the dramatic through line et cetera. So to me the pleasure and the difficulty in doing that film was not falling into that trap. It's something that, quite honestly, I don't think you could do in Hollywood. I know because I tried to do it. I know you can't. I just fell on that sword again in withdrawing from *The Shipping News* (dir. Lasse Hallström). People think there's only one way of doing things.

Everything about that film was presented so that it was just the facts; not coloured: we didn't emotionally colour the music or any other aspect. We presented the facts, and the facts spoke for themselves. And when you're dealing with something, particularly since it was an ongoing case at the time, you can't take artistic flight; it's very difficult because you keep tripping over the truth. See, what most people do is they take the truth and they manipulate it into an emotional reality, which it is not – and I haven't done that. I understand why they do that, but I certainly do not do that.

But what we did find – the thing that did take flight: it's best illustrated by one incident. There was always a lot of talk about how strange Michael Chamberlain was, standing there delivering this message to the crowd that he was praying for them. It was religious but it was kind of quasi-religious, very strange, 'God's will' and all that stuff. Sam and I were struggling with it. He could have just stood there and delivered his speech the way a preacher would and it would have worked. But you're always looking for that deeper thing that gives it another edge, even if it's just to you.

The reports from that night were completely different: there were really three clear impressions given by the speech that he had given. And, you know, the truth was, we found it: he found a way of delivering it which we were hunting for. He would say, 'Let me try this or try that,' and I would say, 'We'll try this or try that.' But, all of a sudden, he just hit a tone, a stance, a strangeness, and the hair went up the back of my neck and we knew, you could suddenly see: some people are going to get one impression, some people are going to get another. It pointed out to us that if you find the right way of being that person you can then understand how many misconceptions could come out of it. So, in other words, you could find the truth of the character, always.

And that became our guiding thing. Every person in the film was told, 'We don't want you to present the pathologist as a bad person, we don't want you to present the prosecuting attorney as a bad person. We don't want that; that's wrong'. We got them to go and talk to and spend time with those people, find out their point of view, find out why they were like that, take up their zeal, their enthusiasm, their belief, and sell it. Say, 'This is what I was like, this is what I actually believe, this is who I am'. Far more interesting. And then let the truth lie where it lay.

Yet the staggering thing is that after seeing the film, people came up and said, 'So what's the real story?' It used to make me so mad I wanted to hit them. Now I just say, 'Go away'.

Seeing Evil Angels *was the first time that some people understood something of the inner personality of Lindy Chamberlain. It was a strength of Meryl Streep's performance. Australians were all caught up in the exotic aspects of the case. Would it have made such an impact if the Chamberlains were not Adventist, if it had not taken place with dingoes at Uluru? That's why it stayed in the Australian psyche.*

And there's such a misapprehension about Seventh Day Adventists and their cultish behaviour and rituals. We think they're cultish. People think they're like Jehovah's Witnesses or Scientologists. And they get all that off-to-the-side religion misunderstanding. And what are the differences with Seventh Day Adventists? Well, their main difference is that Saturday is the holy day, not Sunday. Is that worth fighting about? Because when it's Saturday here it's Sunday over there or vice versa. So number one is that it's a basically decent religion.

The opening scene with the trucker commenting on and swearing about the Adventists is an immediate challenge.

My editor wanted me to take that scene out. The editor and the producer both tried to make me take that scene out again and again and again, and I said, 'When you interrupt the film, it's always going to jar, because you're setting up a different grammar and it's always going to jar, so I don't care, I'm going to jar you, I'm going to really jar you, and then everything after that will be easy'. And I think it's all right. It does confront you.

But the thing I hope comes out of it is that Lindy Chamberlain's faith is very real. She still truly believes that God will help her. Michael, who went around doing death counselling and all that stuff – he's the minister: his belief was more a hope than a belief and so, even though he went round doing the right thing, he wasn't as convinced, or as deeply convinced, as she was that it was alright. He was very easily shaken.

Your overseas films: my favourite is Six Degrees of Separation. *Is it a favourite of yours?*

It's a good film.

There's a lovely scene at the end: after Stockard Channing has talked about the experience with the young man in their lives and reducing experience to anecdotes, she says it was more than an anecdote and, as she's walking down the New York street, you've got her almost leaping and reaching up as she did in the Sistine Chapel: meeting people is like touching God.

Slapping the hand of God; doing the high-five.

You've done a range of the films – Barbarossa, Iceman, Plenty, Roxanne, Russia House, Mr Baseball, IQ *– have you enjoyed making them?*

Yes, I have. Two of them were not as good as I would have liked: *Mr Baseball* and *IQ*. I like *IQ*. The trouble when you do that kind of comedy (unless the star – as say it was with Steve Martin and *Roxanne* – is writing and is really involved in it): you get a lot of interference. Everybody thinks they can help you with those films, so everybody's pitching in. And, as you get maturer, you accommodate a little bit, you give a little here. It doesn't seem like much, it's a one-per cent thing: you give one per cent. Before you realise it, what was a diamond is now a round ball with no personality, no edge. In all honesty, I think *IQ* is a good, funny picture.

The problem was there were two other producers, there was a studio and there was Tim Robbins, and they were all contributing; and Tim Robbins was being difficult because he said in the 1990s nobody would like a character who has a woman fall in love with him because of a lie. That's the whole premise of the film. And it's all right for him to know that and believe it, but he should spend the whole time trying to say, 'Hey, I'm lying to you,' and be constantly frustrated. Because of that attitude, he pulled the film this way, he pulled it that way while we were writing and it just felt messy.

And nobody ever understood the value of those four scientists. And I like the cast that I had, but the other three scientists apart from Walter Matthau were originally going to be Peter Ustinov, Barry Humphries and John Cleese. I wanted them all the way through, but nobody understood how strong they would be. Nobody understood that with a garage and the scientists and this other guy, if you could just stay within that world, if you kept your two lovers together all the time under pressure and you do lots of silly things – there were a couple of wonderfully silly things when they were trying to prove his theory and they kept blowing things up – it had that whimsy about it that would have kept the lovers together and under tension. If they want subplots, they up the stakes and all this formulaic crap – and that's the problem.

Similarly with *Mr Baseball*, which really was just supposed to be about cultural differences using the baseball game, but also there was much funnier stuff. When he goes down to see the father and there's the noodle scene, all of that, that's the kind of humour that could have been throughout the whole film. Again the studio and Tom Selleck had script approval, which I didn't realise when I agreed to do it. I went in to help them out. They didn't understand it, so they pulled it into the conventional. They're not bad films; they're just not the great films they could have been.

Are you going to get Jack Maggs *made?*

God, I hope so. It's proving to be very difficult. I'm actually rewriting and trying to work out why I had a difficulty getting top actors to do it. And the script is complicated. They're not so complicated when they get on film, but they're complicated when they're on the page. So I'm in the process of trying to simplify it without losing any of the good bits.

You've contributed a great deal to Australian cinema, and to world cinema.

I would like to do some more.

Australian Feature Films

1973 'The Priest' in *Libido*

1976 *The Devil's Playground*

1976 *The Chant of Jimmie Blacksmith*

1988 *Evil Angels*

Esben Storm

Esben Storm, *Crash Zone*, 1998.
(Photo: Suzy Wood. The Australian Children's Television Foundation.)

THE AUSTRALIAN FILM AND TELEVISION COMPANION'S *entry begins: 'Storm, Esben, 1950: Interesting writer, actor, editor, producer'. Are you pleased to be referred to as 'interesting' in all those areas?*

It's better to be referred to as 'interesting' than to be referred to as 'boring' or 'uninteresting'.

27A was a strange choice of subject, given the state of the Australian film industry in the early 1970s.

It was a strange choice because there weren't many films being made at that stage, really. *Libido* was the big feature made in Melbourne with three or four directors. But there wasn't much happening.

The main influence on the style of the film was that we knew we wouldn't be able to raise a lot of money. Hayden Keenan, my partner, and I made a little bit of money and had some success with two short films. They'd both won awards at the Sydney Film Festival but we realised that there was no future in short films. This was in the days when you tried to enter a short film in the Melbourne Film Festival and Erwin Rado said, 'We don't show Australian short films' – so it's quite ironic now that there's a short film prize at the Melbourne Film Festival named after him.

If we wanted to make a feature film, we'd have to make it cheap. There was a style at that time – sort of pseudo-documentary with a lot of hand-held camera work: *Culloden* (dir. Peter Watkins), *Cathy Come Home* (dir. Ken Loach) and *Poor Cow* (dir. Ken Loach) – that English Ken-Loach-Peter-Watkins realism. I was drawn to the subject in the newspapers and then went off to investigate and research it. I felt that it would suit that style.

Institutions and the people in them?

A basic theme, which is probably a recurring theme, is that of someone trying to break out, someone feeling trapped within themselves, trapped within the system. That probably drew me to it. Then when I went to research it, I found a broader tapestry.

Response was favourable?

It was favourable. It won a lot of AFI awards. But it was a kind of an art film. Those were also the days when it was very difficult for an Australian film to get mainstream distribution, so Natalie Miller ended up distributing it. Those were also the days before Natalie Miller owned a cinema, when she was distributing 16-mm prints from her lounge room or from her little office at home. It had a good season in Melbourne at the Playbox Cinema. It never really had a season in Sydney. The intention was always to blow it up to 35-

mm. We shot it on very slow stock, so it had a really good grain, but we never got it up to 35-mm.

SBS still screens it.

Yes, it's still alive and quite respected. For a while in the 1970s it was as if we were getting a call every second week for someone to screen it at a welfare workshop.

In view of the developing industry at that time, it enabled some people to think of the social issues that Australian films could explore.

I guess so. It was made at a time when there was no major funding. There was funding: the AFDC – the Australian Film Development Corporation – had been set up with a view to funding feature films. In those days a feature film would cost $300,000 or $400,000, but there was no situation for funding low-budget features. I think we got $12,000 from the interim fund for the Film School. Tom Jeffrey put that in. Then Hayden went out and raised something like $20,000 from different private investors who all put in a thousand each, and the budget was $33,000. That was the total budget.

Then a couple of years later, when people like Gillian Armstrong and Phil Noyce came through the Film School, they were given $60,000 or $70,000 to make films like *The Singer and the Dancer* and *Backroads*. *27A* was 85 minutes. They ended up with 50-minute or 60-minute films, fully funded. So ours was a totally different situation. Films like *Pure Shit* (dir. Bert Deling) then followed that low-budget 16-mm route. *Pure Shit* I think was the best of them. That was a great film.

How did you make the transition, after a number of years, to In Search of Anna?

In between I was asked to do a film called *Angel Gear*. We had won a lot of AFI awards, but then I got a bit carried away because I felt that making *27A* was so hard and felt that people were so unsympathetic to our intent, that when we won these awards, I basically told everyone to get stuffed. Everyone was quite shocked. So my career was down the toilet for a while. I'd never thought of it in terms of sucking up to people, so everyone thought I was an arrogant little shit. But I did get one offer and that was to make *Angel Gear*. It was to be a trucking film. So we spent a couple of years doing that, but it fell through.

Then we set up a business catering to film-makers – cutting rooms, mixing studios and offices – in a big old church manse in Sydney. Hayden and I were still partners. Then I started to think about the past and to get depressed about my situation. I became aware that all the films being made in Australia were period films – *Picnic at Hanging Rock* (dir. Peter Weir), *The Getting of Wisdom* (dir. Bruce Beresford), *Between Wars* (dir. Michael Thornhill). I felt this reflected a society that was unable to come to terms with where it was at. I

Myth & Meaning
M y t h & M e a n i n g
M y t h & M e a n i n g

know you have to look into the past and find your heroes but it seemed to me that it was reflective of a desire not to face up to where we were at.

That also coincided with where I was at personally, in my relationship to women and to Hayden, so I thought I should make a film about leaving the past behind and coming to terms with the present, moving into the future with a positive attitude. That's what I thought I should do personally and that's what I felt Australia should do. It led to *In Search of Anna*.

You took to the road: an actual journey as well as the road being a metaphor?

Yes, there are two stories. One starts with a guy getting out of gaol; someone caught by the system. He comes out and goes looking for what is an idealised memory of love. At the same time he is being confronted, in the form of Chris Haywood, by the debts owed to the past. He's travelling down the road and the past impinges. As regards the structure, you start halfway through a story and then you flash back and flash forward. Eventually past and present build into a climax and spit the main character out. He's able then to pursue his life with the spirit of the present.

We were nominated for six AFI awards that year but we were up against *Mad Max* (dir. George Miller), so we didn't have much chance there. I was lucky to get Best Original Screenplay.

How did the public respond?

The public responded well. The film ran for about eight weeks all around Australia and did really well, relatively. I produced it with Natalie Miller as associate producer. After a while I didn't have any money so I didn't pursue selling it any more. It was time to move on. I was basically broke at the end of it – what can you do?

So you contributed to the shift from period pieces to the industry's looking more realistically at the present?

That may have been true, yes. *Mad Max* probably had more influence, pulled us into the future. But I was very conscious that everyone was making period films. Period's very easy – it's nice and secure, safe and non-confrontational – so it's very easy to feel good about the past.

With Prejudice?

With Prejudice was one of those tax scam movies that ended up being not too bad. We shot it in two and a half weeks. Eighteen days, I think. *With Prejudice* was quite strong and I liked the structure of it: the *Rashomon* (dir. Akira Kurosawa) pursuit of truth, where you enact all the various perceptions of truth. I had a lot of problems with the producer; we fought a lot about how it should be, but it still ended up not being too bad a film.

Esben Storm
Esben Storm

Did it help the cause of the Ananda Marga people and their case?

I think it probably did, a little. It was a little drop on the rock. I was trying not to be too overtly biased. I was trying not to put any colour on it, so that the cops would tell their story and our guys would tell their story. I was trying to direct them so that when the cops told their story, audiences would see it as they imagined that the cops would see it. I was trying to make it so that each side's version of the truth spoke for itself and, therefore, left the audience to make a judgment. And the judgment was fairly obvious.

It's an interesting companion piece to Evil Angels *(dir. Fred Schepisi).*

That's right, the same sort of thing really, except for a lot less money.

Quite a transition, then, to Stanley?

There was a guy called Andrew Gaty who ran Seven Keys. He'd made a film called *The Return of Captain Invincible* (dir. Philippe Mora). Andrew Gaty had made a tremendous amount of money, humungous, a lot of money out of distributing *Tommy* (dir. Ken Russell) in Australia, more successfully in Australia than anywhere in the world. And then he made a lot of money out of soft porn which came into general release. Anyway, he made *Captain Invincible*, which was universally hated. He was hated also by other distributors because he was a bit of an upstart.

He had a chap working for him called Steve Kibbler. Kibbler worked for Grundy's and he had employed me to make a feature film for Grundy's called *Bondi Blue*. I spent a long time after *In Search of Anna* writing this film that I was to direct. We went into pre-production and on a Friday night I went out to Atlab to look at some tests. We were meant to start shooting on the Monday, and Reg Grundy pulled the plug on it that Friday. I had another story called *Dirty Barry*, which was a send-up of *Dirty Harry*. I first wrote it in the mid-1970s and then *Dog Day Afternoon* (dir. Sidney Lumet) came out and it was very similar to that, so I put it aside. Steve Kibbler liked it a lot. By this stage he'd gone to work for Andrew Gaty and tried to get him involved in doing *Dirty Barry*.

Andrew Gaty was a creative producer. He wanted to make a film in the vein of *Arthur* (dir. Steve Gordon) and he asked me to read a script. He happened to be in New York and I was at home. I said, 'It's a piece of shit'. Then I jokingly said, 'Well, either I can come over there and work with you on it there or you can come back here'. The next thing, my wife and I were in New York with him, working on the script with a chap called Stanley Mann from Los Angeles, who's a well-respected scriptwriter. So I worked with him as my script editor, then basically wrote another script which ended up being *Stanley, Every Home Needs One*.

Andrew had certain things that he wanted, which I had to accommodate, but within that I was trying to make a comedy about acceptance and prejudice. But even though it was hugely unsuccessful, it was my first attempt at comedy, which I really enjoyed. Some people still come up and say they like it and have it in their collections and talk about it being hugely underrated.

Was it a send-up of Australian families?

Yes. Stanley is sent to do an ethnographic study of a middle-class Australian family. The family presents itself normally, but then he finds that the father is gay, that the mother is having an affair with the guy who runs the bowling club, the son's dealing dope and the daughter's having an affair with an Aboriginal boy, and the whole family's busy denying all of it.

So what Stanley does for the family is free them so that they overcome their middle-class inhibitions and accept who they are. Dad goes off with the guy and Mum goes off and everyone's happy.

There are a lot of reasons why it wasn't successful. I think the script was okay. It's very hard to do comedy, and it's either funny or it isn't. I learnt a lot about comedy on that one. I think we would've been better off if the budget hadn't been so high, if we hadn't been trying to be so glossy.

Andrew was very intent on making a sort of glossy big-style movie and, in the beginning, the whole thing was predicated on getting an American or an international star to play the lead. We had Tom Conti but they wouldn't let us bring him in.

That could've made the difference.

You also act.

I started acting after *In Search of Anna*. I was so broke and I thought, well, I can act, I can write, I can direct, I can edit, so I'm going to do anything, wherever I can get a job. In the acting business in Australia everyone knows everyone and if you can get a couple of roles a year, that's fine. Because I spend most of my time writing, I often feel cut off. So if you can go out and act for a couple of days, you can socialise a little bit. So I talked Ken Cameron into giving me a part in *Monkey Grip* and that was the beginning. I used to act a lot before I went to Sydney. When I was a kid I did a lot of theatre as a child actor. But when I went to Sydney I thought I was going to become a serious young film director and so I stopped acting, which I shouldn't have done. I don't hang out for it and I don't need it, but when I get asked to do it, it's always a pleasure.

You made some films for television.

The feature was *Devil's Hill*. Even though it was for the Children's Film and Television Foundation, it was a feature, 96 minutes long. I feel quite pleased with that film. It's about a kid who has to go to the top of the mountain to get his cows back. It was set in Tasmania, based on a Nan Chauncey book. I enjoyed Tasmania and making the film. It was someone else's script but it was terrible so I rewrote it. It brought Patricia Edgar and myself quite close and began to cement our relationship. It was the second film I made for the Foundation. The first was *The Other Facts of Life*, written by Morris Gleitzman.

Where did Deadly *emerge from?*

We started writing it about 1987. It was called *The Desert Rose*, then *The Native Rose*. Some Aborigines didn't like the word 'native', so we changed it to *Deadly*. With Aborigines dying in custody, where they're 0.25 per cent of the population and some 18 per cent of the deaths in custody were of Aborigines, it's hugely disproportionate. The whole colonisation process and the invasion and stealing the land from the indigenous people is a weeping sore. I think the country needs to come to terms with this or else it will never be able to move on. The present government probably takes the attitude that, if we starve them they'll die out and there won't be a problem any more, which is pretty much how civilisation works.

So I felt that there was a film to be made about the Aborigines, a contemporary film about Aborigines in Australia. Every time a film touched on an Aboriginal situation, it has not been successful – which everyone kept telling us. It wasn't as if we were suddenly onto this theme: there were three Aborigines in *27A*. When I was researching *27A* in Queensland, one of the things that leaped out was that there was a disproportionate number of Aboriginal inmates in mental institutions. We had an Aborigine, Zack Martin, in *In Search of Anna* but we cut that part out because we couldn't afford to shoot it in the end. Lydia Miller was in *The Big Wish*. She played a school teacher. It wasn't a particularly Aboriginal part, just a character. We had an Aboriginal girl in the second series of *Round The Twist* and we had an Aboriginal boy, of course, in *Stanley*. It didn't matter that the characters were black; they were just another person. That was the idea with the kids' films: they would just be accepted as people; nothing to do with the colour of their skin.

Why did we choose to do *Deadly* as a cop-murder-mystery genre film? Because the problem of racism and prejudice in our society, which is what the blacks have to deal with, is not coming from the enlightened few, the enlightened minority or the concerned minority; it's coming from the great redneck, right-wing mass out there. It's coming from the people who basically don't think about it. The reason the government can afford to take $400,000,000 out of ATSIC is because it won't lose them any votes. Most people don't care, basically.

So the decision was to make a film that would appeal to the people who do not care. You can make an arty sort of film that would investigate the depths of the situation and it would end up at best playing in art cinemas and be shown on the ABC.

This happened with Blackfellas *(dir. James Ricketson).*

Yes, *Blackfellas*, where you got a very strong, positive, critical response, but probably not so many people went to see it. So I was trying to make a film that would go to the heart of the problem. I was trying to make a film that would appeal to the racists and the prejudiced majority.

You have said you wanted a central character audiences could identify with.

Yes. I thought, 'What sort of films do these people watch?' Clint Eastwood. He's an icon of this kind of thing. All his movies are set in the mid-west with rednecks, bounty hunters. The majority of cinema-going audiences love Clint Eastwood movies. So I was trying to make this kind of movie. If I could do that, I would be taking the problem and putting it in the face of these people. If I had a sort of Clint Eastwood-y lead character, who starts as a racist, then basically we're saying this guy is the audience. He goes on a journey and by the end of the film he's holding a black man's hand, he's sort of fallen in love with a black woman and has found within himself the capacity to see that these people are just like him and so has overcome his prejudice. That was the journey I was wanting to take the audience on.

Most people aren't members of the Ku Klux Klan. Racism and prejudice are very subtle, insidious. So it was a conscious thing to make a film that would play to the heart of the problem, and not make a film that would play for success or acceptance where it didn't matter.

You filmed in Wilcannia.

In the early 1990s there was the Royal Commission into Aboriginal deaths in custody. When we came to Wilcannia there had actually been a death in custody and everyone thought we were coming to do a film about that. Originally I wanted to shoot *Deadly* in Western Australia because I like the light. We researched the possibility of shooting it in a town called Kew, which is right smack-dab in the middle of Western Australia. It's a beautiful town, beautiful corrugated iron buildings and really beautiful light. But we couldn't get any money from Western Australia and it was too expensive to go and do it there. Then we did a tour around Victoria and New South Wales and found Wilcannia. Wilcannia's a beautiful old town with beautiful proud old buildings from the time when Wilcannia was a huge port on the Darling River. It has all this history, but it's a town in decay. There had been riots, really bad riots, so once I chose to shoot there, there was a lot of resistance and quite a few – like the people involved in the production of the film – did a lot to try and dissuade me from going because they thought it was going to be dangerous and that we were putting the cast and the crew into a risky situation.

But eventually we did go and there was not really any problem at all. For the four weeks that we were there, the crime rate dropped by something like 95 per cent. The magistrate would come in every two weeks and was amazed that there was nothing for her to do. I had a good time with those people. They were great.

At one stage, Lydia Miller says of John Moore, 'Look, he's a victim, he wants to be a victim, therefore he doesn't have to do anything'. Even in brief moments you continually raise issues.

If you're making a film to preach to the converted or to have artistic praise from the concerned minority, you wouldn't say that. It's very dangerous for a black person to say, 'Don't indulge in being a victim', because a lot them do. A lot of people do indulge in being victims. If you're a victim, you're not responsible for your own life. You're basically saying, 'It's your fault. It's your fault that I am like this'. And as long as you continue saying this, then you're not responsible for your own actions. You have to get to a point where you say, 'Well, I am like I am and it's my responsibility. If I'm going to change or if my situation's going to change, I'm going to accept responsibility for changing it. As long as I'm dependent on others, as long as I say it's other people's fault, then I have no control over my life'. So that's what she was saying to him.

Another thing I was also very conscious of doing was that, when the old black man comes walking down the street and everyone's outside the police station, I was consciously trying to set up a situation where the audience would think, 'Oh, now we're going to get into the old black magic stuff', because what happens in films, theatre and the arts in the portrayal of Aborigines is that they have magic. This allows a white audience to say, 'Oh, well, they are different', which dehumanises them, 'They are not like us'. I wanted to say that they are like us, they're not that different. They don't really have any amazing sort of powers that other people don't have and, when their children die, they cry just as much as anyone else and when they're hurt, they feel the pain as much as anyone else. I was trying to cut through the 'mystic' stuff.

The scene where John Moore carries the wounded policeman was completely unexpected because each of them had said to the other, 'I wouldn't piss on you if you were on fire'. He could have left him there, but you showed him carrying the enemy, saving his life.

Yes. I'm almost crying when you tell me that story. I wanted to make the point that he could kill that man, he could kill him there and then, he could leave him to die, but he was a bigger man than that. With the John Moore character we wanted to create a young, attractive, handsome, active, black person, who wasn't so much about talking but about doing, and who could be more than just Tonto, more than just the token blackfella. He was integral to the climax and the resolution. In doing so was standing up for himself and for his people as well. Carrying the policeman was to say that by doing this he is better than this man and that he has compassion. He has been hurt by him, but he is strong enough to rise above that and be compassionate. So I was basically saying here is a really strong person, a person who's been hurt and who has gone through a situation where he's blamed everyone else, has accepted his responsibility for his own existence and is now doing something about it. I was trying to create a positive, heroic role model.

Caz Lederman's character is about to kill herself but does not because of the child.

The subtext is that you have this tragedy because the cop (Frank Gallacher) is impotent and unable to satisfy his wife. So you've got the forces of evil being portrayed as being impotent, twisted and crippled in their psyches, but having control over the woman. She had been in love with a black man.

The funeral sequence at the grave side. The clergyman (John Gregg) speaks, is interrupted by John Moore, then the song and the symbolic flock of birds. It is very moving.

We went to another town on the Upper Darling to do research and went down to the river where they were all drinking and smoking and told them what we were doing. They said, 'Oh, this boy here, Trumby, he's written a song about this stuff'. So we went back to Trumby's place, picked up his guitar. It started raining and he's standing there singing the song for us and then the cops came down with the paddy wagon and moved everyone on. The song was just fantastic. So we kept in touch with Trumby. Then Gary Foley organised an album called 'Building Bridges' and we got Trumby's song on it, 'Justice Will Be Done'. In the funeral scene I wanted to have a situation where the clergy, the church, was seen to be trying to do its thing and impose its idea of how things should be. John Moore finally stands up and tells him to shut up because this is his family. The minister was saying, 'We can't blame anyone here. No one is to blame and we must accept ...'

'And I'm not angry.'

'... And I'm not angry', yes. And I wanted a black person to say, 'I *am* angry and I *am* pissed off. When I think about my brother, I don't think of him like that; I think of him ... passing the football ...' So I wanted a big speech from John Moore that would put the other point of view, because deaths in custody reports are always about statistics. But here's a guy who died. He's remembered as a footballer, he's remembered as a painter, as a lover, as someone's son, as a human being like you or me, not just a black statistic. And that when they cry; they cry real tears and their tears are just as important as our tears and just as heartfelt and just as full of grieving as ours.

You see black families on TV, someone in an African country crying over their child, but you're distanced from it. It's ethnographic. So you think, 'That's them, it's not us – those poor people'. The medium distances you and you don't think of them as just being another mum and dad. And that's all they are; they're just another mum and dad, just someone's son. That's what I was trying to get to there.

Did you have any denomination in mind for the clergyman?

No, it was just a generic sort of thing.

Subterano.

I have a film called *Subterano*: a sci-fi horror movie set in the future, set in an underground carpark. A group of people get trapped in an underground carpark and get killed by deadly remote-controlled toys. There's a kid in it and he's the baddie. It's about God in a way. It's based on the lines from *King Lear*: 'As flies to wanton boys are we to the gods. They kill us for their sport'. One of the themes is: if there is a God, what if that God is a prick; what if that God is just a bastard? For one of the characters, when he thinks that, it all makes sense. It makes sense of the world; that the world is such a slimy world of greed and selfishness and anguish and pain that the only way that it can make any sense is if the person who created the whole thing is ... It's all a macabre joke.

It's almost the opposite of Genesis 1: 'We were made in God's image and likeness'. If you say, 'We are sinful, horrible, we're in God's likeness, therefore that's what God is like'.

I started thinking about it at the time of Desert Storm, with all the remote-control intelligent missiles, and how war is now remote-control, how a rocket will come down our street and turn left and knock on our door and explode in our face and it will all be on the six o'clock news. It's that sort of thing. It's also about surveillance: a world where everyone is under surveillance. So, how do you communicate your real feelings, what's true and what's an act, what's real and what's not? In relationships, how do you communicate what's real and what's not?

1 3 3

Australian Feature Films

1973 *27A*

1979 *In Search of Anna*

1983 *Stanley*

1992 *Deadly*

Nadia
Tass

Nadia Tass with camera operator David Williamson, *Amy*, 1998. (Photo: Skip Watkins.)

You began work in the theatre and still direct many plays.

Communicating the message of a work is the reason why I choose to do comedy. I grew up in the theatre. Coming from overseas, coming from Europe to Australia, the thing that I experienced most profoundly was that in Europe theatre was very much for the populace.

I went straight into primary school here. I liked reading poetry and reading plays and picking out little excerpts from Chekhov which, as a 10-year-old, were really important to me. I grew up with them. And it was very strange to find people in the school not really responding to this at all. Obviously it's not strange now but, as a 10-year-old, I found it strange because we were used to theatre being very much a part of people's lives; something that the people made, entertaining and communicating some sort of message during the course of the play. And doing Chekhov as a 10-year-old was fun!

For a long time I think I kept theatre and literature for myself and my family (but at school I became a follower of the Collingwood Football Club, wagging school, going to buy fish and chips and Coke ...). Then I continued with theatre through my Pram Factory days and, when my mother owned the Playbox, I found that I was getting right back into, or being consumed by, a type of theatre that was part of the so-called elite. And that just doesn't suit me. It was the main reason why I decided to move into film. I felt that through film I could communicate with and entertain the populace and, by myself, put a stop to this highbrow, 'I'm going to the thea-ay-tre', concept!

You established the Melbourne Film Studio.

At the Melbourne Film Studio we have a lot of people; several Australian producers who are operating out of that space. It's a really good space to be in because we tend to support each other. If one person goes out into the corridor to get a cup of coffee, there are usually quite a few people who will come out. Someone might need coffee but others are being supportive or congratulating. I'm finding the celebration of other people's work is something that actually takes place there.

Of course, there's a degree of healthy competitiveness as well, but a collaboration with other people is something that I had always wanted in creating this studio. I saw it operating with Robert de Niro's company and I would like to do that here. I saw situations or places like this as a young child in Europe as well; mainly within the theatre. So I was thrilled to actually make buckets of money in America, bring it all back here and create the Melbourne Film Studio.

Are you disappointed in Australian audiences and the way they support Australian films?

Well, you can't really force people to go when they don't want to. What we can do is highlight the good things about certain films so that audiences can be attracted to go. We are competing against American product – which is very entertaining in its own genre – plus we're competing with major stars that our audiences do want to go and look at. Disappointed? I can't say that I'm disappointed in the audience. I'm disappointed in the situation.

I'll go back to *Malcolm* and use it as an example. As soon as I finished *Malcolm*, I showed it to a couple of houses. The regular people really, really loved it. A lot of people from the industry came out and said, 'Oh, you'll have to recut it' or, 'You'll have to do this' or, 'You'll have do that'. I think I had the worst review ever from one of the Sydney critics. So I decided that I wasn't going to release *Malcolm* here until I took it overseas. For one, I saw that the film worked with a regular audience. Now, what I wanted was normal people coming to the cinema, enjoying the film. It's a very, very special film for me because it's about my brother – and I didn't want that message, which is about special people, to go unnoticed, and so I took it overseas.

It had a totally different reaction to what it had here. The distributors loved it so much that they paid a heap of money for it – it cost us one million dollars to make and they were paying very close to that just for America. And this was for a limited release so that, in fact, after a time we negotiated a second fee. It was quite astounding.

The critiques were just brilliant. There was one that was bad, and that was from the *New York Post*, on the grounds of morality, the fact that Malcolm and Frank had robbed a bank and got away with it. This critic felt that this was immoral. But he didn't really talk about the production in terms of actual production qualities.

Now it had the stamp of approval from overseas, from Japan and from England. It screened at the London Film Festival. The projectionists, a small group of special people, when they feel that a film in the Festival deserves their recognition, they give it the Golden Sprocket Award. For seven years before that no film had received one, and they gave it to *Malcolm* – which I was thrilled about. Now, it was only after that sort of recognition that we released *Malcolm* here. If I had released it at the time that I showed it to the two different full houses that were orchestrated, both from the industry and outside the industry, I feel that *Malcolm* would have really not worked, would have died, because we really do cringe at our own product. So there is a major problem. How do we overcome this?

My confidence comes from the fact that I grew up with this sense that, when something works for me on the screen or on the stage, I know that it works in the area that I expect it to work. There's nobody who can tell me that comedy and tragedy can't be put together, because my forefathers told me otherwise and they've proved that over the generations. I've seen Aristophanes done by peasants in a Greek village.

Australian films tend to be off-beat. They're more challenging than formula films but a lot of people don't want to be challenged, they want to be entertained.

Yes. If they're off-beat, if they're quirky and they're entertaining, if they genuinely are entertaining, I don't think they need to be supported. I think they need to be reviewed for what they are. If they are entertaining, then I think it's important to communicate that to an audience, so that audiences know that they are going to be entertained when they go.

My cousins, who are not in film or theatre – they're very normal people – for them to leave the comfort of their homes and go to the cinema, they expect to see something that they're going to be – they use the phrase – 'blown away' by.

I'm not saying films have to be comedic in order to entertain. To be really absolutely honest with an audience about what the film achieves is important, so that when the audience comes into the cinema they have expectations which are real, and when they go out they feel that they have seen what they were told they were going to see and they're satisfied that they have got their money's worth. If we tell them that they're going to be seeing something as powerful as William Shakespeare and it turns out to be Louis Nowra – and I adore Louis, I love his work – then their expectations are different.

Stark?

It is wonderful. So was working with Ben Elton. I really liked the message of saving the world and of conveying the message via comedy. The BBC received many calls. If an audience enjoys *Stark*, the underlying message comes across and the point is made.

Pure Luck?

Pure Luck was made in 1991 and I can still live off it. I'm still getting cheques. It did fantastic business in America. It's an American film; it's a studio film. It was successful in a financial sense but not in a satisfying sense. It was congenial doing a Martin Short comedy but American comedy is different from Australian comedy. It is broader. American audiences enjoyed *Pure Luck*, but audiences in other countries did not enjoy it so much with the exception of the Germans. I wanted to do something else with the comedy

Nadia Tass
Nadia Tass

and so did Danny Glover. I would like to have put a lot more pathos and pain into it. But they wanted a comedy for America.

One of the producers of Mr Reliable *says you are the best director of comedy in Australia. Would you prefer to be considered a director of broader range of films?*

Well, to get the comedy right, you've got to have all the other elements right, and if you haven't got the other elements right, it's not going to work, especially in the type of humour that I have in my films. It's not your regular sort of farce or slapstick. I use – I borrow from – those genres at given moments where I stretch and push the concepts to the edge, but I love comedy. I don't mind being called a comedy director. People probably have all these connotations that it's easy to be a comedy director – you make people laugh. That's the hardest thing you can do.

You hit on the quirkiness in Australian experience. It lights up the screen and audiences smile.

People and situations really amuse me. I'm not a funny person. I don't make people laugh by myself – in fact, everybody knows how serious I am – but it's my observation of the human condition and situations that I really love to recreate because I see them as so funny, and then I want to share that perception with the rest of the world.

You show how funny ordinary people are, but not in any put-down kind of way.

No, I love people. I love people so much. I think there's so much goodness in people around the world. It's not just one place. I travel so much and I love relating to everybody.

You invested a great deal of yourself in Malcolm?

Everything. It's my celebration of my relationship with the most special human being in my life: my brother. You see, he could be perceived as such a useless person, shunned, on the outskirts of society, but what I'm pleading for people to do is reassess, look at this human being and see this human being's talent and what he can contribute. Let's embrace these people.

There's a simple goodness in him, which Colin Friels portrays again in a different way in Mr Reliable. *It's a simplicity, an earnestness. These characters might be on the fringes but there is still a kind of … naivety is the wrong word, but there's a kind of nice simplicity which is endearing and which you communicate.*

Yes. I look at the world we live in today and we are so sophisticated, or we think we have made it sophisticated. Yet if we just peel off those layers of sophistication, what we'll find underneath is that simplicity that we all come out with.

From Malcolm *through* Rikki and Pete *and* The Big Steal *to* Mr Reliable, *you're often on the wrong side of the law, so to speak.*

Yes, I know. I'm just a constant questioner of authority. It's not so much that I want to be a rebel. No, I don't. But when rules are set, I want to find out why those rules are there. And I think my brother used to do that, too. We both did it together. 'Why? What was wrong before?' Sometimes, as in bureaucracy and in the establishment, we create rules for the sake of simplicity ... for the sake of what? More harmonious bureaucratic functioning? Right. But not for people. It's at the expense of the individual. It's at the expense of human nature, and that's where my bane is. And I think, let's not do this. Let's find another way.

The only newspaper in the world that found *Malcolm* immoral was that *New York Post* review which said, 'This is an immoral film'. Now, I understand where that man is coming from, and that's fair enough. He was 70 years of age – but it's not the age, it's just that the man was totally and utterly set in obeying the rules that were set for him in the American states.

He didn't see the funny side of the film?

And couldn't actually see the humanity of it. This is what's sad. I don't mind, but it gave me an insight into how sad some people are. He couldn't see that Malcolm, before he was introduced to this criminal and his girlfriend, was so lonely, so isolated, so unable to communicate. And through his liaison with these two other human beings who were criminals – or one was a criminal and then the other one joined – this man started to blossom internally. What I'm saying is: it's because he was rejected that he wasn't able to blossom.

Now, in this situation, we have a criminal befriending him. In the situation where we, as a society, embrace this man, he's going to blossom again.

Have people made comparisons between Malcolm *and* Forrest Gump *(dir. Robert Zemeckis)?*

Yes, they have. *Forrest Gump* is a story told in the American way. In sentiment I think it's very similar.

Then you moved to Rikki and Pete. *They're not quite outside the law but there's a kind of larrikinism there. There's a distinction between larrikin and hooligan. Hooligans are vicious but larrikins are lovable. Is* Rikki and Pete *a comedy of Australian larrikins?*

Yes, and they were again questioning; questioning authority. But what they were questioning initially was their father. It was through their father that the system was represented very strongly. Rikki says to the father about Pete, 'You made him what he is. You're the one that's to blame', because the father was so immovable, not prepared to see Pete as a person who had individual needs; as a person who needed love. That's what the father never gave.

Pete became a radical and destructive. He was a passive-aggressive. He was demonstrating his anger in the most obtuse way because of this inability for him to be angry over so many years toward his father, for not getting what he needed from the father figure.

A significant Australian theme?

It is. But, you know, I believe that if *Rikki and Pete* had come out first, before *Malcolm*, it would have been recognised a lot more in Australia than it was. *Rikki and Pete* was the one that was recognised most in America. The reviews there were glowing – I was so embarrassed – and I think it's because it deals with the middle-class platform.

The dysfunctional family?

Yes, which is very, very common in America, and they were able to identify with that so much more than Australians.

What about the nice larrikins in The Big Steal?

Oh, love 'em. I love them.

The two families are quite different. Is it still the middle-class platform?

It's still that pursuit of middle-class values. Claudia Karvan's father actually gets there. He establishes himself as a middle-class person and imposes all these middle-class values on his family. We can juxtapose the purity of Ben Mendelsohn's parents. It's my constant pursuit of finding the purity of the real human being.

The purity of the real human being?

Because when we deal with other cultures and with other social platforms, we're dealing with a lot more sophistication. We have to unravel so many more layers in order to get to the essence of the human being.

Mr Reliable.

Terry Hayes was absolutely brilliant. He gave me a script to read which was written by somebody else and I said, 'Okay, I love the story, I love the concept, the characters. I can see making a movie based on this concept, but it needs to be rewritten', and he said, 'Okay. How do you want it rewritten?' and I said, 'Like this and I want you to rewrite it'. And he said, 'Fine, I'll do it.' He rewrote it and then, basically, he just left it with me. He was one of the producers. I was three weeks into my shooting in Queensland when he arrived and he said, 'This is so different to what I saw, but it's fantastic'.

The original writer is still credited as one of the writers but he was not a writer while I was working on the film. It's because I felt that I could get what I needed from Terry, and if I was going to make the film, I needed to know that the script was going to be what I wanted. Otherwise I wouldn't know how to direct it. Not that he had to give me the stamp of approval, but he was my producer and I guess he really had to give me some sort of confidence in my work.

There was a story about the promotion of Mr Reliable?

One of the other producers on board was playing with the money via Polygram. Now, that producer was loosely attached to *Priscilla, Queen of the Desert* (dir. Stephan Elliott). Michael Hamlin came on board as well because he is also Polygram and he was the one who responded to the script and said, 'Okay, we'll go into this'. So he is one of the producers, as he was with *Priscilla*. I saw the trailer for *Mr Reliable* and it said, 'From the producer of *Priscilla*'. Now, if an audience hears that on the trailer and they go to see *Mr Reliable*, they're going to be so damned disappointed, because it's not a *Priscilla*. It's a film that's made by me. I'm talking about people's emotions, I'm talking about people's pain and pathos and then allowing the audience to laugh – pushing them to laugh at certain moments – and then pulling them back into the drama and into the pain of life, whereas *Priscilla* doesn't do that. *Priscilla* is a different genre.

So my point is that we, by saying to the audience – by luring the audience into the cinema with the idea that *Priscilla* worked, made X number of dollars – and that the producer of *Priscilla* produced this, we're deceiving the audience. We're giving the audience different expectations of what they are going to see in *Mr Reliable*. It's the morality aspect for me. It's really that I don't want to lose my audience. I want the audience to know exactly what they're coming into to see with my work.

In Mr Reliable *we get the sense that writer and director have been upset by the events, the effect on the victims and the stupidity of the bureaucracy. Yet so much of the film is funny, celebrating the genial side of life. But there is some edge with Barry Otto's portrayal of the Premier, the villain of the piece, machinating.*

Barry plays the Premier, who is Askin. I did a fair bit of research to find out about this character. I couldn't find too much that I liked there. Hence the sort of character that you saw in Barry Otto. I was thrilled with what we arrived at with Barry – and I needed that sort of stand from this political figure for the rest of the characters to play against him.

A question about religion. There is almost no religion in your films except for Mr Reliable. *At one stage, Colin Friels as Wally Mellish asks Beryl whether she had got religion and is relieved when she says, 'Oh, no, no, I haven't', and yet the clergyman chaplain played a significant role at the wedding, as a witness and at the end. Is religion significant?*

Me? I'm a Greek Orthodox, Russian Orthodox from my father, and my children are Greek Orthodox. They've both been christened and some years ago we went to church in my village. Every time my children go into the church they say, 'We're going to get that wine again, Mummy', and then I explain, 'Well, this is what that wine means', and they go, 'Oh, but we hate the taste'! So my position with religion? I want my kids to have religion as something they can use when they need it, something to fall back on when they need it.

Perhaps the film shows the ocker attitude: 'Religion we don't need, yet the minister we do'?

Yes. What is in the film is really a reflection on the society that I'm working with and the opinion of the characters in that situation.

One of the major themes of Amy *is grief. You say that grief is all-powerful.*

It's insidious and immovable to some people, and they're the very people who are less likely to seek help.

Rachel Griffith's performance in Amy *exuded tension, even during the scenes when she was happily married.*

Yes, because, as a rock-and-roller's wife, she was always going to have those moments where she questioned how long she was going to last. That's part of the deal, really. The fact that her husband was just such a loving person for her and for Amy is almost irrelevant from the individual insecurities that a rock-and-roller's wife would have. She tells us that 'There's only one of me', when that very thing is questioned by the Kym Gyngell character. The reason I felt a need to put that in there was because that is a question that's always in the fore of wives' minds when they know that their husband is so incredibly popular, that there are screaming girls around him all the time. It's inevitable. It's a bit like Mel Gibson wherever he goes, and it takes a really special type of wife to be able to deal with that situation.

So the suddenness of his death made the grief all the more profound?

It makes it incredibly profound because those times that could have been completely and utterly full, she was spending being worried whether she was going to stay there forever.

We are reminded of Malcolm *with the suburban street. You certainly create inner Melbourne suburban streets peopled by interesting characters.*

It's mainly because I grew up in that type of environment and I find myself incredibly comfortable in bringing back all those characters that were so familiar to me as a child. The wonderful thing about a working-class environment is that as soon as they embrace you as a community or as being a part of the community, it really becomes a support system for when you need them.

Initially they're hostile because that's how it works. To have, as one of the boys says, aliens come into your street: it's not something they're going to be happy about. You can imagine the criticism so often with someone like the welfare officer in the suit coming through. They look down their noses because it's as if they have to be at the beck and call of everybody in a suit. Well, the question is 'Why should they?'

You didn't gloss over the domestic abuse.

It's pretty obvious in our society. That was the reason, plus the couple of swear words that are very, very background, that gave us the M 15+ rating, which doesn't quite make sense to me. Are we supposed to not show the public or not show children the very thing that they know about? So many children have seen the film now, and they come out and feel relieved. One comment I had was, 'I didn't know that it happens to other people'.

The little boy who befriends Amy dramatises that.

And that was a tangent that I really wanted to bring into the film because, if we're going to be working on a canvas like the street, we can't avoid it. Not to include it is ludicrous and it's dishonest.

It's a blend of the sadly serious side with the humorously eccentric: the fellows fixing the car and the strange character of Ben Mendelsohn's sister.

She clearly had a very big problem. And that's exactly what it was meant to be, that blend of different genres, because life is a blend. Life doesn't go on just in the drama or just in the tragedy or just in the comedy. It's fascinating to see how much of all these different aspects actually creep into any one of our days, and to what degree.

Most of the time what we do is homogenise our stories because we are at the beck and call of Hollywood. A Hollywood which says, 'If we create a very simple through-line that's linear, then we will be able to appeal to the majority of people out there who will come and see the film'. Which means more money. So it becomes the product. I'm not interested in 'the product'. I'm interested in actually saying something about the world I live in.

Helping people to share the experience?

In *Amy*, because the mother couldn't deal with her problem, Amy was not able to deal with hers. She developed elective mutism. If she was able to talk to her mother about her incredible pain inside and the fear that she had – not just fear, but the conviction – that she herself was responsible for her father's death, it would never have escalated to such heights or pain.

It was effective that the solution wasn't revealed until towards the end, so that while we had a hunch that something like that had happened, we weren't actually sure until we saw it.

I think it was necessary to take the audience through the searching before giving them the solution.

The search for Amy and the surrealism of the singing: how have people responded to that?

Usually audiences erupt in applause and exhilaration, it being the favourite scene of the majority of the people who have seen the film. Filmically, the reason I put it in that position was to open up the audience even more, to give them relief from the pain that had accumulated inside them, the sadness to that point, just before I come in with Amy's revelation – which means, hopefully, it's going to hurt a lot more.

Screenings I've been at, both in Australia and in New York, have been absolutely amazing. It actually unifies different ends of the world, because it's something we all experience. Whether we like it or not, grief is a part of living.

You've moved, with Malcolm, who was more than a bit on the edge of society, and with Amy, who unwittingly puts herself through experience on the edge of society, from the celebration of the comic to the celebration of the comic with grief.

When you put it that way, that's absolutely intentional; however, it is bizarre. I understand how quite ridiculous I must seem in some situations because people don't normally talk about things like this.

Ben Mendelsohn made it all credible with the way that he sang and listened to Amy. We could believe him and respond to Amy through him.

That's his position in that story. He's a voyeur; he's a facilitator for what the other characters need to develop or unfold the story, and one step back is the audience as the voyeur. I've never seen Ben better.

He's a very, very deep, sympathetic human being, but the characters that he usually is given to play or he accepts don't have these layers in them. He can play the larrikin, whereas in fact Ben is incredibly intelligent, sympathetic and he's got an amazing ability to be empathetic with the outcasts of society.

Your collaboration with David Parker over the years has seemed to strengthen.

We still basically work in the same way we started off: he created the idea of actually telling a story about this condition of Amy, and I responded to it very strongly. So he went off and wrote the script, came back. I looked at it, then we talked a lot about what he had written, and then he went off and started writing again because we need to keep refining the script. This went on for eleven years. During that period we were trying to find finance.

People do not want to know about grief, and financiers want to know even less about grief. Financiers are also told by Hollywood that a mixing of genres stylistically on the screen is more than likely not going to give them their money back. So this is why it took such a long time to actually make this film. But in that time David and I had the opportunity to keep refining and reflecting on the type of society or the canvas we wanted to create. We used it in a positive way and I think the fact that we did take such a long time to find the money has helped us in the maturity of the project.

We did go back to David's original draft – over the years people would say, 'Well, what if you simplified it, then we'll give you the money', and our reaction to that was, 'Well, how do you think we should simplify it?' One response, 'Well, maybe you should take out Tanya's huge breakthrough outside the cafe', which just doesn't make sense to me; the guy didn't get it. Another one was, 'Well, maybe you should take out the singing'. What are you left with? You've got no reason to tell a story. Then another person said, 'Well, take out all the comedy'. Okay. Then what we're dealing with is a drama tragedy. It doesn't make sense.

The people in the street and their support after their hostility gives a great quality to the appreciation of the grief.

And the power of the little girl's purity of spirit and how it can actually change people's lives in a street. By the time she is actually lost, she has created wonderful relationships, opened up these people's hearts through her singing, and they're all out there searching for her.

Even the crotchetty lady watering the footpath ...

Exactly. Doing the absolutely unthinkable, which is singing to find her. I mean, how ridiculous is that? In my way of thinking, it's totally ridiculous, yet these people are out there doing it, which is what I'd be doing if a little girl down the street was lost. So it's the very condition that touched people and opened them up as human beings which created the musical aspect of the movie.

You make films in the United States.

Just to do a film and then come back home again.

Better experiences than for Pure Luck?

I hope so. I take every necessary precaution to make sure. Another thing I realised is it's absolutely not necessary to be aggressive at all about these things; it's just a case of negotiating, which probably is a lesson that comes with maturity anyway. I think I was just hot-headed and young back then.

Australian Feature Films

1986 *Malcolm*

1988 *Rikki and Pete*

1990 *The Big Steal*

1996 *Mr Reliable*

1998 *Amy*

Michael Thornhill, *The FJ Holden*, 1977.
(Documentation Collection, ScreenSound Australia.)

In the 1960s and 1970s, when you were working on film reviews and lecturing, did you imagine that there was going to be an Australian industry?

I was basically a propagandist. First of all, I didn't have a formal education, although I'm spasmodically well read, and I actually started as a technician, not as a critic. I started as an apprentice film editor, for want of a better description, so that in my twenties – you have to remember contextually that this is before there were any film schools or anything like that; there were a few tech college courses – I started writing articles. So I had a concurrent career, as it were, as a film editor and a film reviewer.

I didn't get the film-reviewing job straight away; I did it part-time, filled in, and then I was offered a job as the reviewer on the *Herald* and got fired eight months later. Then I was immediately hired by the *Australian*. I saw my position as pro-active on two fronts: one was fighting censorship and two was trying to do anything to help get an Australian film industry established.

I think the people who did the real groundwork were Sylvia Lawson and Cecil Holmes, and that Phillip Adams and Barry Jones have taken all the credit. I think the intellectual framework had been laid. Basically, I tried a new tack: I was very influenced by, in left-right terms, the kind of left liberal attitudes which were not just Marxist, but left liberal anti-Americanism. I always thought that was crazy in this country because I actually thought that various American administrations and various Acts of Congress had been far more radical than anything that was proposed by a kind of cranky left liberal Marxist push, any nationalistic thing. What I started to do was to look at the Sherman Anti-Trust Acts of the 1890s passed by the U.S. Congress. My form of attack as propaganda, basically, was an attack on the vertically integrated nature of the industry which, incidentally, was outlawed in the U.S.

So that was where I came from. I also believed what Truffaut said in an interview, 'If you want to be an artist in the afternoon, you have to be a businessman in the morning'. (That's in pre-feminist terminology.) What I was doing in my kind of reviewing, in commenting on the industry, was not pushing the 'This is our birthright' line, but pushing an economic rationalist line, which was that the marketplace is not free.

Now, I think that position is far more sophisticated than pushing a purely nationalist point of view, so that's really what I consider my contribution, humble and modest as it was. I think that kind of thing freaked them all out a lot more than the left liberal tub-thumping.

When you started to make films yourself, how were you able to work within the context that was developing in the 1970s?

Well, it's all gone backwards now, of course. But I believed in the Lyndon B Johnson theory of being inside the tent pissing out, rather than outside the tent pissing in. So, I thought that a combination of public and private support was essential and that you were not going to get finance just through public support. I thought that the thing to do was to get the distributors involved, if not investing and putting up guarantees, at least putting up money against distribution rights.

The other thing that I did was to distribute a film myself, so I learnt about the deal side of it and the advertising side, all of that. I think I'm fundamentally an art-house film-maker trying to survive in a commercial world, and that means convincing people that you've got something that is commercial when, in fact, you don't have a Megaplex or Multiplex film, you've actually got a smaller film. Basically, I never saw myself as making mainstream populist films. I've got nothing against mainstream populist films, because they keep the thing turning over.

You collaborated with Frank Moorhouse over many years.

We've got to put this in context. He collaborated with a lot of people. We did one short film together and we did two feature films, of stuff that got made. I executive produced but didn't direct a TV tele-feature that he wrote, *The Disappearance of Azaria Chamberlain* (dir. Judy Rymer). He's an ideas person, I think. He doesn't earn and has never really earned a living writing screenplays, although he's collaborated with other people on various projects. I really saw him as a far better, more succinct ideas person than I was, and that was the basis of the relationship.

Everybody evolves in different directions. I evolved. My work, small as it is, is now evolving towards a more modernist, collaborative approach. I think the most interesting Australian films are the modernist films – and there are very few of them.

Mad Max (dir. George Miller) was really interesting because it was apocalyptic, raw, morally primitive, a combination of moral primitiveness in an aesthetic sense and a kind of Greek revenge tragedy, and that's a one-off special event.

The other interesting Australian films for me are *Bliss* (dir. Ray Lawrence), *Love and Other Catastrophes* (dir. Emma-Kate Croghan), *Kiss or Kill* (dir. Bill Bennett). They're what I call modernist things, the antithesis of Prologue, Act One, Act Two, Act Three, Epilogue television-inspired drama, which a lot of Australian films still are. So, my collaboration with Frank was right for the time, where what I was attempting to do was to solve mise-en-scène problems with ideas.

Now I'm trying to do something quite different, which is to create something from the ground up, with ideas and with actors. My latest project has, probably, a 65-page rather than a 110-page script and, while some scenes are totally written out, others are not and, therefore, I keep changing it. When I know what actor may be playing what role, I rewrite it completely to fit that actor. And even then there will be a two-week reading rehearsal period where we will keep push-pulling characters. That's basically where I am at the moment.

How do you see Between Wars *now, almost a quarter of a century later?*

I think that it's got – to use the sort of neo-classical dramatic terminology which I don't like using now, but will for the purposes of communication – I think it's got a very weak Act Three. The last third is too compressed; it's not elongated, the characters are not elaborated enough. I think it's got a very powerful Act Two and an okay Act One. I think Act Two has captured something beyond the ideas. It captured certain emotional vicissitudes of the country in the way that Act One and Act Three didn't. Act Two is successful because it's measured and it's lyrically lackadaisical – whereas Act Three is almost all about imparting information. Act One has interesting moments, but Act Two, between the wars, is the most successful because it goes beyond a narrative expression of ideas. It goes into the feelings, both personal and wider community feelings, and that's why I think Act Two is quite successful. Also it's far more successful in getting the feelings of innate conservatism rather than directly expressing it.

Presenting those ideas in the 1970, of the liberal and the conservative, the exploration of psychology in the context of World War One and then what happened in the 1930s, was unusual.

I think Frank was more interested in looking at the evolution of a psychiatric practice than I was. I was more interested in a kind of social psychosis, so there were two different things going on. He had a lot more knowledge than I did of Havelock Ellis and stuff like that. Also he had researched case studies that I was unaware of, and he had a much more profound and better knowledge than I did. I was more interested in how you translate or, a better word, how you 'realise' ideas. I was much more interested in the peripheral aspects of it all. His major contribution was that he came up with ideas that I could never have come up with; but having said that, I think Act Three doesn't work. I think it's too compressed and it needed to be double the length and we needed to slow down. Instead of taking big ideas, we should have taken one idea and expanded that rather than having three or four ideas and compressing them.

You take one idea and you toy with it and play with it and tease it rather than having a series of thematic things that you've got to get into a series, which makes for compression. I think the most successful thing in the film is Arthur Dignam's performance as the other doctor because what it did was show the urbane side of a colonial society. With a less urbane actor, that wouldn't have been possible.

With the nostalgia films of the time, it's interesting that you were going back to a more recent past but really wanting to show – your phrase – social psychosis. With The FJ Holden *and* The Journalist *you became contemporary.*

Well, *FJ Holden* was probably the one people liked the most. I think the academics have got it all wrong. There have been reams of stuff written about it being social realism. I don't see that it's social realism at all. My idea of social realism would have been to document unemployment – which there was quite a bit of at that stage – do all that sort of stuff, kids sticking up camera shops, the whole ethnic mix. Whereas I actually saw it, and still do, as a dreamlike, poetic kind of thing. I had more French poetry than British social realism. I never saw it as being factually accurate. It was always fascinating to me how you can just get it totally wrong in terms of perceptions. Everyone saw it as social realism. And I still think they're wrong.

People look at it now, they review it now and they see it totally differently. They see it now more like I saw it. But then it was seen only as searing social realism. And it caused a lot of censorship carry-on.

You see, I think some of the content got in the way, so that people were looking at the narrational content rather than actually feeling what was in front of them. The thing still works because it's not rushed. There's some quite fast montage, but the linear thing is not rushed. It also captured a series of what I call monosyllabic feelings rather than articulate feelings. I'm talking about the visual style as well; not just the characters but the actual milieu of the whole film.

The Journalist was a misfire completely and I think it was my fault entirely. We should never have had Jack Thompson. He was just miscast. He's not a comedian. He's a serious, solid actor. We should have had Sam Neill in the lead role and you would have had a debonair roué; it was meant to be a debonair roué. It was meant to be a piece of fluff – a piece of effervescent fluff that came out feeling like lard.

Again people do a content analysis, like they did with *FJ Holden*. If you could imagine, say, Sam Neill in the Jack Thompson role and Arthur Dignam as he was then in the Sam Neill role, I think you would have an entirely different perspective on the film. I don't think it ever had anything particularly profound to say, but I think – and I'm not saying this by way of defence, because I'm saying myself it doesn't work – it would have been more effervescent.

I also thought that the women were all better than the guys, and I think female actors are less prone to nationalistic, stereotypical behaviour.

The Everlasting Secret Family screened on television recently.

You didn't watch it in a strip, did you? You watched it full screen? You should look at it in letterbox format. It's shot on Super 35. *Titanic* (dir. James Cameron) was shot on Super 35, which is a format that blows up into an anamorphic squeezed image. When you see *The Everlasting Secret Family* in a strip version – and I've had people actually look at the full screen and then the strip version – in the strip version it's far more analytical and far less character-driven. It's unbelievable, the difference. In the strip version it's far more distant. On cable television now, especially Channel 32, they play the films and alternate between the strip version, letterbox version, and the full-screen version.

Now, with an ugly directed film like *How to Marry a Millionaire* (dir. Jean Negulesco), it doesn't make much difference. But when you see *The Longest Day* (dir. Ken Annakin, Andrew Marton, Gerd Oswald, Bernhard Wicki, Darryl F Zanuck) in a strip version – okay, it's all been superseded now by *Saving Private Ryan* (dir. Steven Spielberg) – you actually get to see, despite all the guest stars and all the rest of it, you get to see how unimportant each individual person is, and it's a series of tableaux. Full up, it seems like a character-driven thing.

Now, that's the same with *The Everlasting Secret Family*. In full-screen with 20 per cent of the image missing off either side – in other words, 40 per cent of the image missing – you've got a different film. I'm not comparing this to the 'Mona Lisa' or something, but you could go in and chop the 'Mona Lisa' down the middle and take 20 per cent off the sides and you get a face like ... ! So I think you need to see this film on the big screen.

In retrospect, especially now, with lurid headlines, royal commissions and judges in court, was it ahead of its time?

But you see, the trouble – in my opinion what I screwed up really badly – was that the finance fell away and came together and I lost some technical people that I originally wanted. Now, if I had my way, the film would be far more stylised than it is. It's a bit stylised, but it looks like a regular film, and I wanted it more stylised. So I think it has nothing to do with any reality.

I get people leaving messages – 'How did you know all that?' But it's bullshit because that's not what it's meant to be about. It's more like a medieval thing. It's a gothic horror.

And the gay community is split down the middle. I was on the phone doing radio interviews all across America, some from here, some from London. And I reckon it was about one-third got it and two-thirds said it was homophobic. One-third said they knew exactly what was going down and they didn't think it was homophobic. They thought it was a sort of medieval fantasy or what-have-you.

It was always meant to be funny. I don't know about Frank. I can't speak for him but I'll speak for myself: it was always meant to be funny, humorous. It was always meant to have a dark, humorous side. But on television that comes out a lot more than it does in the more abstract letterbox format. By the way, it ran 16 weeks in London in one cinema. It just died the death of a dog here and David Stratton said it was the worst film ever made. I actually went to *Variety* and demanded another reviewer do it for them. So, although the film didn't get a good review, it got a reasonable review in *Variety* compared with what David Stratton would say.

But to answer your question, I think that the mistake was, it wasn't stylised even more. Even though that wouldn't have worked in Australia, it would have worked internationally. There's no social documentary aspect, I wasn't making a documentary about Oxford Street. But people keep saying, 'How did you know that?' And I say I didn't. 'Oh, no, you knew about all this.' I say, 'Look, it's not about that', but no one believes me. I mean, I say, one, I wasn't poofter-bashing and two, I wasn't attempting to do a documentary.

I say to people, 'Let's take out the gay thing and let's put in a heterosexual Masonic issue, okay?' I say, 'It's the priesthood, it's the Masons, it's the police, it's any kind of society'. What do you think was going all through medieval Italy? There was more 'protestantism' in medieval Italy than anywhere. It's about secret societies. And people still say, 'Oh, no, it's about this gay judge', or something. There's nothing I can do about that.

That's interesting in view of what you were saying about your other films: your emphasis on feeling and on the visual, drawing the audience into that experience rather than just simply focusing on or eliciting an analysis of the content. Is this true of your television, Harvest of Hate *and* The Robbery?

Harvest of Hate was a gun-for-hire job. I didn't complete the film. They re-edited and I just walked away.

Robbery has been extremely successful internationally. I mean, it was made for two and six: that was at a time when you could get much more interesting projects through the television system here than you can now. I'm pleased with *Robbery*. It's a film noir that people didn't understand here as a film noir. Its basic theme is the revenge of the underclass and what the French would call the 'petit bourgeoisie', and what we might here call the 'lower middle class', who are led by a disgruntled leader. It's a kind of revenge-film-noir thing, and because it's in four to three – 1.33 to one – it's made for television and that means the framing's exactly right. So I think it stands up rather well, actually.

It doesn't get shown much here. It does overseas. It's continually playing on cable systems in France and England. The French dubbing is fantastic. In

M y t h & M e a n i n g

French voices it's all that spivvy, mock ironic spivvy lower-middle-class petit bourgeoisie stuff, while the officers have Ecole-Nationale-type voices. It even went out on video in the States.

I like it; I'm not ashamed of it: I think it's a nice little thing. But, because here it's seen as a B-genre thing, you've just got to put up with that, roll with the punch, not bitch about it.

The Disappearance of Azaria Chamberlain?

I executive-produced it. I executive-produced a number of TV things. I don't have strong opinions about it. There are quite a few cheats in it, but at least what it did do – I'm not emotionally close to it – was put the audience in the view of 'I, the Jury'. It has an enormous following in northern Europe. I think Judy did a terrific directing job. I think it was interesting but, again, it's not a personal project.

The work you're doing now?

I've been working on consultancies and scripts and things but what I've decided to do is to try to make a film for about a million dollars on the latest digital technology. The camera we're going to use has only been in the country two months. There's a test sitting there – a hundred feet – which we've transferred to 35 mm and non-technical people can't tell the difference.

I guess where I'm going is to combine aspects of genre with post-modernism. That's what I'm interested in. I'm not interested in telling a story. I'm interested in the audience. I'm wanting to strip melodrama out of the thing and I'm interested in the audience experiencing emotions. Whether, for instance, it's *Pulp Fiction* (dir. Quentin Tarantino), *The Sweet Hereafter* (dir. Atom Egoyan), *The Spanish Prisoner* (dir. David Mamet): these are all films where you don't identify with the characters, therefore you're not being sucked into the vortex and going on that kind of journey. It's a journey, rather, where you're responding to the emotional situation in front of you. But you're not being hooked onto prologue, Act One, Act Two, Act Three, epilogue-and-Bruce-Willis-saves-the-world sort of thing – though I've got nothing against that. I see all those movies.

I think *Saving Private Ryan* is a most interesting film. It's an Act-One-Act-Two-Act-Three film: it's really *The Dirty Dozen* (dir. Robert Aldrich) revisited, where we take the eight or ten people and go behind lines to save this person, Act Two is that journey and Act Three is a fantastic battle scene where everybody loses. So it's quite a conventional film except for Act One. If there's a major war, this film will be withdrawn like *All Quiet on the Western Front* (dir. Lewis Milestone), because its major thing is its first 25 minutes, no more than twenty lines of dialogue, tops – but that's what it's like to be in war.

Now, if it had continued in that vein ... I thought the only good thing about

Michael Thornhill

it is the first 25 minutes before it becomes a far more conventional film. It's getting harder and harder because the distributors want Megaplex films, which means that you can take a film that takes three million at the box office and still not earn a cent, because it's all gone in exhibition percentage plus cost of promoting the film.

With the Scott Frank-Steven Soderbergh film, *Out of Sight* (dir. Steven Soderbergh), the audience goes along and is confused because it's not a traditional narrative film. It only gives the appearance of being a traditional narrative film. And David Mamet: he just fights the system. He does a script for Hollywood – John Sayles is the same sort of person: they do a script for the mainstream and then they do their own thing. In *The Spanish Prisoner* it's not the scam, it's the journey along the way. Therefore, the journey along the way, in a non-Megaplex film, has not to be about identifying the characters and sucking you into the story. I would say that in *The Spanish Prisoner*, people sit there for half an hour wondering what's going on but slowly getting sucked in. So a hundred minutes later they are totally mesmerised. Being mesmerised – as distinct from being hooked for a hundred minutes – those kind of films have refrigerated questions. A refrigerated question is something where you have a cup of tea or a couple of beers and say, 'Hey, *that* didn't make sense and that didn't make sense'.

Too late!

Australian Feature Films

1974 *Between Wars*

1977 *The FJ Holden*

Stephen Wallace

Stephen Wallace with Greta Scacchi, *Turtle Beach*, 1990.
(Photo: Jim Sheldon, Laker-Merewether Film Company.)

YOUR EARLIEST FILM WAS Love Letters from Teralba Road?

I'd made a couple of short films before. *Love Letters from Teralba Road* came from a series of letters that I found in a flat in Birchgrove. It was a 19-dollar-a-week flat – basically two rooms, three rooms – and I found these letters in a drawer under newspaper. I had a quick look at them and noticed that they came from Teralba Road in Adamstown in Newcastle, where I come from.

I didn't actually read them. I put them away. They were about 10 years old at the time. Anyway, Dick Mason from Film Australia asked me about a year later if I wanted to write a story about the city – they were making dramas at Film Australia. It had to be half an hour long. I said I'd got these letters – four letters, I think – and a note, and the note said, 'Get your dinner, your dinner's in the oven'. Blah, blah, blah. 'Eat it yourself. Got home, found you weren't here, and left'. It was a note from him to her; a really rough note. Then all the letters were from the woman to the man.

So I read the letters – they were set in 1959 – and they were very painful. They were about the man trying to get his wife to come back to him. I thought this was a great idea for a story about the city. I didn't really think about all the implications. I wrote the story and used the letters and realised I didn't know the ending. So I thought I wouldn't have an ending; I'd leave them in limbo. I tried to, from the letters, make out who he was. But I knew these people, I'd come from Newcastle – I felt I knew them – and my mother came from that same sort of background. I never showed the letters to anybody; just got excerpts from them. I thought it was a good story about a man coming down on a flight to Sydney to see this woman who's obviously been bashed.

I also wanted to make a film about something that really came from me. When I was making it, I lived in Erskineville. I had this negative attitude about my life and I lived in this really tough area in Erskineville – deliberately lived there, so that when I made the film, I would feel like them. I thought the film shouldn't have anything fancy about it. When I cut from one sequence to another, no fancy cuts, no fancy camera movement or dissolves. I wanted to reflect the true feeling of working-class people, battling people. I wanted to get the absolute feeling of their situation.

David Stratton refers to it as a story of an ordinary Australian bloke.

Yes. We got Bryan Brown to play the role, but I actually wanted someone different. I was looking for someone different, for a short little guy – I think this would have been more like the real guy – a short little guy who had hair sticking up at the back: blonde hair. He was short, tremendously insecure, violent, and you couldn't talk to him – but very vulnerable. I couldn't find an actor like that, and still can't. I didn't want a big handsome-looking guy. Bryan was the nearest we could get, and I'm glad we did.

Captives of Care *was a documentary drama?*

It was always going to be a drama. Rosemary Cresswell showed me the book. I trusted Rosemary and had a good relationship with her. 'What do you think about making this book into a film?' They took me to meet the author and, when I met him and talked to him, I said, 'Yes, we'll do it, but we'll do it with the handicapped people and we'll build actors around them'. They had a scriptwriter who really couldn't write it, and we struggled and battled with the script, trying to get it right. In the end it was a bit of a mess and the producer took over writing it. But they raised the money through 10B(A) and through the bank. It cost $110,000, and we decided we would improvise with the actors.

I wanted to do it because I liked what they were trying to say: very articulate people. In the end the handicapped people were much more interesting than the non-handicapped people to talk to. It was a good subject, but it was a nightmare to make, a very difficult film.

The handicapped people weren't the problem. It was really more the production. I realised I was dealing with very inexperienced people, and I was a bit inexperienced myself, and I was unused to not having support. And the producer was very inexperienced. Although it was 10B(A), we couldn't get any cameramen, we couldn't get a sound person, so we had to use a documentary guy from Byron Bay, the only person we could find. The sound person was very inexperienced – I was actually teaching them things on the job – and I got very angry with the DoP because he wasn't doing it properly: he was treating it like a documentary. And we had to experiment with improvising – how do you link the sound up when you never know when people are going to talk?

So that was why it was difficult. The amazing thing is we shot for three weeks, and the entire last week we didn't use. We completely wasted a week's work. We put the first cut together and it looked appalling. Then the editor and I – we had a very good editor – we said, 'We're going to throw out the script and we're just going to cut it'. Because we shot a lot of documentary material and because there was a lot of good stuff in it, we said, 'We're going to throw out the script, we're just going to hack it around in our own way'. We put it all together and, somehow, it started to work. It was just magic that it worked.

Everyone thought Julieanne Newbold was the wrong person for it, but I always loved Julieanne and I thought she was right because she's a very warm-hearted girl. I know she's a little bit soap opera, but I think it was right for her. Anyway, it worked in the end, but it was a messy film to make, very messy.

You focussed on people on the margins. That brings us to Stir.

The Prisoners' Action Group approached me: would I make a film about Bathurst? I said 'No, I can't do anything'. We didn't even have a script. Then we went to see Bob Jewson, the writer. He was an ex-prisoner and he gave me a whole pile of stuff to read, completely formless, just a lot of dialogue he had written in prison. And when I read that, I said, 'This guy can write, and he's seen it all'.

I think it's my problem in life, in a way, that I've always been very sympathetic to people and wanting to tell their stories. I've always felt a bit on the fringes myself – I don't know why – and so I identify with them very strongly. But, at the same time, I didn't want them to be unfair to the warders. It was a great struggle with the Prisoners' Action Group because they thought all the warders were brutal. And I said, 'That just isn't true'. It's like in the French Revolution: all the nobles weren't awful people, yet everyone wants to believe that, and all the revolutionaries weren't good people. So you've got to take a balance.

When I went to Italy, a girl came up to me and said – and it's the most insightful thing anyone ever said about it to me – 'It's a good film, but if you only realised, you could have made it into an exceptional film: it's Dante's *Inferno*. If you had made Dante's *Inferno*, you would have got a film that got beyond that'. It's very hard when you've got the Prisoners' Action Group and bashed prisoners around you looking at the script and saying, 'Aren't you going to represent us properly?' They wanted a polemical film. So that was hard. I thought you could have both. Now I could probably do it. I couldn't do it then.

The riot scenes and the oppression had the Inferno *atmosphere about them. But there's Bryan Brown again, early in his career, embodying the ordinary Australian victim of injustice and prisons.*

Bryan Brown has always embodied, to me, something very special. He hates me when I say this, because he doesn't want to know, but there's no other actor that I've met who embodies what I feel in the way he acts. Whether I have or not, I always feel I've got tremendous integrity, and Bryan Brown has it in his face. At the same time I feel very ordinary. I had very ordinary parents. I come from an ordinary background, although I was sent to Scots. But I feel ordinary underneath, yet with lots of energy, and I think Bryan has got that. I've also got a lot of suppressed energy and I think Bryan has got that. And underneath it I feel very sensitive. I won't argue the point, but I feel sensitive and I think Bryan underneath is very sensitive too. And yet at the same time he's a larrikin; he's what I'd like to be: a larrikin. I feel I'm a larrikin underneath but I can never express it, but Bryan expresses it. That's why I like him. And that's why I liked him in *Stir*.

Max Phipps was excellent as the embodiment of smouldering authoritarianism.

Yes, the neurotic authoritarianism. I've always liked Max Phipps. I was in ensembles with him years ago. I always thought he was an exceptional actor under-used, and I fought very hard for him in that film. I never had the same rapport with him that I did with Bryan.

Critically Stir *was acclaimed; what of government response?*

The Liberal Party was in power when the riots happened; when we made the film the Labor Party was in and Neville Wran came to the opening. The man in charge of the Police Department at that time – he became the Commissioner – told me, 'Keep making films like that'. He was one of the honest commissioners, Avery. I know the New South Wales Prison Department use it now as a training film.

Bob Jewson said one thing – and I think this is what we tried to make the theme of the film, although it was very hidden – that riots don't happen out of the blue. The prison authorities make you believe that all these criminals that are incarcerated are at all times dangerous and they're trying to get out. But Bob said that's never true: most of them have accepted their lot and they're trying to serve their time. They only get into a riot situation when they're treated badly and unfairly over a long period. He said most people don't want a riot; they know what it's going to mean: longer in gaol.

The public's response?

They came to it. It cost $460,000 or $480,000. I know it's made a profit. It ran for six or eight weeks. That was the time when Australian films were taken off as quickly as possible. It had a run on television and it sold quite well overseas.

So your next film was more autobiographical?

The Boy Who Had Everything, yes, was pretty autobiographical. I was always very unhappy about it because originally I had a different story. He was older, 27, at university, struggling, couldn't pass. He had been a star at school and he had a girlfriend, his same girlfriend. He was going to prostitutes, and trying to resolve things about his life. Dick Mason and Sandra Levy wanted him to be younger and Dick said, 'We can get the money for it if you make him younger. Everyone's interested in a young boy; they're not interested in a 27-year-old.' I thought, 'Give me a break'.

So I said 'Okay'. And they said, 'Can you set it in a college?' I had been to St Andrew's College; I didn't really want to make a film about St Andrew's College, but I knew about the system. So I did. It was meant to be about, well, the people I'd seen at the school. It wasn't exactly myself, but it was people like my brother, people I'd seen at Scots – and partly myself – who had been stars, had all the material goals, had achieved these, but everything else had been left undone. The boys themselves didn't know what was happening to them later on in their lives. They didn't know why things weren't satisfying for them.

I knew this happened. It happened to me at St Andrew's. I'd been a top rower, footballer, but when I wanted to give it all up and do drama, everyone got very upset. Even though the film itself is not the greatest film in the world, it sold very well, particularly in Europe. I think most people get the message. Everyone in Australia hated it because it didn't reflect a lot of things accurately. But that theme was something I wanted to make. I want to make films about things I think are important.

You can't just expect someone who's a prefect at school and is good at sport – all those things are easy at school – to succeed. When you leave, life is much more complex. I've seen them fall apart time and time again. Originally I had the father in the film, as well as the mother, was supposed to be very working-class, but all of it just went by the wayside because there was a lot of commercial pressure.

It was very glamorous with Diane Cilento.

She tried to play working-class, but it just didn't work. Robyn Nevin wanted to play that part, and I think she should have. Jason Connery was very young then, very nervous about the film and thought it would ruin his image, and he was never very friendly to me. He did the film, but he thought I was ruining his career.

It contributed, along with John Duigan's The Year My Voice Broke *and* Flirting, *to a rethink during the 1980s and 1990s of the Australian male image.*

Yes, I had hoped it would because I had struck so much of it. I found that I couldn't talk to men my own age much – still can't, really. I can a bit more now but, in those days, you could never talk about anything. It was what football team you were in and how you did. Everyone went to university and did Law and did brilliantly and nobody grappled with anything. It's wrong because a lot of men want to talk about these things and why should this be left to the women, which is what happened.

I often wish that I could do *The Boy Who Had Everything* again and make it the older man, because the issues could come out ... but maybe they were right: it wouldn't be so entertaining and you wouldn't get the college life.

Christina Stead and For Love Alone?

The French liked *For Love Alone*. Again, it wasn't very popular in Australia. It ran here for six weeks, got some scathing reviews. Mainly they're criticising the script, but I collected all these reviews from women's magazines. Women's magazines and the feminists hated it. They thought I had murdered Christina Stead, that I'd simplified it beyond belief. Patrick White liked it, though; he went to see it and said, 'It's better than the book'!

I don't think the feminists really liked Christina Stead's attitude to men because she was praising of men and praising of love. I met her and talked to her quite a lot. She did not believe in feminist separatism at all. She believed that men and women should be together and that love between a man and woman was the very best thing that could ever happen to anybody, that love did exist and it lasted a lifetime. And I believe in that. I didn't then. I asked her, 'Do you really believe that?' And she said, 'Yes, it happened to me'. I think most women would acknowledge that now. They had to go through that storm-trooper period.

I couldn't understand it; I was shocked. They attacked it so viciously. So I guess it wasn't a totally competent film. I know it was a bit slow and clumsy and I have to accept that.

Did you enjoy going back into that period of Australian society?

Yes, but I think it was a bit arch. I enjoyed it but I don't think I ever really got a handle on it. I don't think it was that different from now; people weren't that different. I think I tried to make them a bit too different. But I did enjoy it. I liked the theme. The reason I made the film was that I read the book and, while I thought the book was very clumsy and awkward, there was a moment when she was sitting on the train, talking about love and what love meant to her. That moment on the train was why I made the film: her attitude about love, how she'd worked out what it meant. This man had loved her and given her the freedom to go and sleep with another man. This was a blooming moment for her and I thought it was worth making the film for that moment. That's what I was trying to get. I thought the feminist critics could have been a bit more understanding, but they weren't.

In terms of criticism, Blood Oath *and Australian memories of the War?*

A lot of people criticised it, I think, because it wasn't as accurate as it should have been – and it was a bit melodramatic. I think that was all true in the script. I thought I could overcome some of that, but I couldn't really. In America and in Japan they didn't criticise this at all; in Australia they did. But the people who had actually been there didn't. They said it was an exaggerated version of what really happened.

I grew up at a time when soldiers who had returned from the War were talking about Japan and the hatred of Japanese and what they did. I was happy to make the film, whatever the final result is. I wanted to make a film about the Japanese treatment of our prisoners of war. It wasn't Japanese soldiers fighting – that was fair enough; they fought ruthlessly, but no Australian ever complained about that. That was war. What we complained about was the way they treated their prisoners of war, and we thought that was unfair because they were helpless. You don't treat prisoners of war like this, no matter who you are.

There were criticisms of the accuracy. The original writers brought the script to me after they worked on it a lot. They would have been better to have stuck more to the actual truth. It's much more interesting.

The character of the Christian Japanese prisoner was unexpected.

Yes, that was true; absolutely true. He came from Nagasaki or Hiroshima. He was executed with the Rosary in his hand. He was a Catholic and did voluntarily give himself up like that, although he was innocent, in exactly those circumstances – although it wasn't radio messages that got him, it was just his confession. He wasn't actually executed until six months later. We had him executed the next morning and it was New Guinea; he was taken to New Guinea and executed. But there were many protests on his behalf, including the priests in Nagasaki. But he was executed along with a lot of other people. The other guy was executed; he didn't commit harakiri.

It made it a bit more complex for an Australian audience thinking about Japanese cruelty, and suddenly you've got this theme of Catholicism. How do you reconcile the atrocity and justice?

The theme was true and the Australians found it very hard that this guy was actually a Catholic, a Christian, and that he had been told to come and do the execution. He did do the execution. He wasn't lied to so much as he just didn't ask any questions. He sort of knew it was wrong and he knew that they were innocent, that they hadn't been tried properly. And he said that. He gave himself up because he believed in God, Christianity and justice, and he got punished for it.

When he was blindfolded, all that was absolutely accurate. A priest was there and he said to him, 'I don't need a blindfold; I'm not afraid of death'. 'I'm sorry, it's regulations'. That's exactly what was said.

So he becomes almost a Christ figure in that sense?

Yes, he does. I wish we had made more of that. It's an interesting theme.

The Americans?

The Americans were never in the original story about the Ambon trials. I don't think there were any Americans there. The leader of the Japanese did get off like that. In fact I think he's still alive in Japan, a very old man – probably running Mitsubishi or something. A lot of critics said it was simplistic and, in a way I suppose it was. But the point is, it's true. Americans are always doing that. In the Tokyo trials, the Emperor got away and a lot of other people got away. The Americans wanted to run Japan properly and they didn't want to make the mistakes of Germany.

I don't think many people realise how horrifying the killing of the six hundred on the airfields was. Basically they were bayoneted to death on the airfields and buried. And the Commander knew about it. And he wouldn't come back and face trial because the Americans were protecting him. So we wanted to dramatise that somehow. In my bloodthirsty way I said, 'I'll tell you how we're going to start the film. You're starting is no good. What I'm going to do is have six hundred men all lined up on the airfield. I'm going to track down as each one of their heads is cut off, so people realise what we're dealing with there'.

We found that young Australians weren't very interested. They didn't want to know about the War. They didn't want to know about the Japanese. The film didn't do all that well here but it did very well in Japan. The Japanese soldiers at Ambon came to see it, had a big dinner and they said they were very glad the film had been made. It had been worrying them for years, what happened at Ambon, and they were glad it all came out.

You went back to Asia for Turtle Beach.

I loved the book and I really wanted to make the film. I think in the end the script really wasn't good enough and I had a terrible run-in with the producer on it. It was just a nightmare. I wanted to make a film about Asia again, because I thought Asia was misunderstood in Australia and I thought the more light we can shed on Asians, the better. I wanted to make a film about Australians up there and us dealing with Asians. I thought this was central. It's a much bigger issue now: us dealing with Asians. We have got to deal with Asia and Asians and Asian-ness. That's why I liked the book.

But unfortunately in the film, it all went haywire because I think Greta Scacchi was wrong. I got offered *Turtle Beach* straight after *Blood Oath* because they were thrilled with the film – the same people who had funded *Blood Oath*. It looked like a big step forward. I read the script and said 'It's not for me because it's not good enough; it doesn't work'. Then my wife read it and said it's a wonderful opportunity. But I was right in the first place: the script wasn't good enough. And I was too tired to make it. I was exhausted from *Blood Oath*. Anyway, that's all by the by. I went ahead and did it.

The producers all wanted to make *Pretty Woman* (dir. Garry Marshall). I said, 'It's not *Pretty Woman*, it's a film about Asia'. I had to fight to get an Indian to play the Indian; it was a struggle from start to finish. There was plenty of money, but I kept compromising on it. I kept compromising about the place where the beach was, about the roughness of the set. I wanted it really rough.

Then there was this whole thing about the disco place, which was actually Matt Carroll's idea – something he'd seen in Thailand. I hadn't researched enough on Malaysia. If I had researched on Malaysia, I would never have had the disco scene, because it just doesn't exist in Malaysia.

Also the massacre on the beach. Everyone was worried: the massacre had to be built up, whereas the massacre was wrong – emotionally and morally wrong. All this was pushed and I felt I'd lost control of the film.

I fought with the producers all the time and, as soon as they got the director's cut, they removed me and the editor from the film and then finished it, I thought, in a most appalling manner, and I should have taken my name off it. I got advised by my agents not to, but I should have. I don't feel the film is mine. A lot of the shots are mine, but extra stuff was shot and my name is on it, so I've got to take responsibility for it. But it's the one film I've made that I feel ashamed of.

And you haven't made a feature since.

I haven't made a feature since, no. It had a big emotional effect on me. I was never offered another picture. I was sent various scripts but I didn't really want to do them. I think if I'd just made *Blood Oath* I could have gone on, getting offers from America. Making *Turtle Beach* stopped everything. People were totally cold on me. That's why I should have taken my name off. It was Matt Carroll who made it.

I still don't know if I'm going to be able to do this – it's been nine years. But, if I was going to make films, I'd go back to *The Boy Who Had Everything*, only not compromise like I did on *The Boy* and just try and make the films that I really want to, or work with writers that I really want to. I've worked with Keith Thompson and developed two scripts of my own and I'm hoping I'm going to make one very soon. We're trying to raise money.

You have spoken about Scott Hicks and Rolf de Heer and how they broke through expectations with personal films.

And it happened with Peter Fisk when he made *True Believers* for television. Scott Hicks had made two or three features before *Shine* and Rolf de Heer had made two before *Bad Boy Bubby*. These directors are making quite competent films, nothing special, and sometimes not so good. All of a sudden, out of the blue, they make a film which startles everyone. It's just extraordinary. And my question is: why? What's happened? Something different has happened for them. It happened to Bob Connolly in documentary. He had been working for years at the ABC on *A Big Country* and *Four Corners* and had made nature documentaries, documentaries in Tasmania. All of a sudden he made *First Contact*.

Basically, what happened with Rolf de Heer and Scott Hicks is that they decided they would make a film they really cared about, that came from their hearts, came from inside themselves, and they weren't going to compromise. They would wait years to make it, if necessary. I think they found their voice. You've got to have a bit of freedom and you've got to fight for it and it's got to be something you really care about, something central to you, something about your life, a deeper film. And still try to make it entertaining. That's what's happened to them: they found their vision and their voice. And once you do that, you've got something special and people respond to it.

In your television material there's a strong voice, again with compassion for those on the fringe. What attracted you to your segment of Women of the Sun?

I liked the story of the Aborigines being put under pressure and standing up. I suppose I always like those stories of people standing up for their rights. I love the story of the French Revolution. A lot of things went wrong, but I like people standing up for their rights. I liked the fact that the Aborigines all walked off; that sort of frustrated gesture of defiance. I suppose that's true: I do like people on the fringes battling. I used to think I wasn't like that at all. But I came to realise that I am actually quite political, even though I don't think I am. I don't think of myself like that, but I do like those stories because I think they're the heart of our life.

Mail Order Bride *again has the Asian connection.*

I wish it had been made a bit better. I got sent three scripts by the ABC; I could do one of them. They were very generous to me in those days. It wouldn't happen now. But that's the one I wanted to do. The Ray Meagher character always reminded me of my brother, who's a sort of inarticulate Australian with a loving heart. There's an awful lot of them about: big yobbo-looking guys who've got soft hearts. It's very typical of Australia and something that I can identify with very strongly and I never have any problem with it. Talking to Ray Meagher I said, 'What does this guy want in his life? What's driving him?' And he thought about it for a long time and he said, 'He wants to build a home; he wants a home' – and it's something you can't say to another guy: 'I want to build a home'. But that's what he does, and that's what a lot of Australian men want. They want a home, they want a wife, they want a woman, they want some love in their life, but they can't talk about it.

Filipino groups sometimes express concern about treatment of Filipino brides in Australia.

Filipinos didn't like the film very much. They thought it was insulting. They didn't want anyone to see the film. They were ashamed that this woman would be called a whore, but I don't think they understood the western subtleties of the film because it wasn't doing that. The woman who played the role understood, but she'd been living out here a long time. I think they just felt that they didn't want this sort of thing even to be said. But that's the impression I got. They liked the film, but they were very uncomfortable about it.

And with Louis Nowra, Hunger?

I never wanted to do that film. I got talked into it. I always thought it was a bit strange about this guy doing a hunger strike. I got attacked by the Communists, saying that I should have been more loyal to Romania. I kept saying, 'Loyal to Romania? Do you know anything about it?' And most of the Communists said, 'Oh, no, but we can't be seen to be attacking the left anywhere'. I thought, 'I can't stand this'. The one thing I've never been is a rabid Communist or a rabid left-winger, ever. I said, 'You have to see it for what it is, otherwise you start believing in Robespierre. You've got to see the truth of the situation.' The truth of the situation is Romania was in a shocking state, even if it was a Communist state. I felt it was a good story, but I thought it was a bit static.

Then Olive.

Yes, *Olive* has had a tremendous effect on people. People still talk about *Olive*. Olive was a woman dying. I thought, 'Oh, God, I can't make another one of these dreadful films', but I met the husband. I actually didn't want to make the film until Olive told me – and I couldn't tell this to the husband – but Olive was an actress. She had come to Australia from South Africa, and she really wanted to break away from her husband. Her husband was a good, decent, ordinary guy. A woman therapist told me that a lot of women are married to good, decent, ordinary guys who don't do anything wrong, yet they want to break away and they can't. So a lot of them, to get away, die. And, in a way, that was my theme for the film. The husband said, 'You can have that theme if you want to, but I can't accept that'. I thought this filming the process of dying was a painful thing to do, but maybe was worthwhile; a painful film to make, even though we were acting.

You did a science-fiction story for the Winners *series?*

Yes, that was Tony Morphett, and he had religious themes as well. I was very religious when I was younger – Church of England – but I broke away because too many questions couldn't be answered for me. But I like people who are religious and I like things with religious themes, because I think it's all connected to humanity. So he put all that in, basically: Christian themes of bonding. The trouble was we ran out of time to shoot it properly. It rained and it was a nightmare, but I'm glad I made it. It's still running in Europe.

'Gordon Bennett' in the Bicentenary series of Willesee's Australians?

It wasn't great. We had to shoot those films in two weeks. They actually lost a director, rang me up on Friday to start on Monday, then two weeks later I was shooting. The thing about it was that Gordon Bennett was a decent man but much maligned in this country. The film comes down heavily on his behalf and – although people still argue – the Army still acknowledges him as a hero. He was a very good general but he was castigated because he left his troops. But it was such a quick job it's hard to comment on it.

The last contribution to a series was one of the Seven Deadly Sins.

Yes, 'Envy'. That was with Keith Thompson. Keith was working-class and it's a good story, but I always felt it stopped halfway through and started on a new film. The best thing about it was I was trying to do interesting things with the style, but I was always cross that he didn't follow the theme right through. I thought it would have a bigger effect than it did, but I think it got a bit lost in its cleverness. It's about a girl who's a loser. She was supposed to be a mouse – they described her as a mouse. I remember saying to the casting agent at the time, 'One of the interesting things about this is to cast a mouse'. But they said they didn't want to cast a mouse. They wanted a sexy girl who plays a mouse. I said, 'I'm going to cast a mouse and you watch the shit hit the fan'.

So we cast this mouse, Ross MacGregor's daughter. She was a very good actress and she looked exactly what the film said: a mouse, a girl who will never get a man. But she's got this guy and she's going to hang on to him, and that's what turns her nasty. And Bob Weiss, the writer, the person who had written it turned on me, and so did Penny Chapman. They reckoned they were never going to accept this girl under any circumstances. So we had to find another girl in Melbourne who was sexy. They never said that. She was a very good actress who has since done very well, so perhaps they were right. But I always felt the film didn't have any impact because of that. They turned her into a neurotic girl to make it work. The mouse thing couldn't work with her because she wasn't a mouse. I thought, 'If they kept it as a mouse, we would have had an extraordinary film', but to this day Bob Weiss says, 'You were wrong, Stephen, you were wrong'. I said, 'Well, I didn't have a chance, did I, because basically I had to leave the film if I wanted that girl; I had to resign'. But I decided in the end I would do the film. The other girl wasn't that far off it, but she was far enough to make the film unmemorable. And what's happened to the film? It's been totally lost. I reckon that's the reason.

Since then?

I've just done things like *The Flying Doctors* and *Water Rats*. *Water Rats* is fun. It's all over the top. I quite like it but I don't take it all too seriously.

But it does mean that over twenty years you have done a great deal.

Yes, I've done a lot. Sometimes I think I've done nothing.

Your themes have been humanity and social justice, and in the Australian context of decent people and integrity – and marginalised people.

I think that's true but I want to go a bit further than that, a bit into the terror of life. Someone said, 'You're always showing dignified people maintaining their dignity no matter what'. I think it's really about ordinary people who are battling in life, who find a way through, because that's how I see myself: an ordinary guy battling my way through to find a voice, to say something in the society, to be important. They aren't extraordinary people, but they're trying to be part of society and be decent people. They've got a decency about them. I feel that very strongly in Australians: that's what they're like, their greatest quality. Like my mother. She was very insightful. She thought she was ordinary but she was a very insightful, strong character who was – she always used to say about her family – poor but honest.

Australian Feature Films

1979 *Love Letters from Teralba Road*

1980 *Captives of Care*

1980 *Stir*

1985 *The Boy Who Had Everything*

1990 *Blood Oath*

1992 *Turtle Beach*

Simon Wincer

Simon Wincer, *Crocodile Dundee in LA*, 2000.
(Photo: Jasin Boland.)

It's always a very difficult question because it's a bit like asking a parent which is the favourite child – and I suppose that's a fairly standard answer. *Phar Lap* is very dear to me because it's a wonderful story and Phar Lap represented so much of Australia to so many people. I was also a great admirer of Tommy Woodcock. He was such a wonderfully genuine human being who was, I think, an old-fashioned Australian hero who had wonderful old-fashioned values. That's very dear to me. But I suppose every film is like giving birth. You live with them for so long – each one takes at least a year of your life – that it's hard to say which is the favourite. I suppose *Phar Lap* might be slightly more favoured. It was also the film that got me recognised internationally and set me on the path to a much wider career with a lot more options.

You made Quigley *with an American in Australia and* Lightning Jack *with an Australian in America.* Quigley *was originally written as a western?*

It was, and it was actually written a long time ago. *Quigley* was written originally and developed for Steve McQueen's company, but it floundered when he passed away. Then, I think, Clint Eastwood's company, Malpaso, picked it up and kept it for quite a while. The first I heard of it was when Kirk Douglas thrust it at me when he was out here doing *The Man from Snowy River* (dir. George Miller) and said, 'What do you think of this?' It was a pretty average sort of script, very American.

When MGM was reformed under the direction of Alan Ladd Jnr, he sent it to me (it was just after I had made *Lonesome Dove*) and said, 'Look, we know the script needs a lot of work but Tom Selleck's attached to it and we think he would be terrific for this character'. I was very anxious to do something in Australia and I liked its potential, so Ian Jones, the Australian writer, and I reworked the script to fit it into an Australian historical context.

I also think it presented an important side of Australia. But I know the film was absolutely damned in Australia (which I was very upset about), probably more than any film I have ever been involved with. I was more upset that it was totally dismissed in Australia because I thought it had something very important to say about the treatment of Aborigines and genocide because there was nothing in the film that did not actually happen, although the story itself was fictitious. All the Aboriginal people involved in the film were really great fans of it because it showed a side of history that so many Australians just aren't aware of. My children learn history from Australian history books now, but when I grew up, I learnt Australian history from a British history book. The bias was totally different and we didn't hear about these events.

Simon Wincer
S i m o n   W i n c e r
S i m o n   W i n c e r

There are some striking sequences in Quigley: *scenes of Aboriginal massacres. They are difficult to sit through, but all Australian audiences need to face them. One of the massacres was of shooters firing on the Aborigines (but perhaps we are somewhat used to this from American westerns). But the other was of the Aborigines being herded to the top of a cliff and being pushed over.*

It's very powerful and quite confronting. Probably why it was dismissed here was because people didn't want to see an American come to Australia, be the hero, and solve all our problems. But on the other hand, Australia in that era was not really so much 'Australian' as it was a British colony and populated by a melting pot of races from all over the world. First-generation Australians were probably not involved in anything like this because they were growing up in the major centres. But the outback was still populated by all sorts of ruthless people, very much rulers of their own little kingdoms.

There is another brief, telling sequence where Tom Selleck meets Alan Rickman, the landowner. At the table it emerges that Rickman wants Selleck to hunt Aborigines rather than dingoes; the elderly Aborigine who's serving at the table stands silently listening to the racist statement that the American Indians have no word for 'wheel'. Later there is vindication with a vengeance with the death of Rickman and the Aborigine walking silently from the homestead. This had a great deal to say to a wide audience.

Yes and, in fact, the film was well reviewed in America, particularly in the trade magazines, because they thought it was a frontier classic. It did pretty well theatrically and in America it has done very well in video release. So I was really disappointed in the way it was just dismissed in Australia.

The contrast, then, is the Australian in the United States. How do you see Lightning Jack *within those western conventions?*

I was not really involved in the genesis of *Lightning Jack*. Paul Hogan never saw it as a fish-out-of-water story in terms of comparing it to *Quigley*. *Crocodile Dundee* (dir. Peter Faiman) was, of course, a fish-out-of-water story but I think *Lightning Jack* is simply a western. It doesn't depend on Paul being Australian or anything like that. He is Australian. You can't get away from that. In fact, when he wrote it, he was thinking of just being an American cowboy, but I think it was Greg Coote of Roadshow who said to him, 'Paul, don't be silly, you've got too big a persona, you can't suddenly be doing accents and stuff', and he was absolutely right.

But the genesis of *Lightning Jack* was, in Paul's thinking, bank robberies. We always see a bank robbery in a western with the guys either riding off or getting shot, or, maybe, the third cowboy from the left gets away. Who is this char-acter? What does he do? What is he like and what happens to him after this? So that's really how *Lightning Jack* came about, the sort of mystery guy who's an underling in a bank hold-up – and he happens to get away. These char-acters, like anybody else, have flaws, have egos and so forth. That was where Paul really took it from. He wanted to poke gentle fun at the western genre.

He also wanted to make a more traditional, old-fashioned sort of classic western that was not revisionist like, for example, *Unforgiven* (dir. Clint Eastwood) or *Lonesome Dove*. It wasn't too dusty or too sweaty or too bloody or anything like that. There was more of the feeling that John Wayne could ride over the hill at any moment or canter down the street. So we actually went to all those older classic western locations. I think you can see that, visually, there's a great deal of familiarity with the more traditional westerns and with slightly larger-than-life baddies and heroes, virtually no blood, and a more up-market saloon than the reality of those days.

So that was the approach. In fact, Paul really wanted to get right away from the fish-out-of-water thing because he felt he had already covered it. And in the 1880s there was not a huge difference between what was happening in America and what was happening with Australia. They were both in the hangover period of gold rushes and land grabbing.

Reviewers commented on racial themes and the character, Ben, played by Cuba Gooding Jnr. They thought the portrayal and the mannerisms were racist and a retrograde step. In radio interviews Cuba Gooding denied this. Paul Hogan has said that this was not the intention and that, in fact, he hadn't thought of it at all.

We were floored by some people's comments – probably more so in Australia than in the United States – about the sort of 'Steppin Fetchitt approach' criticism. First of all, the part of Ben was written not for a black actor, nor for a white. We just happened to cast Cuba because we felt he was best for the role. In fact, I think the first actors we considered were Christian Slater or Johnny Depp, actors like that. They weren't available.

There was not a line of dialogue or piece of business changed for Cuba. But it all takes on a totally different meaning, of course, when suddenly there's a black actor and everyone is so politically sensitive. It had never even occurred to us and I think we were all a bit hurt by some of the comments. For example, criticism was made when Cuba shoots himself in the foot and rolls his eyes. If you shoot yourself in the foot, I defy anyone not to put on some weird expression. Of course, on a black face the eyes look that much wider and that much whiter. While we were all a bit hurt, we have to live with that sort of criticism because certainly nothing was intended by us. At some of the preview screenings we questioned black members of the audience and they didn't seem to have any problems with the film at all.

Simon Wincer

Was it successful in Australia?

It has done well in Australia, yes; very well. It's interesting because it took off with a big bang and it was, I think, the twelfth biggest opening of all time in Australia and did very solidly over the Easter period and then gradually, as all films do, started to fall away, then levelled off. Later, older people were still going as well as people who take four or five weeks to make up their mind to go to the movies. I think it grossed eight or nine million dollars in Australia, which is pretty solid, and the film, will, I think, break even throughout the world. I think America was a bit disappointing because again it opened really strongly but the distribution company, Savoy Pictures, didn't have the muscle nor the financial resources to really support it.

The earlier films, Snapshot *and* Harlequin, *were local thrillers. In* Harlequin, *Robert Powell portrayed a character who was based on Rasputin: a diabolical figure, a Devil figure.*

In the earlier days of the Australian film industry I had been working at Crawford Productions with the writer, Everett De Roche. We were toying with some ideas for movies and he often said he was fascinated by the Rasputin legend; that it would be good to do a story on it. I said that it would be nearly impossible to do something Russian and in period. He said, 'Well, why don't we do an updated version of the story?' That's more or less how it came about. We were very lucky to get Robert Powell because he had gained a huge following, particularly in Catholic countries, through his portrayal of Jesus in *Jesus of Nazareth* (dir. Franco Zeffirelli).

Robert, I think, is an extraordinary actor because he has a great stillness, which is almost frightening. He can simply twitch the corner of the lip or move an eye. I think a lot of the strength of that character in *Harlequin* is so effective because of the way it's played by Robert: terrifying and yet fascinating. In a way, it's a little like Ralph Fiennes' character in *Schindler's List* (dir. Steven Spielberg). Amon Goeth is an appalling character but you can't help being drawn in by him because he's just so awesome. Interestingly, *Harlequin* was most successful in, of all markets, South America – again because of the popularity of Robert Powell.

It's a long time ago, and if I were to remake that film, I think it would be pretty different now – simply because of growing up and experiencing a lot more of life. In those days production was really hurried. I think that film was made in five-and-a-half weeks, or something like that.

The particular angle, the diabolical figure, as part of our Australian screen fiction is an interesting highlight.

It is, yes. Everett really has to take the credit for that rather than me. I was the one who put it on film but it's his creation. I suppose I steered Robert in the direction we thought it should go, but I can't claim credit for having created the character. But it is interesting to create characters like that – there was something about him that women found very attractive too.

In talking about values and devilish characters, are you interested in any explicitly religious themes? Do you have some religious background?

Not really. To give you my background: I'm sort of middle-class Church of England, went to a private school in Sydney and was pretty happy – a very similar background to Peter Weir's. I grew up in Rose Bay and he grew up in Watsons Bay and he went to Scots College, which is up the hill from Cranbrook, where I went to school. My only dealings with Catholicism in those days were football, when we played CBC Waverley or Joeys (St Joseph's, Hunters Hill) or some school like that. They were always tough and they always seemed to have hairy legs.

I was, of course, confirmed and Liz and I still occasionally go to church – at Easter time. And quite often, in Los Angeles on a Sunday morning, we'll get up and go to Church; she's a Presbyterian and we just go because we enjoy the experience. I regard myself as a Christian – not what you'd call 'deeply Christian' – and I've tried to instil those values in my children, who have all been brought up Catholics because their mother was Catholic.

As regards religious themes, *Operation Dumbo Drop*, a job for Disney, delves very slightly. It's about a rag-tag group of soldiers that have to escort an elephant across Vietnam – a true story and wonderful story – and they suddenly realise the religious significance of this elephant to the group of people they're trying to take it to. There's a very powerful scene where the young boy who's attached to the elephant as a *mahout* walks into a temple in the middle of the night. It's somewhat overgrown by the jungle. It's an elephant temple. I've been into some of these temples and they're extraordinary. The group realise the significance of this being, an eye-opening experience for them.

You made The Girl Who Spelt Freedom, *another Disney feature?*

That's right. George and Prissy Thrash were Baptists from Chattanooga, Tennessee. Through the church they both felt they had a calling and took on the care of a Cambodian family, all of whom I've met: a most lovely group of people. I'm sure Lin Yan would be capable of running America one day, she is so bright, so articulate.

That was a very interesting experience. When I cast Mary Kay Place and Wayne Rogers and all the kids, we were filming one night at Vancouver Airport, which is where we made the movie because there is a large Cambodian population there, and the real Thrash family came up with Lin Yan's family from Chattanooga. They all met each other that night and it was fascinating because they all turned out to like each other and be so like each other. The only difference was that George Thrash is actually quite small and Wayne Rogers is very tall, but Mary Kay Place and Prissy Thrash are almost identical and they just hit it off at once.

These are more serious-minded Disney films.

That's interesting because when Michael Eisner and Jeffrey Katzenberg took over Disney in late 1984 they decided to get back into this sort of movie for the Disney Sunday-night movie and this was the first of them. I thought it was such a good one because it was really the story of children of the killing fields; a true story about a little girl who had never been in a classroom in her life, got to America and became the shining star in the spelling bee and got to meet the President. I think it was a wonderful, heart-warming story.

Values, legends, myths seem to appeal to you. What is your approach to myths in doing the Young Indiana Jones *films? And you have explored, especially in* Phar Lap *and* The Lighthorsemen, *the Australian ethos and myths.*

Yes, and it was the same for my involvement with *The Man from Snowy River* (as Executive Producer). I suppose we all like to dream about being the best or creating the best. I remember at school wanting to be the best at football; the one that people looked up to. I've always looked up to people so, I suppose, legends and heroics go back to that sort of thing. But I am fascinated by this. I guess; I don't quite know why. It's always easier for the critic to look in and say, 'Well, this is probably why', than for me to be analytical about it. I've always liked the classic story and the mythic proportions. I've had a few conversations with George Lucas about this – an extraordinary person that I really enjoyed working with.

I bought him a beautiful bronze Lighthorseman as a 50th birthday gift, because I did an episode in Turkey about the Australian Light Horse, a sort of remake of *The Lighthorsemen*. It's from a different perspective, where young Indy's in Beersheba as a spy, trying to save the city from being blown up as the Australian horsemen come in. Cameron Daddo played the leading Australian character – delightfully too.

So you have made The Lighthorsemen *twice?*

Revisited it, yes. What happened, in fact, was that George Lucas actually bought the film from RKO in America so he could use footage from it. So we've intercut footage from the original into the new. It was very interesting because we had Turkish horsemen playing the Lighthorsemen. It's fascinating to see them dressed up as Australian: the men that were firing the guns at them out of the trenches. Anything heroic gets the old heart beating – and that's a heroic story: eight hundred men who galloped across a three-mile open plain into Turkish cannons, machine guns and entrenched Germans. They didn't question what they were doing but did it because they were told to. To me these are wonderful values that seem to be fast disappearing from this sad world we live in.

You invested Phar Lap *with something of that same kind of drive for success. Tommy Woodcock had it.*

Phar Lap was an icon to the Australian public, especially during the Depression. There was something about that horse: he came from the wrong side of the tracks, he was half owned and trained by a battler, he wasn't part of the establishment – he was a working-class horse, if you like, and he became an icon because people knew they could go to the course and put a bob on Phar Lap and they would get their money back. I think that has very deep roots in the them-and-us thing which has always been big in Australia. I suppose that goes back to the convict days because not only was Phar Lap trained by a battler and half owned by a battler, but the other half owner was Jewish and American to boot, so that was really shoving it up the establishment and the squattocracy.

Do you think that the editing of Phar Lap *for the American audiences altered its dramatic impact?*

We talked about this a great deal. Everyone in Australia knows the horse died and we wanted to deal with that and get it out of the way and end the film on the note of his greatest triumph rather than his death. I preferred the film the Australian way, but obviously in America it's not a well-known legend. It took the film a while to get going over there. But, again, if I remade the film now, it would be interesting to see the approach we would take. We just learned so much over the years. David Williamson and I talked for ages about it, and with John Sexton for ages. That's the approach we decided to take because we knew that otherwise the audience would be sitting there waiting for the final death scene. I said we wanted people to leave the cinema up rather than down.

I would love to work again with David Williamson. I'm a great admirer of his, but nothing has presented.

And Harley Davidson and the Marlboro Man?

After doing so many period films, it was nice to do something that's very contemporary. I do like doing action films, films with a lot of action, and so I guess that's the reason I did it. Probably the script could've been a lot better. But it's interesting that when it was shown on Australian television, a lot of people who didn't see it in the theatre here – it did okay but not great – particularly of my son's vintage, came up and said, 'I really enjoyed that film'.

Simon Wincer
S i m o n   W i n c e r
S i m o n   W i n c e r

I had just got back from the U.S. opening of *Lightning Jack*, and was quite surprised that all sorts of people came up and said how much they enjoyed it.

Finally, Free Willy?

Again, it's them and us: it's the good triumphing over evil. What appealed to me about it (and all my films apart from, say, *Harley Davidson and the Marlboro Man*) is that they're all pretty much family-based films. They have very broad appeal. I like every kind of film as part of an audience but also as a film-maker. Because you have to live with something for so long, I'd rather live with something that I personally enjoy. I love ending films on a note of triumph. If all my films have a common thread, it's that they have a very strong emotional thread – all of them.

You received unanimous favourable reviews for Free Willy.

Yes, pretty much everywhere. When I read that script, I knew if we could deliver that moment of the whale jumping over the wall we had a movie. It's a very strong story: the little boy, the parallel stories. What appealed to me about the film was the theme of family: the boy who has no family, trying to come to terms with foster parents and new family, and the whale that has been plucked away from his family, the two of them being drawn together and having a similar background and, somehow, forming this unusual friendship. It really appealed to me a lot.

Australian Feature Films

1979 *Snapshot*

1980 *Harlequin*

1982 *Phar Lap*

1988 *The Lighthorsemen*

1990 *Quigley*

1994 *Lightning Jack*

Peter Malone

Father Peter Malone.

Interview with Fr Peter Malone by Director Nick Parsons

Films and the Church are not things that most people would normally put together in their mind. Do you think that you look for the same thing in both of them?

Well, the Arts have always been significant in mainstream Catholic tradition and, despite some Church officials who always seem to work on the presumption of suspicion first, ultimately all the Arts have found a place. Film probably has a much stronger status in parts of the Church than even some Catholics realise. The International Organisation has had juries at Venice for 52 years, Cannes for 50 and various others and, as time has gone on, they have become ecumenical. In Berlin we have five Catholics and five Protestants on the jury, and this jury is accepted as part of the Festival's official juries.

What made you start interviewing directors?

I started reviewing in 1968 for a magazine, *Annals*, designed mainly for Catholic families. Although they were fairly controversial times, it was interesting that the magazine itself was moving into schools for discussion of religion and values. The first films that I reviewed, for instance, were *To Sir with Love* (dir. James Clavell) and *Far from the Madding Crowd* (dir. John Schlesinger), then *The War Game* (dir. Peter Watkins), *The Graduate* (dir. Mike Nichols) and *2001* (dir. Stanley Kubrick). It was a period in the Church when people were writing books about values. In fact I did one myself in 1969, *The Film*, and one in 1970 called *Films and Values*.

When the Australian film renaissance started, which I never thought would happen, I suppose I got more and more interested in Australian films and what we were actually doing. It was only when *Black Robe* came out in 1991, and Bruce Beresford was available for interviews, I put my name down and had what I thought was a stimulating conversation. He got interested and started talking about his research, for instance, and his reading all the Jesuits' letters and thinking through Mission activity as understood in the seventeenth century compared with now. And I thought, 'This is something that I could perhaps contribute to Australian cinema consciousness'.

So in 1994 I started to interview seriously. By the end of the year, I had done about a dozen and, whether this is a character defect or quality, once I had started I became obsessive. Whenever there was the opportunity. The last person I interviewed was Ana Kokkinos, and she is number 76 of the Australian directors.

How many overseas directors have you done?

Only about a dozen.

Do you think, comparing the overseas directors and the Australian directors, are there common themes or concerns that emerge with the Australian directors that set them apart?

I think so – or whether it is the kind of questions that I ask – but I am interested in how they perceive their contribution to filming Australian identity, and I find —

Are they conscious of that?

A number of them are, or they become articulate about it once the question is asked. Bob Ellis talks about Australian Catholicism, quoting Les Murray, as 'a country of the mind'. He explores what he understands as the Catholic ethos, for instance, shaping the Australian consciousness. And I noted that, say, Phillip Noyce said that Irish Catholicism and establishment Anglicanism are the two shaping forces of Australian culture throughout the nineteenth century into the twentieth. I suppose because I'm a Catholic they start to talk that way, but Phillip Noyce suggests that Australian Catholicism, because of its working-class Irish background, would probably be the more stimulating. And Fred Schepisi talks in this way as well: he says that when a society is going smoothly the art that emerges has nothing much to say, but in recent years the shift from religion to spirituality has actually generated quite a number of questioning movies and stories.

It is interesting that you mention that shift from religion to spirituality; I wonder if there has been a change in the concerns of films from the 1970s through to the 1990s and now into the year 2000, in terms of the way that the Church and religion and spirituality are presented. It is a surprisingly common theme for such a secular group of people, and yet it comes back again and again. You can pick almost any Australian film, it seems, and at some point there is a representative of religion in there.

I saw *Soft Fruit* (dir. Christina Andreef) recently: suddenly the mother and daughter are cleaning the church. They see the nun who taught them and the daughter hides in the car. They always say that Australia is a secular society but the census would indicate that it is not. My example of a secular society would be, say, post-Lenin Russia – or Romania, as John Smith at the God Squad in Melbourne found when he went there soon after the collapse of the Soviet empire. He was talking to university students who didn't have a consciousness of transcendent metaphysical questions. He was very surprised; he thought that they would have. Whereas in Australia even an atheist like Tim Burstall, in his interview, said that, although he was brought up by atheist scientific engineering parents, if he were to become anything then he would become a Catholic. Now, where that came from I don't know, but I have tended to say that we are 'secular*ised*'. Our behaviour and many of our attitudes look secular, but underneath there is something transcendent which is basically, if not religious, then at least spiritual.

I was just thinking about the issue of spirituality and religion. Do you think the established Church, as an image in the Australian psyche, has been associated with Europe, and therefore with the mother country that, I suppose, in a sense rejected us in the first place, and that what Australians have been searching for in their movies all along has been something which is linked to the country itself? We sort of flirted with Aboriginal spirituality but in the end you have to be Aboriginal to buy into that.

In a sense your question would apply pretty well to the representation of, say, the Anglican Church in the 1930s. (Although Ken Hall has hardly anything on religion or Church, which I find quite extraordinary.) In the early days a film might include the monk and the Church or the monk and the woman. You have *The Silence of Dean Maitland* (dir. Raymond Longford) (which Ken Hall did remake, but it has more of a *Thorn Birds* quality to it). So in the 1930s in our Australian industry there is practically no religion or Church, or it is merely a formality ...

Although the bush is really the Church of that period.

Probably the closest you get is *The Man from Kangaroo* (dir. Wilfred Lucas) with Snowy Baker as the minister who is the regular bloke, the boxer and all the rest of it. So in a sense, as the bush was being sanctified and the city was so evil, *The Man from Kangaroo* works well that way.

But with the Catholic Church, Pope John XXIII, for whatever reason, at the end of the 1950s must have sensed that the world was changing. We didn't dream the 1960s were going to be like they were, but with the Second Vatican Council there was an assembly of over two thousand bishops collaborating to rethink the image of the Church as not just Roman but universal. And it did mean then that the Church had given permission for Catholics to rethink, reshape, create, critique, and we did. Now, I think Schepisi breaks through for the Australian version of that with his short story in *Libido* (dir. David Baker, Tim Burstall, John B. Murray, Fred Schepisi). It rang so true in 1973 when it was released that a priest was contemplating leaving his vocation and asking a nun to leave and to marry him. That sort of thing was really happening, and Keneally's dialogue is so real, even the incidental chatter of Arthur Dignam with the nuns, which was like, 'What will the Bishop think?'. And Schepisi did the same, but more so, with *The Devil's Playground*, which everybody did go to see, sometimes with embarrassment for the Catholics. I had to go a second time to see it for itself rather than in the context of what was happening in the Church and how it was examining the past. But for whatever reasons,

Peter Malone

Schepisi was actually contributing to the movement of the Australian Catholic Church from an authoritarian Irish mould – as John Maloney from ANU used to refer to it – to 'What is Australia like? What kind of people are we? Does the very stern Jansenist spirituality make any sense?' And, as you say, there was a breaking free. But the breaking free was not to say that the Church was necessarily wrong, but that the Church needs to adapt. That idea carries right through to, say, *Brides of Christ*. Schepisi, I think, enabled Catholic issues to come to the surface in all kinds of ways, like in *Soft Fruit*. You get all kinds of variations, like Chantal Contouri as the mother and mad kinds of characters in *Metal Skin*. Now, all this contributes to Catholic film culture and I think it enables other denominations to do the same.

So from the 1970s to the 1990s, I think that what the films were doing with culture was really trying to dramatise the question of national identity, hence the return to the past, *Picnic at Hanging Rock* (dir. Peter Weir) or whatever, balanced by the caricatures like Barry McKenzie. By the time we got to the 1980s some of the more contemporary stories were being told. I am thinking of the winners at the AFI awards in the 1980s: *Careful He Might Hear You* (dir. Carl Schultz), *My First Wife* (dir. Paul Cox), *Bliss* (dir. Ray Lawrence), *Malcolm* (dir. Nadia Tass), *The Year My Voice Broke* (dir. John Duigan) – there is quite a range of films and acceptance, I think, of identity and of the culture and exploring its dimensions. There were still the quirky comedies. I saw *Muriel's Wedding* at the Melbourne Film Festival opening, and everybody roared laughing at the ABBA imitation, but six months later when I saw it again, all I could focus on was Jeanie Drynan and the pathos of her death. And that exemplified for me that the one film could caricature the characters and the culture, yet underneath it can still say a lot about dysfunctional families and relationships. There is a greater depth to it.

But I am not sure where we are at the moment, because I suppose with all the hype surrounding Australian film, and yet without having had blockbuster success in the last three years, we are now looking to make more modest films. And it is the nature of these films to adopt a more exploratory, questioning stance. If I can just cite one example – and this will be throwing it back to you – *Dead Heart*. Ernie Dingo's character actually dramatises the problem of being caught between two worlds. Which begs the question, 'What is Aboriginal spirituality?' Has Bryan Brown's character got any? Or what? Or Lewis Fitzgerald and his earnestness? We have arrived at the year 2000 with a lot of questions, and to answer them I think is a religious task, basically, and a spiritual task.

Index

Myth & Meaning
M y t h & M e a n i n g